How to
Behave So Your
Preschooler Will, Too!

ALSO BY SAL SEVERE, PH.D.

How to Behave So Your Children Will, Too!

How to Behave So Your Preschooler Will, Too!

SAL SEVERE, PH.D.

VIKING

VIKING
Published by the Penguin Group
Penguin Putnam Inc., 375 Hudson Street, New York, New York 10014, U.S.A.
Penguin Books Ltd, 80 Strand, London WC2R 0RL, England
Penguin Books Australia Ltd, 250 Camberwell Road, Camberwell, Victoria 3124, Australia
Penguin Books Canada Ltd, 10 Alcorn Avenue, Toronto, Ontario, Canada M4V 3B2
Penguin Books (N.Z.) Ltd, Cnr Rosedale and Airborne Roads, Albany, Auckland, New Zealand

Penguin Books Ltd, Registered Offices: Harmondsworth, Middlesex, England

First published in 2002 by Viking Penguin, a member of Penguin Putnam Inc.

10 9 8 7 6 5 4 3 2 1

Copyright © Sal Severe, 2002
All rights reserved

CIP data available

ISBN 0-670-03108-9

This book is printed on acid-free paper. ∞

Printed in the United States of America
Set in Adobe Garamond
Designed by Jessica Shatan

For my parents, Mary and Tony, and

my children, Anthony, Leah, Alyssa, and Dominic, and

*my wife, Dianne, who taught me the most
about parenting preschoolers*

Preface

The idea for this book occurred to me while I was doing an interview for National Public Radio, when the host of the program asked me at what age discipline really begins. This was a question I had heard many times before, not only from talk show hosts but also from many parents. My answer was always the same: "The sooner the better!" Then came the revelation: My next book needed to address discipline issues of preschool children. Why? Because patterns of behavior that are formed during these precious, developmental years are the foundation for later behavior, attitudes, and relationships. So it is essential to establish positive patterns from the beginning. Furthermore, preschoolers are unique in that their behavior is so strongly influenced by their level of understanding, their ability to comprehend and use language, and their temperament. And because the mind of a preschooler absorbs everything around it, parents need to be completely aware of their own behavior. Therefore, parents of preschoolers now have a *How to Behave* book written especially for them.

I have spent the last thirty years working with behavior-disordered children. Early in my career, I realized that working with these children solely during the school day was insufficient. I needed to get their parents involved. It's been my experience that when a child's family life is improved, all other aspects improve as well. So I began sharing my experiences with groups of parents. Groups became workshops. Since 1982, more than 30,000 parents have attended these workshops. Nearly half were parents of preschoolers. I report this to you because I believe that I have learned more from these parents than they have learned from me. Every time I heard a new strategy or solution to a common problem or an entertaining story I would write it down. This book is a collection of these strategies, solutions, and stories.

—Sal Severe

Acknowledgments

A well-written book depends on many people besides the author. I wish to thank one of the best preschool psychologists I know, my wife, Dr. Dianne Heckman, for her inspiration and constant encouragement, as well as her invaluable contributions and assistance with the research for this book. Since readability is as important as content, I am especially grateful to my editor, Jane von Mehren, for her brilliant insights and refinements. Special thanks to my agent, Laurie Liss, and Tim McCormick, my first publisher, for bringing *How to Behave So Your Children Will, Too!* to Viking and the world, which made this book possible.

Thank you to the professionals and proofreaders who gave their valuable time and advice: Lisa Merrin, Ph.D., Robert Atwood, Ph.D., Bonnie Neil, M.S., Robin Howell, Sandra Peacock, and Jennie Pham. Thanks to Gaye Vaterlaus for her expertise and help with the children's-book list in the appendix. Above all, thank you to the parents and children who have shared their stories so that others may become better parents.

Contents

Preface   vii

Acknowledgments   ix

Part I • Introduction   1

1   What Preschoolers Need from Their Parents   3

Part II • Developmental Factors That Affect Behavior   15

2   How Language Affects Behavior   17
3   How Temperament Affects Behavior   38
4   How Self-Esteem Affects Behavior   45
5   How Motivation Affects Behavior   53
6   How Preschoolers Learn   62

Part III • Better Behavior Principles   77

7   Quick Start Strategies   79
8   You and Your Preschooler Learn from Each Other   93
9   Being Consistent Is Seldom Easy, but It Is
    Always Worth It   103

Part IV • Putting Better Behavior Principles into Practice   115

10   How to Build Positive Behaviors and Attitudes   117
11   Use Charts and Checklists to Teach Accountability   131
12   Use Rules to Provide Guidance   139
13   Managing Your Anger   155
14   Alternatives to Spanking   164
15   Correcting Misbehavior with Time-Out   171
16   Planning Improves Misbehavior   197

Part V • Applying Better Behavior Principles
          to Everyday Challenges   207

17   Common Challenges   209
18   Sibling Strife   224
19   From Comfort to Coping   231
20   Preschool Fears   241
21   Behavior in Public Places   250
22   Preschoolers, Aggression, and Anger   259
23   Choosing a Preschool   268
24   Children with Special Needs   271
25   From Cookies to Car Keys   277

Appendix: Children's Book List   281
Index   303

PART I

Introduction

1

What Preschoolers Need
from Their Parents

 I remember an occasion when our daughter Alyssa was four. We were going out for dinner, and decided to go to our favorite Mexican restaurant. Alyssa loved having a quesadilla and a side of rice. We have learned that it is always better to go to restaurants where your child has a favorite selection. We ordered our food and nibbled on chips and salsa. Then it happened. As the waiter began placing our meal on the table, Alyssa got up on her knees. There was something strange on her plate. The cook had placed a garnish next to her rice. At first she just stared at the pile of green stuff. Then she pointed an accusing finger and announced, "What the hell is this?"

We looked at each other with frozen stares of disbelief. Did we hear that correctly? Before we could decide, Alyssa looked up at the waiter. So did we. His expression was just as frozen.

"What the hell is this?" she asked again.

"It's lettuce," he replied.

"I don't like lettuce, don't you know that?" Alyssa admonished.

We apologized to the waiter and held our breath. We removed the lettuce. Alyssa proceeded to eat with her usual vigor. After dinner, we explained to Alyssa that *hell* is not a nice word. To this day, we still do not know if she knew what she said.

This kind of baffling, sometimes embarrassing outburst is not uncommon during a child's preschool years. You must be ready for any contingency; life with a preschooler is filled with unpredictability and backup plans. There are times when you feel elated and proud, and others when you feel challenged and embarrassed.

Preschoolers have a spirited desire to rule the world. They are on a quest for autonomy. This emergence of independent thought causes preschoolers to appear self-centered, demanding, and annoying by adult standards. Even the slightest disappointment or frustration can turn into an uncontrollable emotional outburst. Preschoolers behave without regard to consequences, which is why they test limits, often just to see what happens. Although many parents see these behaviors as a never-ending test of their devotion and patience, which often wear thin, these behaviors are normal, predictable, and part of every preschooler's journey from infancy to childhood, from reliance to independence. Parents who understand these natural behaviors will have more appropriate expectations for their children and will be less likely to misinterpret these behaviors as deliberate misconduct.

Being the parent of a preschool child requires a wide variety of personal qualities and technical skills. You need the combined talents of a teacher, recreation director, mediator, psychologist, spiritual mentor, chef (gourmet and short order), medic, consoler, and monster eradicator. Other basic skills include being able to craft an alligator costume without warning the night before the preschool play and stretching a recipe for twenty-four cookies to twenty-seven. You will need to memorize a medley of lullabies, all the hand gestures to the "Itsy Bitsy Spider," and at least a dozen verses of "The Wheels on the Bus."

For the purposes of this book, a preschooler is a child between the ages of three and six. This stage of development is commonly referred to as early childhood, and it encompasses the nursery or preschool and kindergarten years. During these years, children begin to become surprisingly independent as they learn to apply communication and problem-solving skills in social situations. The preschool years are a critical time because the behaviors and attitudes that are shaped during this period last a lifetime.

Parents are perhaps more important at this stage than any other. And in this book, you will learn how to be the most effective parent you can be. At this stage, children need parents who understand that discipline is a teaching process. I believe that discipline includes everything we do to teach our children to think for themselves and make good choices.

Successful parents learn to teach, practice, and reinforce the rules of good behavior, rather than simply announce them.

At this point in their lives, children need parents to be good models. That means you use manners to teach manners, and practice self-control to teach self-control. And since preschool children naturally trust their parents, maintain that trust by being affectionate and warm, yet firm and consistent. Appreciate the unique world of your preschooler by seeing situations from your child's point of view. Focus on positive attitudes and behaviors in your child, and use verbal encouragement that builds internal motivation and self-esteem. Correct misbehaviors by redirecting your child to positive replacement behaviors; for example, "My ears don't listen to whining. Please ask using a polite voice." Be proactive. Minimize the opportunity for misbehavior by keeping your children engaged. Avoid conflicts by giving children choices. Provide activities that are structured yet involve the child's interest and imagination. Plan ahead by establishing routines and schedules. Prepare children for transitions. Rehearse situations and explain proper behavior.

Stay calm when your child is testing you or pushing your button; anger only gets in the way. Be patient. Recognize that needs and wants drive your children's behaviors, and at this age, children communicate and express emotions with their behavior. Learn the difference between mischief and misbehavior; not all irritating behavior is misconduct. Your child's intent is not always willful, and a parent must distinguish between deliberate misbehavior and behaviors that are the result of other factors, such as the child's inability to communicate clearly. Behavior can also be a reflection of fears, stress, fatigue, hunger, mood, time of day, type of activity, peer influence, and more. Knowing the difference between behaviors that are deliberate and those that are not takes experience and a remarkable sense of judgment. And when correcting misbehavior, do so without belittling your child.

Most important of all, be consistent. Follow through, especially when you don't feel like it. Teach your children how to predict the outcome of their choices by using clear and specific expectations and consequences.

Your child's preschool years are a time of great learning not only for your child but also for you, especially if your preschooler is your first-born. The time and energy you spend learning about your child's development and ways to teach good behavior are well worth it. The behavior patterns that are developed during this stage can last a lifetime. It is a critical time. Most preschooler parents believe that this stage of child rearing may be the most difficult yet the most rewarding job you will ever have.

What Preschool Parents Have in Common

All preschool parents have the same goals and aspirations. We want successful children who are happy and well adjusted. We want our children to feel good about themselves, confident, inquisitive, and eager to learn. We want children who are loving, respectful of others, well behaved, and self-motivated. Our children are a measure of our success and worthiness. We judge ourselves by their success and achievements. We want them to have all of our finest qualities and none of our flaws.

Most preschool parents confront the same behavior problem: not listening the first time, or the second or third. We become annoyed repeating everything three times, or having to raise our voices to get our children's attention. We become drained listening to them whine and plead. We feel guilty for getting angry, but it appears to be the only way to get results. We blame ourselves and feel ineffective for not knowing what to do.

The truth is, like it or not, a certain amount of misbehavior is normal. What is essential is knowing how to react; responding correctly and consistently will reduce misbehavior now and in the future. Reacting incorrectly will only increase misbehavior. What is difficult is that our natural inclination is to react in one of two ways. Sometimes we react passively, giving in to misbehavior because we don't know what else to do or we simply do not feel like confronting the problem, at least not right now. At other times we react with anger. You will learn why both giving in and reacting with anger make misbehavior worse.

Knowing how to react to misbehavior is important. Knowing how to prevent misbehavior is even more important. You can escape many misbehavior episodes by setting up a few guidelines in advance, and by taking the time to teach your preschooler how to behave.

As part of my research for this book, I have read a number of excellent books about preschoolers. All of these books do a marvelous job of explaining why preschoolers behave, but offer limited analysis of how a parent's behavior is related to their preschooler's behavior, and less about specific solutions—what you say and do. That is what makes this book different. It goes beyond providing a framework for understanding your preschooler's behavior—it explains how your behavior, your words and actions, affects that behavior.

How This Book Will Help

This book will help you appreciate how preschoolers see the world and how they learn to make sense of what they experience. As a result, you will be able to make some sense of your preschooler's behaviors, even the irritating behaviors that seem completely illogical. Finally, you will learn positive strategies, not only for helping your child learn to behave but also for building a strong relationship that helps your child succeed in the world.

To achieve these goals, you will learn strategies to deal with specific issues, such as:

- How to get your preschooler to listen the first time you ask him to do something.

- How to explain situations to your child so he will understand why it is important to behave.

- How to get your preschooler to behave without your getting angry.

- How to prevent problems by determining the purpose behind your preschooler's behavior.

- How to redirect misbehavior into correct behavior.

- How to be more consistent.

- How to use incentives without bribing.

- How to use consequences that teach.

- How to correct your children without conflicts and power struggles.

- How to manage nagging, whining, and tantrums.

If you already have well-behaved preschoolers, thank your higher power. This book will help you too. It will make you more aware of the successful strategies you are currently using and show you how to maintain good behavior. In addition, it will prepare you for any future problems you may face.

The success of any type of discipline depends on your understanding of the developmental factors that affect and influence a preschooler's behavior. It is important to understand how preschoolers learn, how language develops, how temperament is related to behavior, and how self-esteem affects behavior. Since the primary focus of this book is behavior, however, you may want to consult the many other resources that are available. There are books that will help you gain a deeper understanding of your child's development, as well as other resources that provide a more detailed analysis of specific developmental milestones, such as toilet training. Even though most children are toilet trained by age three, except for occasional accidents, there is a discussion of helpful strategies for toilet training in part V of this book, along with a discussion of bed-wetting. In preschool-age children, these two common issues may involve physiological factors. If you have concerns in these areas, consult your pediatrician or a pediatric nurse for strategies and preferred reading material.

There are a number of theories about parent and child behavior. Most authors accept one theory, and try to convince you that their ideas work for every parent and every child. After trying this approach early in my career, I decided it was insufficient. Since every parent and child is unique, why not use a variety of methods? Use the best from every theory. This book offers hundreds of ideas. Not all of them will work all the time; select the ideas that make sense to you. They will help you enjoy your preschooler to the fullest, make the most of these precious, critical years, and build a positive relationship with your preschooler that will be a strong foundation for later childhood and adolescence.

You do not need to read this book from beginning to end. The chapters are designed to be read alone and even out of order and still make sense. This is helpful for a parent who has little time to read—which is probably the case if you are a preschooler's parent—but wants help with a specific problem today. However, because the chapters have been written so they can be read separately, key concepts are sometimes repeated.

You will find reminders to be positive, consistent, and patient in every chapter. If you are in a hurry to get started, I would suggest reading chapter 2, "How Language Affects Behavior," chapter 6, "How Preschoolers Learn," chapter 7, "Quick Start Strategies," and then any other chapters that interest you. If you are concerned about your child being too stubborn, active, or shy, add chapter 3, "How Temperament Affects Behavior." If you get angry easily, read chapter 13, "Managing Your Anger." I strongly suggest that you avoid jumping ahead to chapter 15, "Correcting Misbehavior with Time-Out." Time-out is only useful as part of a total discipline plan. It will only work in combination with all the positive strategies this book suggests. Please read the other chapters first.

How We Learn Parenting Behavior

At a recent workshop, a mother talked about her anger with her four-year-old, explaining how she yelled and screamed at him all the time. When I asked her if she knew why she did this, she answered without hesitation, "That is the way my mother raised me. All she did was yell. She was always mad at us." What a remarkable awareness—the first step toward making a change. Have you ever said something to your children and then realized you heard these same words when you were a child? "Be careful, or you'll break your neck." "Be quiet and eat." We tend to parent the way we were parented. We tend to discipline as we were disciplined. Becoming more aware of this influence enables us to pick and choose our methods. Things we like, we use. Things we do not like, we do not use.

We also learn by watching other parents, and talking with friends about their experiences. They learn from our experiences. We share techniques that work.

We also learn by trial and error. Much of what we do with our children is based on our best guess at the time. You begin using trial and error the moment you get home from the hospital with your firstborn child. The baby is crying. What does it mean? Hungry? Lonely? Wet? Too warm? Too cold? Trial and error also applies to discipline. If your preschooler responds to a positive strategy once, you will probably use it again. Some things work; some fail. As time goes on, you will have more experiences to draw from.

The beliefs that you already have about parenting and discipline are fine. Learning from your parents and friends and learning by trial and error is normal. Add judgment and common sense, and you have the substance for a solid foundation. This book will build on that foundation.

When Parents Disagree

It is quite common for parents to have some differences of opinion when it comes to discipline, as well as other aspects of raising their children. These differences are natural, since you and your spouse did not have the same parents and were raised in different homes, neighborhoods, cultures, and so on. Since consistency between parents may be the single most important factor in successful discipline, it is important that your and your spouse blend each of your parenting styles into a unified set of beliefs. This book will explain how different strategies can work in different situations, so you can take advantage of the parenting skills that each of you bring to your family. More importantly, this book will give you and your spouse a common foundation on which you can build your cooperative approach to discipline and child rearing. There is an added bonus when this happens. Your children will learn from your example that compromise and cooperation are helpful ways of solving problems.

Parents often ask what to do about a spouse who needs a little gentle encouragement to try new ideas. Bobby Jo would cut articles from magazines and magnet them to the refrigerator. Her husband would see the headlines, become curious, and read the article. Several pages in this book can be used the same way. Copy them and hang them on the refrigerator or other conspicuous place as a reminder to you and an inspiration for your spouse.

Love Does Not Always Light the Way

Today, many parents never experience being around babies and small children until they have their own. Too many parents have the false belief that if they love their children as much as possible, misbehavior will someday improve. Love, warmth, and affection are essential. They are fundamentals, but they are not enough. Children need trained, competent parents who have understanding, judgment, and skills. Most of us don't go to school to learn to be parents, so we may feel that we don't need training. This book will help you get the training you should have: pulling together all the good ideas you already have, providing strategies and direction for skills you need to improve, and creating a framework and structure for your role as a parent. As you learn that what you are doing is right, you will gain confidence, and more confidence means more self-control, less anger, less guilt, and less frustration. It also leads to more respect from your children. Without confidence, many parents are afraid to correct their children, worrying that their children will not like them, or being afraid they might harm their children emotionally.

Parenting has never been easy, but it is more difficult now than ever before because of changes in our culture. Today many couples are both employed outside the home, which means Mom and Dad come home stressed, with short fuses. The stress in their lives affects not only their parenting but their marriage as well. If the marriage doesn't survive, the children suffer. In some schools, four out of five children have experienced divorce. And because extended families are now rarely available to help care for children and to pass along family values and traditions, parents, whether married or single, often feel isolated.

Influences outside the family also threaten our values and the way we parent. You show your preschooler how to solve problems with words instead of fighting, yet many children's programs and cartoons promote fighting. You teach polite language; most movies contain cussing. You teach honesty; public figures lie. You teach respect; professional athletes spit at referees. These influences confuse children and create problems for parents.

Problems are more complicated. Even though today's parents are the richest and most-educated group in history, the solutions are not always easy. That is why parenting books, magazines, and television programs have become popular in the past decade. If you want to be a successful parent, you have to know how to discipline children in today's culture. Love is not enough.

Changing Your Behavior: How to Begin

Any change has three steps: awareness, commitment, and practice. Be aware of what you need to do differently. Are you repeating your parents' style? Do you have habits you would like to change? This book will help you become more aware of your parenting behavior so you can decide what aspects you need to change. Once you have the awareness, make the commitment to change—not only to yourself, but also to your children. Putting in the energy now is worth the rewards that come later.

As you read the ideas in this book, you may think, "Sounds great. That will really work for us." Reading about a new technique is not the same as doing it. Any change that is worthwhile requires practice. Every parent must practice. Even I have to practice—my children do not care that I teach parenting classes. When I'm home, I'm Dad. I get tested just like you.

Changing behavior means changing habits, and habits are not easy to change. Old habits are comfortable, new ones are not. As you continue with this book, you will be reading about strategies and techniques that you need to use more, as well as counterproductive behaviors that you should avoid. You will also find that many of your present ideas are fine and need no change. As you read, make a list of your behaviors that you need to practice *more,* behaviors you need to practice *less,* and behaviors that are appropriate and should be *continued.*

Behaviors I need to do *more.*

_____

_____

_____

Behaviors I need to do *less.*

_____

_____

_____

Behaviors that are appropriate, which I need to *continue.*

_____

_____

_____

Since it takes about a month to develop new habits, review your list two or three times a week for the next four weeks. This review will help you solidify your new habits more quickly.

Promise to have *courage* to be open and accept new ideas. If what you are doing is working, stick with it. If not, then have the courage to try something new. Promise to have *patience*—plenty of patience! Preschoolers need plenty of time to learn and develop proper behavior patterns. This is where most parents fail. We have gone from one-hour dry cleaning to one-hour photos to one-hour eyeglasses to thirty-minute tune-ups. Microwave food, cellular phones, e-mail, and express lanes have conditioned us to expect instant gratification. Technology has taught us impatience. We believe that because we are trying a new idea, changes should take place overnight. A few days is not long enough to test a new idea; some methods take weeks to show improvement.

Preschoolers learn good behavior. A well-behaved child is not the result of luck. Be encouraged—if behavior is learned, then it can be taught. Parenting behavior is also learned; you can learn to be a more successful parent. The way you behave toward your children affects the way they behave toward you and everyone else. That's what I hope to teach you in this book: how to behave so your preschooler will, too!

PART II

Developmental
Factors That
Affect Behavior

2

How Language Affects Behavior

**Language comes so naturally to us that it is easy to forget what
a strange and miraculous gift it is.**

—STEVEN PINKER

Language allows us to take a thought from one person and put it
into the thoughts of another. Not only do we communicate with
language, we think with language. We develop everything from abstract
concepts to practical innovations with language. We are able to cure disease
and venture into space because we have language. The most dynamic component of a child's development during the preschool years is language.

The process of learning language is nothing short of miraculous. Infant brains unscramble sounds, picking and choosing the ones that are
part of human speech while ignoring the sounds of the dog's barking.
Then they match sounds to meaning, which is rather difficult. Consider
how many sounds have multiple meanings: for example, "two," "too,"
and "to." Think also of the trickiness of language: "The man cuts the
tree down. Then he cuts it up."

In his recent book *Words and Rules,* MIT professor Steven Pinker describes the astonishing acquisition of words:

Children begin to learn words before their first birthday, and by
their second they hoover them up at the rate of one every two

hours. By the time they enter school children command 13,000 words.

Once a child begins assigning meaning to sounds, the next task is to combine them, putting a string of sound together to create an intelligent communication. The arrangement of words matters. "Run the dog see" may have the same words as "See the dog run," but only one phrase is meaningful. Next, children begin to fine-tune communication with grammar and syntax, a feat that is not fully accomplished until later childhood. In spite of all the complexities, about 90 percent of the sentences spoken by three-year-olds are grammatically correct.

Language from Birth to Three

Infants communicate by crying, cooing, laughing, and making sounds and squeals. By exchanging sounds with their parents, infants gradually begin to imitate their speech. When the parent responds with a smile and more sounds, the infant responds by using more sounds. An infant's babbling develops into repetitive sounds such as "dada" and "mama." As they continue to imitate and experiment with new sounds, they begin to echo simple adult words such as "bye-bye" and "hi." Parents have fun trying to guess what different sounds mean; infants, however, may not attach meaning to all sounds.

At approximately one year of age, a child realizes that words refer to people (sister), objects (ball), or situations (night-night time). A one-year-old begins to link words with gestures to get his wants and needs met. For example, a child will say "Milk" and point to his cup, or a child will say "Up" as he reaches his arms to be picked up. Language develops rapidly as toddlers understand the meaning of more and more words they hear being used by their parents and siblings. Expression begins with simple words. A single word may have different meanings. "Mama," for example, can mean "Help me," "More milk," or "I want that," depending on how and when it is being used.

By approximately two years of age, children use word combinations to express their wants and needs. "No, mine" and "Me do it!" become favorite expressions as they assert their independence. Toddlers often have strong feelings that they do not know how to express. When they become angry or upset, they express themselves physically, sometimes with tantrums, outbursts, or aggressive behavior. A toddler may push, hit, or bite because he has a limited ability to use words to express feelings and resolve conflicts.

The following table was adapted from the Manhattan Museum for Children. It is called the Evolution of Conversation and shows how all children follow the same path to language.

THE EVOLUTION OF CONVERSATION

Eye contact: Hmmm. I am not alone!

Smiling: When I smile, she smiles back.

Gurgling and cooing: Is that me making those sounds?

Pointing: Hey! When I point and make sounds I get attention.

Babbling: She keeps copying my sounds. I must be doing something important.

Words: Mama, dada, no, mine, juice. Words are cool.

Sentences: Baby go store. I really have power now!

Reasons and explanations: Why? Why? Why? He told me to do it.

Arguments: I want to go to the park. Not later. Now!

Language During the Preschool Years

Language development peaks during the preschool years as new words are acquired at an astonishing rate. Also during this period, a child's brain develops rapidly. Preschoolers learn about their world by observing and discovering what happens when they interact with the world and people around them. They begin to build complex, informative sentences that link ideas, events, or pieces of information. Preschoolers learn to categorize items. They understand that an apple belongs to a larger group of objects known as fruit. Preschoolers also begin to develop an awareness of time and sequence. They use words such as "before" and "after" to clarify the order of events. "I go to bed after you read me my story."

Preschoolers continually practice the social skills involved in using language, such as taking turns, listening, and judging the effect of their words on listeners. Use language that teaches and encourages your preschooler to learn correct social skills. Billy and Justin are drawing with crayons. Billy asks to borrow one of Justin's crayons. Justin is reluctant. Mother intervenes, "Justin, Billy would like to borrow one of your crayons. What a wonderful opportunity you have to share. Sharing is what good friends do."

A child's ability to interpret and understand the meaning of words and then use words for self-expression affects every aspect of a preschooler's life, especially behavior. As they develop better understanding of their world through language, preschoolers begin to learn how to control their behavior and how different behavior results in different outcomes. This understanding of the relationship between cause and effect is a prerequisite for learning self-control. "What happens when I pout, whine, or have a tantrum?" "What happens when I do not listen?" Preschoolers begin to understand intentions. The concept of "by accident," as well as the idea of doing something "on purpose," becomes clearer. "What happens when I hit?" "What happens when I take somebody's toy?" Because children at this age now have some ability to sequence events and understand the result of their behavior, you can begin to teach them responsibility and accountability, key ingredients for teaching children to make correct decisions.

There is an important caution. The ability to understand language, sequence events, and comprehend cause and effect increases greatly with age. A three-year-old's ability to understand language and right from wrong is much less than a six-year-old's ability. These abilities also vary among children the same age. An older three-year-old is typically more capable of understanding than a younger three-year-old. Since every child's rate of development is unique—even twins develop at slightly different rates—be sensitive to your preschooler's level of language development and comprehension. Be patient. Your child's language *will* develop.

While there is a wide range of normal development, there are, however, some children who demonstrate behavior problems that are in fact the result of hearing impairments or underlying communication delays that interfere with their ability to understand, use, and process language.

If you have concerns about your preschooler's communication skills, or if he becomes frustrated and angry when he attempts to communicate, seek the assistance of a speech and language pathologist through your school district or health services. Early intervention is important in preventing future learning problems and negative behavior patterns. For more information about children with special needs, see chapter 24.

When preschoolers are unable to use language to express feelings, needs, or desires, they often use their behavior as a method of expression. These behaviors are often annoying and sometimes defiant and disobedient, yet they are not always intentional. Some may be due to a young child's inability to communicate and express himself. By understanding typical language development, you will be better able to tell if your child's behavior is intentional or reflects his inability to understand, express, or process language. Each situation requires completely different strategies. Let's explore what they are.

"Please Use Your Words"

Lynn has finished all her milk and wants more. She begins to cry.

"Please use your words, Lynn. Say *more*," her mother asks.

Lynn stops crying, looks at her mother, and says, "Mo."

"Good. Here is *more* milk. Thank you for using your words."

After a child is a year old, it is time to introduce the concept of using your words. This means that your child needs to use words rather than whining or crying when he wants something, such as "up" or "more."

Young children may not always articulate the exact sounds correctly. That is normal. Some sounds are not mastered until the age of seven. In the beginning, accept any sound your child makes, but you may want to repeat the correct word, "more." This is how children learn correct pronunciation.

The purpose of this technique is to teach children that using words to express what they want is better than whining or crying. You can introduce this technique when your child is as young as one year old, but even if your child is three or four, you can introduce this technique successfully. For example, three-year-old Mark runs into the kitchen, crying.

"What's wrong?" his mother asks.

Mark continues to cry.

"Please calm down and tell me what happened. Take a deep breath. Please use your words."

It may take several months of consistent teaching before your child understands when and how to use his words, and even after getting the basic concepts down, all children will need cues and reminders throughout the preschool years and even into later childhood. As your child matures, you may want to modify your approach as well. Take the case of three-year-old Beth.

Beth: (Begins to whine because she cannot unzip her backpack.)

Robin: "I cannot understand what you want when you talk like that. Use your big girl words, and I will be happy to help you. Say, 'Mom, can you help me, please?' "

Teaching preschoolers to use their words also applies to their relationships with siblings and peers. As children grow older and learn to play independently with other children, words allow them to navigate social situations. Words help them get what they want without conflict: "Could I please have the boat after you, Bryan?" Words help children learn to share: "Taylor, would you like to trade Barbies with me?" Words help them express feelings: "I don't like it when you tease me, please stop." When children become upset while playing, remind them to think about the words they could use. Don't hesitate to tell your child, "Your words are powerful. Think about what you need to say."

Communicating When a Child Is Upset

Parents often forget that when young children are upset or angry, they are experiencing strong emotions that create a lot of internal mental "noise." Children are not good listeners when they are upset. As a result, they are not able to comprehend long sentences, which run words into one another. Use simple words and phrases that your child understands in order to increase your child's understanding of what you are asking. Let's see how Melissa and Kent's mother put this strategy into practice.

Melissa and Kent are arguing about their toys. Mother sees that both children are upset. Rather than beginning a long discussion about the merits of sharing, Mother intervenes with simple directions. "Please stop. Calm down. Please share the toys." These short, simple sentences help children focus on what it is that they need to do. Be specific about what you want your child to do. Do not dwell on what it is that you do not want him to do. This is essential when a child is upset, and an important rule to keep in mind whenever you are communicating with a child: Focus on positive behavior.

Using Language to Teach Correct Behavior

Development of language and understanding is what makes it possible to teach preschoolers appropriate behavior. A child needs to understand intention before he can learn right from wrong. A child must be able to generalize before he can take what he learns in one situation and apply it to a new but similar situation. All of these abilities rapidly develop during the preschool years.

Most preschoolers misbehave because they have not yet learned self-control. Successful parents use language and reasoning to teach their preschoolers behavioral self-control. This is hard work, requiring dedication and commitment. It is sometimes easier to control your preschooler than to take the time and energy to teach him to control himself. Remember that discipline is everything we do as parents to teach our children to think for themselves and make good decisions. So take the time to teach. The following sections will show you how to use language to teach your preschooler to think through situations and then choose the correct behavior.

How to Teach "Good Listening" Skills

Four-year-old Travis seems to be in a world of his own. He does not listen when his mom asks him to get dressed. He does not respond when Dad calls his name. He has difficulty paying attention for long periods of time. He hops from activity to activity and toy to toy. At times he is so involved in what he is doing he shuts out everyone. At other times Travis's parents feel he behaves this way just to upset them: "Sometimes he listens fine. Then there are times we have to yell to get him to hear us."

Travis probably does not have an attention deficit. Travis is most likely not misbehaving. Travis is a preschooler, and his "not listening" is typical. Preschoolers have difficulty attending and listening because their brains and nervous systems are still developing. It may be several years before these skills are fully functional.

Travis is exhibiting common behavior for a preschooler; in fact, the question I am frequently asked by parents of preschoolers is, "What should I do when my child does not listen?" Children have been "not listening" to their parents since biblical times. Most parents believe that their preschoolers have selective hearing—they hear fine when they choose. If you believe your child's ability to listen needs improvement, there are things you can do. But first, remember some basic principles.

Listening skills need to be taught as part of language development. Listening requires attention. Since attention skills are just developing, preschoolers use much of their mental energy when they engage in activity. They can attend to one thing at a time, and it is often difficult for them to shift gears to attend to something new. Think about when your child is playing a game or watching television. His attention becomes riveted on one thing. When you call his name or ask him to do something, do you sometimes feel your child is deliberately ignoring you? In many cases he isn't, but his brain is so absorbed in one thing that he does not process the words you are saying. This may appear to be deliberate ignoring, but it is not. The brain builds a barrier against outside events so the child can stay engaged without distraction. This is typical preschool behavior. (It can also appear in older children and some spouses!)

To improve your child's ability to listen, model good listening. Show your preschooler how to be a good listener. When your child talks to you, stop what you are doing, and listen. Put down the paper or mute the television. Look at your child. Make eye contact. Repeat what he says. This shows him how to listen and also lets him know that what he is saying is important to you. Be a "good listening" example.

Use positive verbal feedback. Look for good listening. When you call her name and she responds, recognize her listening: "Thank you for being a good listener." When children follow your directions, it is important to reinforce them: "Thank you for picking up your toys. Good listening." This technique is simple but extremely potent. It teaches children that it is important to be good listeners and do what they are asked.

Mona used the fortune cookie technique to promote better listening. Her family would often go out for Chinese food. Mona would read her daughter's fortune cookie: "Always listen to your parents to bring good luck."

What to Do About Not Listening

No matter how positive you are about reinforcing good listening, there will still be situations when your child does not listen. There are several factors to consider before deciding what to do when your child does not listen to you. In most situations, when your child intentionally ignores you, he is misbehaving. Techniques such as redirection or time-out may be needed. Redirection is discussed in chapter 7; time-out, in chapter 15. Knowing when your child's behavior is intentional is not easy to determine, but the following techniques will improve behavior.

Preschoolers often become entranced when watching television. Maddy becomes so involved in some television programs that she blocks out everything around her. This is not a problem unless one of her parents needs her attention. Their strategy involves calling her name, waiting about ten seconds, then calling her name again. If Maddy does not respond, then Mom or Dad uses the remote control to turn off the television. The first time her father tried this, Maddy got angry and wanted to know why her dad had turned off her show. He explained that he had been calling her name, but she hadn't heard him, so he turned off the television so she could listen better. He promised that when they were finished talking, he would happily turn the television on again. Maddy's parents have repeated this several times, and she has been learning to listen, so they need to turn off the TV less and less. Now when her dad has to turn off the television, she will turn to him and say, "Yes, Dad," and he will explain what he needs. These parents are teaching their daughter that even though she is watching television, she still needs to listen for her name.

Many parents are tempted to raise their voice or shout when children do not listen. This may break through the attention barrier but can lead to more unnecessary yelling. Your children will learn to yell at you to get your attention. Use cues to get your child's attention when he is deeply engaged in an activity. Nonverbal cues work well. Walk up to your child and touch him on the shoulder. Say his name. Sometimes saying his name in a whisper will break through to his attention better than raising your voice. Tell him you need him to listen. Ask for eye contact. Sit in a chair or squat down so that you are at your child's level.

When you have eye contact, you are more likely to have his attention, which increases his comprehension and understanding. When Jason's mother needs his attention, she uses this approach:

"Jason, I see that you are really enjoying your book. That's great. Could you please look at me for a minute? I have something important to say to you, and I need you to be a good listener."

Another technique to build better listening skills is to have your child repeat what you say. "Jason, it is time to pick up your toys. Tell me what I said?" Accept any reasonable approximation. The point is to check for listening and understanding. If your child cannot repeat your request, tell him again, "It is time to pick up your toys. What do you need to do now?"

Patterns of inattentiveness often occur when children experience emotional stress. When parents separate or divorce, children have increased anxiety, worry, and fear. The death of a family member, such as a grandparent, or of a pet can be very difficult for a child. Other sources of stress may come from a car accident, sudden family illness, or significant changes in a child's life, such as moving into a new home or the birth of a sibling. These kinds of situations create an emotional imbalance in children that interferes with their ability to attend and listen. Be especially sensitive to your preschooler if he has had a stressful experience. Stay calm and be patient. Talk about the issues if you can. Most preschoolers can adjust to these situations, but it takes time.

If you have older children, be cautious. Joyce has three children, aged eight, six, and three. Because her two older children were well behaved and good listeners, she expected her preschooler to listen as well as the older children. Once Joyce realized that she needed to adjust her expectations for her preschooler, she found the younger child's behavior much less irritating.

Communicating So Your Child Can Listen

Just as your preschooler sometimes has trouble switching gears when fully involved in an activity, she may have trouble taking in lots of information at once. Do not overload your preschooler with too many requests or directions at one time. For example:

"It's time for bed. Get your pajamas on. Your blue ones are clean. They are in the top drawer. Brush your teeth, and I'll be in to tell you a story."

If your child fails to complete all of these directions, it is not because she is not listening, it is because there are too many things for her to remember. Give young children one instruction at a time. As a child's ability to attend and remember develops, give two or three directions and see what happens. If your child can complete your requests, reinforce her for doing a good job. If it becomes frustrating for her, try again another day.

Remember that your preschooler's understanding of the world is very basic. If you tell your child to clean up his room, for example, he may understand the concept but not know what to do first. Be more specific: "Ian, it is time to clean up. Can you start by putting all your cars in the bucket?" By giving him an idea of what to do first, he will be more likely to get started.

Being able to communicate to your child also depends on your child's emotional state. Children who are upset or crying are not good listeners. Their attention is preoccupied by whatever is upsetting them. Help your child calm down first. Then get his attention. Then talk.

You are at the playground, and it is time to go home. Leaving fun activities is seldom popular with children—is it with yours? Here is how you might handle this common situation: "Celia, come here, please. It is time to go home."

Celia begins to cry, and her mother asks again.

"Celia, I am sorry. We have to go now."

Celia still cries, and her mother helps her calm down by acknowledging her feelings: "I know you are sad because we have to leave. I am sorry we have to leave, too. But it is time to go."

Next, the mother must get her attention: "Celia, please look at me. Please be a good listener."

Then explain why you need to leave: "We have to go because it is time to meet Daddy. We will come back to the park another day."

This a time to be aware not only of how we communicate with our preschoolers, but also of how they speak to us. Preschoolers use the words they have in their language memory to express themselves. When you ask them to tell you how they feel when they are ill, you get remarkable responses. "My brain is cracked" describes a headache. "I have crickets in my throat" tells you his throat hurts. "My nose has glue in it" describes a stuffy nose.

Sometimes your child responds to your requests with words that are completely unrelated to the subject. This may be because she understands that a verbal response is required, and she is using words she knows rather than providing no response at all. When this occurs, acknowledge your preschooler's response. Then repeat your request. "Liana, please go get your shoes." "Here is my doll, Mommy." "Your doll is very pretty. Please go find your shoes."

When your child does not have the expressive language needed to respond to a request, provide the appropriate words for your child to imitate. This is an excellent way of minimizing frustration that can escalate into an emotional reaction or misbehavior. It is also important to give preschoolers additional time to think. It is okay to ask a young child, "Do you need more time?" or, "Do you need my help?"

Learn the Danger Signals

Look for situations or circumstances that may agitate your preschooler or create inattentiveness. The most common of these factors are hunger and overtiredness. This often occurs when children arrive home from their day at preschool. They may be cranky or in a poor mood. Create a daily routine for your preschooler, including a snack and a calm activity, such as watching a television program or reading a story. Once your preschooler's physical needs are met, he will be more able to attend and listen.

Another common issue is sweets. For example, Julie becomes very active after eating chocolate. To reduce this problem, her mother limits her intake. Some children become too excited when they play certain games, engage in certain activities, or play with certain children. This is typical and should *not* be considered a problem unless your child's behavior becomes out of control. If you can predict when these situations may occur, talk privately with your child before play begins. Remind him of the rules and tell him you want him to have fun, but you expect proper behavior as well. Remind your child to be listening for your voice. "When I call your name, you need to be a good listener. I know you can do it!"

Birthday parties are often the perfect combination of too much sugar and too much excitement. Talk with your child before you leave the house. Explain how you expect her to behave and be a good listener:

"Amy, I want to talk with you before we leave for Gracie's party. I want you to have fun playing with your friends. I also want you to remember to listen to Gracie's mom and me. Listen for my voice. If I call your name, say, 'Yes, Mom!' "

When You Are Ignored

There are times when preschoolers intentionally do not listen. They hear you but ignore you; sometimes they even put their hands over their ears to emphasize the fact that they are not listening to you. This is usually a preschooler's way of getting control. She may be upset with you for something that happened earlier, and now she wants you to be upset. Perhaps she did not get her way; now she will make sure you don't get yours.

If you believe that your preschooler is deliberately ignoring you, stay calm. If you get upset or angry or start yelling or nagging, your child wins his bid for control, and you will have engaged in a power struggle. When you remain calm, you are better able to think through the situation and persuade your child to listen. Figure out what your child is upset about and recognize his need for control: "I see that you are upset because you could not watch your show. I know you really wanted to see it. I get upset when I cannot always do what I want to do."

Give your preschooler time to think. Explain the consequences of not listening: "If you don't take your bath now, we won't have time for a story." Then add encouragement. "I hope you make the right decision. I really want to have time for the story."

Provide clear and concise expectations. Use simple words. Speak slowly. Repeat your directions. Remember that children have more difficulty listening when they are engaged in activities or when they are upset. If your child seems to be ignoring you while he is playing, use a cue to gain his attention: "I am not sure you heard me because you didn't answer me." Always help calm an upset child before talking to him. Even when you practice these strategies consistently, your child will not always listen to you. Manage these situations as misbehavior. It may be necessary to interrupt your child's playing and redirect him to pick up his toys. It may be necessary to carry your child and leave the park while she is screaming. But as a long-term strategy, you should always consider your child's ability to understand and use language as a way of building better listening skills. Most importantly, when your preschooler listens the first time, recognize the good listening. "Thank you for being a good listener." When your preschooler follows directions the first time, recognize the correct behavior: "You followed directions. Good for you!"

Use Positive Directions

Bill Cosby tells the story of God and Adam. What did Adam say when God said, "Don't eat the apple"? "What apple?" When you tell preschoolers not to do something, it plants the idea of doing it. It often arouses their curiosity. Instead, you need to use words that teach your preschooler correct behavior. Tell him what to do rather than what not to do. Give positive directions rather than negative directions. This is difficult for many parents. It is contrary to the way many of us were raised. Yet positive directions teach preschoolers to think about what you expect from them. Positive directions plant the idea—do the right thing.

Four-year-old Brad and his father enjoy playing catch. Dad is always encouraging Brad to "throw the ball." One day Brad was holding an apple over his head as if to throw it. Dad shouted, "Don't throw that apple." Brad immediately threw the apple at Dad. Was this deliberate disobedience or a misunderstanding? While this situation could easily be viewed as deliberate disobedience, it probably was not. Brad heard the word *throw*, which triggered an apple launch. After all, Dad and I like playing catch. Brad missed the word *don't*. Dad always says, "Throw the ball." He does not say, "Don't throw the ball." A safer instruction would have been, "Please bring the apple to me," or "Please put the apple in my hand," or "Please put the apple on the table."

Meanwhile, three-year-old Jessica was sitting on the kitchen floor eating cookies while reciting the rule: "No cookies before lunch." Jessica could repeat the direction, but she did not understand it. When she saw the cookie jar, she thought about cookies, since that is what she understood. She missed the part about not having cookies until after lunch. By stating directions in positive terms—"Cookies after you eat lunch"—preschoolers learn correct behavior more easily.

This strategy helps—but it is not flawless. Most three-year-olds cannot wait until after lunch for anything, especially a cookie. A good rule to teach your child is: "Ask Mom when you want a cookie." Then you can decide at that moment if a cookie is okay. If it is not, you can explain why. Explain the reasons for your decision: "I am afraid that if you have a cookie now, you may get a tummy-ache. You can have a cookie after you eat your lunch." If you take the time to explain and reason with your child, she will be more willing to comply with your request.

Poopyhead

Any preschool teacher will tell you of the amazing, almost magical power of the word *poopy*. Say it in a preschool classroom, and it hurls every child to the floor, laughing hysterically. Words like *poopy, peepee,* and *poopyhead* are more contagious than a virus. Preschoolers are fascinated with poopy or potty words. Parents are extremely embarrassed by them, especially if it is your child who starts the epidemic in class.

Preschoolers enjoy repeating words to each other that they believe they shouldn't be saying because it excites them and gives them power. When a preschooler uses a potty word or even a stronger cuss word, he learns that the word has a strong emotional effect on parents and teachers, especially if we react impulsively and dramatically. Preschoolers learn that they no longer have to actually do something to get your attention; they can simply say something. You cannot shelter your children from foul language, but you can respond to it appropriately when it occurs.

The best response is to ignore it. Do not overreact when you hear the first potty word flowing from your child's voice. You will have to fight off your inclination to laugh, cough, choke, scream, or faint. This is difficult to do, but it is important that you stay calm and rational. Keep a straight face. Use positive directions by redirecting your child with appropriate words:

Susie: "You're a poopyhead!"

Sarah: "You're a poopyhead!"

Mom: "What's wrong, children?"

Susie: "Sarah took my red crayon. It's mine."

Mom: "This is a good time to be taking turns and sharing."

Susie: "But I want it."

Mom: "Try this. 'Can we take turns, Sarah? Please.' "

Susie: "Can we take turns, please?"

Mom: (Speaking to both children.) "*Poopyhead* is not a polite word. You are always so polite. Mom and Dad do not use words that are not nice, and we hope you don't either."

Mom deals with the real issue first—a disagreement about sharing. Mom helps Susie use other words to solve the problem before addressing *poopyhead*. The more attention you give the potty words, the more often they will be used. Do not lecture your preschooler about the morality of bad language, as it will only make them feel ashamed or guilty. Simply explain that the word is not nice or not polite and then ask them to not use the word again. Remember to encourage polite language: "Susie, you have been very polite to your sister today. Good for you. I know you are a polite person." Most importantly, be a proper role model and set a good example. If you cuss, your children will cuss, and a thousand positive redirections won't help. There is more on being a good model in chapter 6, "How Preschoolers Learn."

A mother recently asked if it was illegal now to wash a child's mouth out with soap. It is not illegal, but it is inhumane and ineffective. Do not put soap or Tabasco sauce or pepper in a child's mouth when he uses a bad word. This would be painful and confusing and create fear and shame, and it would not teach anything useful. Some parents like to use a made-up word as an expletive. You can ask your children to make up a word, such as *glubbie*. Then everyone in the family can use *glubbie* rather than inappropriate words.

Tips for Potty Words

- Don't laugh, no matter how funny you think it is. If your preschooler thinks he can get attention this way, he will, regularly. If you ignore potty words, they will likely fade away.

- Don't overreact. Your child may use potty words to get you angry.

- Explain that some words offend people. It is not polite. "You are a polite boy. Please do not use that word. It is not polite."

- Teach substitute words, such as "oops" or "shucks."

- Do not expose your child to improper language on TV or in the movies.

- Teach the correct words for body parts. Children will feel important and be less intrigued with improper alternatives.

- If you are with your child when they hear a bad word, talk about it and remind them that it is not a polite word.

- Teach by example. Use polite language yourself.

Are You Whining?

The purpose of discipline is to teach children to make good decisions about their own behavior. Since preschoolers are not always aware that their behavior needs to be corrected, the first step is to help a child see that his behavior is inappropriate and needs to change. Rather than confronting your child about misbehavior, it is sometimes more strategic to pose a question about his behavior. This causes him to think about what he is doing.

Linda is whining to her mother about wanting to watch another cartoon. Mother asks, "Are you whining?" Linda thinks for a moment. If Linda has learned from previous experiences that you do not give in to whining, she will probably stop. The key to this approach is consistency. Linda must know that you are consistent and will not give her what she wants when she whines. Here are some other questions that help preschoolers think about their behavior:

TEACHING PRESCHOOLERS TO "THINK ABOUT IT"

- Are you whining?

- Are you crying?

- Are you teasing?

- Are you playing softly with your brother?

- Are you using a quiet voice?

- Are you being a good listener?

- Are you being a good friend?

What Is This on My Ear?

Preschoolers love to bother or interrupt you while you are on the phone. In fact, it is a concern I hear from preschool parents everywhere I travel. Why this is such a prevalent behavior is hard to define, but there are a number of key factors. Young children want your undivided attention, always. They are familiar and comfortable with your talking and listening to them, so when you are on the phone talking to an invisible person, your preschooler may think that you have forgotten who to talk to—me!

Be realistic. You cannot have long conversations with preschoolers or toddlers around. If you need to make a lengthy call, wait for naptime or use distraction. Have plenty of toys and activities ready to keep your child engaged. If your have a toy phone for your child to play with, it is a good way to teach her about the phone. If you work from home or need to make long calls regularly, have a baby-sitter care for your child during your busy time.

Do not let a phone call turn into a power struggle. Teach your preschooler not to interrupt. Tell him how you expect him to behave before you make an important call. "When I am on the phone, Mommy needs to speak to someone else. You need to wait your turn. I will talk to you when I am finished. I promise it will only be a few minutes." Some children need more assurance. "You can stand here and hold my hand (or leg) while I am on the phone. But you need to be quiet until I am finished."

Be consistent and do not get angry if your child continues to interrupt. Stay calm and remind him to wait. Most importantly, when you finish your call, thank your child for waiting. "You did a good job waiting. You were very quiet. Thank you. Now it is your turn. What would you like to talk about?"

Some children will still need a reminder. Roxanne has taught Shawn to wait her turn when Mom is on the phone. Occasionally, Shawn will interrupt. Roxanne reminds her with a question.

Roxanne: "What is this on my ear?"

Shawn: (Pauses a moment to think) "A telephone."

Roxanne: "You are right. What do you need to do?"

Shawn: "Wait my turn."

Roxanne: "You are right. Please wait. I will be finished in a minute. Thank you."

This approach is similar to "Are you whining?" It reminds children to think about their inappropriate behavior and then self-correct it.

Learning Self-Control: What Preschoolers Need

The goal of successful discipline is to teach your children self-control, which is a long-term and ongoing process. Children need certain abilities before they can control their own behavior. Here is a list of the readiness skills that preschoolers need in order to learn self-control. These skills are developmental, which means they emerge during the preschool years and then grow with guidance and teaching throughout childhood. Nurture these skills as they appear, and your preschooler will more easily learn to control his behavior.

The ability to pay attention and listen.

An understanding of the vocabulary you use to explain what you expect.

An understanding of the behavior that you expect.

An understanding of how he chooses his behavior.

An understanding of cause and effect.

An understanding of how his choices have outcomes.

The ability to use words to express his needs, wants, feelings, and confusions.

How to Teach Good Listening Skills

Model good listening. When your preschooler talks to you, stop what you are doing and listen. Look at your child. Make eye contact. Repeat what he says.

Catch your preschoolers being good listeners. When you call his name and he responds, recognize him for listening: "Thank you for being a good listener." When preschoolers follow your directions, recognize them: "Thank you for picking up your toys. Good listening."

Use cues to get your child's attention when he is deeply engaged in an activity. Nonverbal cues work well. Walk to your child and touch him on the shoulder.

Say his name. Sometimes saying his name in a whisper breaks through better than raising your voice.

Tell him you need him to listen. Ask for eye contact: "Look at me, please."

Sit in a chair or squat down so that you are at your child's level. When you have eye contact, you are more likely to have his attention, which increases his comprehension and understanding.

Communicate with your child at his level. Ask your child to repeat what you say: "James, it is time to get dressed. Please tell me what I said?" (This does not guarantee that he really understands what you want.)

Do not overload your preschooler with too many requests or directions at one time: "It's time to get dressed. Get your clothes on. Your red pants are clean. They are in the top drawer. Your T-shirt is on your bed."

When your child does not have the expressive language needed to respond to a request, provide the appropriate words for your child to imitate. Say, "Yes, Mom."

Being a good listener also depends on your child's physical and emotional state. Children who are tired or hungry are not good listeners. Children who are upset or crying are not good listeners.

How to Give Positive Directions

Preschoolers need to understand what behaviors are allowed and which ones are not, and why. Emphasize the correct behavior by asking children to do what you want instead of telling them what they did wrong.

INSTEAD OF SAYING:	SAY:
Stop crying.	Please dry your tears. Calm down. I know you can do it.
Stop fighting.	Please share your toys. Please take turns. I know you can work this out together.
Stop teasing.	Please ask in a polite voice. Use nice words.
Stop whining.	Please use your words. Use a big-girl voice.
Stop squirming—sit still.	Quiet legs and arms, please. Let your legs and arms rest.
Stop screaming.	Use a quiet voice. Use an inside voice. Can you whisper? My ears hurt. Please use a soft voice.
Stop hitting.	Please keep your hands to yourself. Use a gentle touch, please.
Stop throwing toys.	Toys are for playing.

3

How Temperament Affects Behavior

As toddlers approach their second birthday, it becomes obvious to everyone around that their temperament is beginning to emerge. This is the time when toddlers develop *their* way of doing things and begin to assert their will on you. Parents begin to identify their own personality traits in the behavior of their children. These traits are often most noticeable when children are very happy—or very upset. For the astute parent, this is a time of great personal insight—you begin to see yourself in your child!

Temperament refers to the aspects of our personality that are inborn. Do not be concerned that you did something right or wrong when your child was an infant. Temperament affects the way we interact with the world around us. It describes how children behave rather than why they behave. Temperament affects the way children learn, their personal relationships, the way they solve problems, the way they manage frustration and anger, and the way they meet the challenges of growing up.

While temperament remains relatively stable over our lifetime, it can change or develop with experience and maturity. Diversity in temperament helps explain why children behave differently. Most experts in child development view behavior as a relationship between temperament and environment. Behavior is the result of the child's inborn attributes fitting into the world around him. Your child's behavior is often the result of the interaction between his temperament and your parenting style.

The Different Types of Temperament

Although there has been considerable research on temperament during the past four decades, opinions differ regarding the specific characteristics of temperament. Some studies view temperament as a simple concept—some children have "easy" temperaments, while others have "difficult" temperaments. Some studies refer to children as "tranquil" or "spirited." Or perhaps you would agree with Bill Cosby, who says that there are basically two types of children: difficult and impossible! Other studies describe temperament as having many characteristics.

1. Children have different activity levels. Some have more physical energy and are always on the go. They tend to be loud. They have difficulty sitting still. Others have less energy and tend to play quiet games, draw, and watch television more.

2. Children have different types of moods. These range from pleasant and friendly to more reserved and shy. Some children cry more than others do.

3. Some children are more emotional than others. As a result, some are easy to soothe, while some remain upset for long periods. Some children are cooperative, while others are more disagreeable and stubborn.

4. Children have different levels of flexibility or adaptability. Some children are more regular or predictable than others. Their life has routine. They fall asleep, wake up, eat, and nap at much the same time each day. For other children, each day is different. Some adjust to changes in schedule better than others.

5. Certain children seek adventure and excitement. They will taste new foods but may also be the child to jump out of a tree. Other children are more withdrawn and reserved. They are more cautious about new situations and new people.

6. Some children are more persistent. They keep trying. They stick with it. Other children give up more quickly. They are more easily frustrated when a task is difficult.

7. Some children are more distractible. They have shorter attention spans and get diverted by everything nearby. Others are able to stay focused and block out distractions.

Temperament is not good or bad. Certain characteristics can be positive in some situations and challenging in others. On some days, persistence creates a "can-do" attitude. Other days it creates a "won't do" attitude.

We learn about our children's temperament by observing the way they respond and relate to the world around them. Being responsive to the different aspects of your preschooler's temperament empowers you to accommodate her uniqueness while guiding her inborn traits in a positive way. This results in a better "fit" between your child's temperament and your parenting style.

Over many years of doing workshops for preschooler parents, I have found that three temperament types emerge as being the most common. These are the types that have generated the most questions and concerns. I refer to these as *energetic, persistent,* and *shy.*

Energetic Temperaments

Dustin was a very active four-year-old. He would run around the house, jumping from toy to toy and from one activity to another. His mother, Judy, would get upset and reprimand him: "Dustin, please stop running. Stop making so much noise. Find something to do and be quiet." Due to her frustration, she found herself nagging Dustin. The nagging did not change Dustin's behavior, but once Judy understood that her son had an active temperament, she was able to adjust her parenting style. She planned physical activities for Dustin, taking him on bike rides or walks to the park or playground. On days when scheduling did not permit trips away from home, Judy would find time to play with him in the backyard. By keeping Dustin engaged in activities that were planned, she made sure that his energy was productive rather than irritating. Judy and Dustin spent more time together and increased their positive interactions—they began to have fun.

An energetic child can be a challenge. If your preschooler has abundant energy and runs around the house getting in trouble by knocking over lamps and bumping into furniture, do not punish him by sending him to his room for long periods. Restricting him to a confined space will frustrate him and may induce a tantrum or angry outburst. Being filled with energy is not misbehavior. By understanding his active temperament, you can channel his energy into a more appropriate physical activity. Build routines into his day that allow him a constructive way to release his energy. Exercise is a great release for parents and children. Several parents have told me that they have a daily routine where their children exercise. There are children's exercise programs on television, and children's exercise videotapes. This is an excellent way to teach healthy habits, spend time together, and channel your child's energy.

Persistent Temperaments

Based on my personal and professional experience, I have found that children who are bright, verbal, and stubborn may be the most difficult to manage. I refer to these children as attorneys-in-progress. They love to argue their point. They always have a better reason than you why they should or should not do something. In recent years, these children have been referred to as "strong-willed." Children with persistent temperaments can wear you down because they do not give up.

Four-year-old Lucy always refuses to pick up her toys (actually, this is very common for this age). She begins by saying no and arguing: "I don't want to. No." Then she cries, sometimes throwing herself down and kicking her feet. Within moments of Mother's request, Lucy is emotionally out of control.

It would be easy to view Lucy's behavior as defiance or deliberate disobedience. Many parents might take the position, "I'll make her behave or else." That would be a mistake, and probably make the problem much worse. It would create more conflict and encourage Lucy to be more persistent and argumentative.

Persistent children do not like surprises or changes. They do not switch activities very well. Lucy's behavior appears to be defiance, but in fact it is part of her persistent temperament. Lucy needs plenty of time to prepare herself for change, even with reasonable requests like picking up toys. I have heard hundreds of parents wonder, "All I did was ask her to pick up her toys, and she went ballistic."

Lucy needs time warnings. (See strategy 6, "Anticipate Transitions," in chapter 7, and "The Difference Between Threats and Warnings" in chapter 9.) "Lucy, in a few minutes it will be time to pick up your toys. I will set the timer. When it goes off, I will help you get started." Helping Lucy get started helps her make a better transition. Use ample encouragement as you start. Give her a reason to pick up toys: "You are doing great. Good for you. Your toys will be in your toy box when you need them." This strategy works well to guide persistent children into being more cooperative, but that does not happen overnight. It is a long-term, proactive approach, but much better than constant conflict.

Do not get trapped into arguing with persistent children. Use warnings to help prepare your child for transitions. State your requests clearly and consistently. Stay calm. If you get angry, you are being defeated. There is a bright side. Even though children who are bright, verbal, and persistent may be difficult to manage as children and adolescents, they typically do well in life. These are the achievers and leaders of the world. Having this to look forward to may help you get through their childhood a little more easily.

Shy Temperaments

Shyness can be due to fear, stress, and anxiety. Almost all preschoolers show some shyness in new situations or with new people. It is normal if your child often acts shy during the first few minutes of a new situation. Once your child sees that you are not afraid, he will begin to feel comfortable and less shy. Children who are excessively shy, however, do not make this adjustment in a few minutes.

Alice thinks she is ready for Nicole's first day of preschool. She has done everything imaginable to prepare her daughter. When mother and daughter enter the school, Nicole wants to please, yet within seconds she has wrapped herself around Alice's legs. She does not want to go. Nicole is not grasping at her mother for attention or control, but because she is shy and probably afraid. This clingy behavior reflects her need for reassurance. She will need time and encouragement.

Start by being proactive. Shyness decreases with practice. Take your child to places where she can practice meeting new people. Role-play and rehearse what she can say when she meets people. "Hello, my name is Nicole. I am four." Do this slowly. If you push, you will create more anxiety. As your preschooler gradually learns to interact with others, she will gain more confidence and become less shy.

Do not criticize your preschooler for being shy. Do not label your child as the "shy one." If your child feels shameful or guilty, it will make his shyness worse. A clinging, shy child may stand out. People may comment, "She is just being shy." Minimize this situation. You could smile and say, "She is fine around people she knows."

Explain to your preschooler that it is okay to feel shy. Empathize with his shyness or fears. Use stories from your childhood about situations where you may have been shy. There are a number of excellent children's books about shyness. (See the reference list in the appendix.) Read stories about shyness with your preschooler. Always discuss the moral in the story and how your child can apply the message.

Encourage outgoing behavior. When Alice would see Nicole talking to other children, she would recognize her for being brave: "I saw you playing today. It looked to me like you were having fun. I knew you would enjoy meeting new friends."

Parents of shy children worry about social development. Will she ever let go of my leg? Will he ever have friends? While parents are often embarrassed by their shy preschooler, remember that most of these children grow up to be perfectly well-adjusted and successful adults.

Use Strategies That Match Your Child's Temperament

By understanding your preschooler's temperament, you can develop more effective discipline strategies. Knowing your preschooler's temperament helps you determine if your child's actions are intentional misbehavior or a natural part of her disposition. Knowing that some behaviors are due to temperament helps you feel less guilty and more confident. For example, you can perceive a shy child's behavior as embarrassing and feel guilty, or you can see shyness as characteristic and feel confident that your positive strategies result in improvement.

Many problem behaviors reflect your preschooler's inborn temperament. Do not punish your preschooler for his temperament. Instead, be proactive. Try to circumvent recurring problems by planning activities and routines that fit both your child's and your needs. If your preschooler has difficulty with transitions, plan extra time in the morning— get to preschool early. If your preschooler is shy, don't expect him to be the life of the birthday party, even if it is his own birthday party. Don't tell your cautious preschooler that Santa won't bring her any presents because she refused to sit on his lap at the mall. If your preschooler is easily frustrated by new tasks, don't buy the 400-piece building set. Encourage your child's natural interests, and you will all be happier.

Create an environment that matches your preschooler's temperament. As your child grows and matures with your support and confidence, he will learn to regulate his temperament so that his behavior matches your expectations. Put your own ambitions aside. Parents who try to force their preschooler to fit the image of "my perfect child" often end up frustrated and discouraged.

Recognize your own feelings. No one has children because they want to add stress, frustration, and anger to their lives, yet at times children can cause them in abundance. Talk about your feelings and frustrations with other parents you trust. This will help you remain calm and patient. You may also get some good ideas to help you deal with the problems you are facing. Being able to vent with another adult will help not only you but also your preschooler.

Accept children regardless of their temperament. Whether your preschooler is tranquil or spirited, easy or difficult, you can be successful. Understanding your preschooler's temperament improves your judgment—but it is not magic. Understanding temperament helps you adjust your parenting style so that you can teach your preschooler self-control and guide him to become a happy person. It helps you nurture your child's nature.

Remember: adjusting your parenting style to accommodate your preschooler's temperament is a productive strategy; labeling your child is not. Children believe what you tell them. If you tell your energetic preschooler that he is "hyperactive," he will be. If you tell him that he can't control himself, he won't. Knowing that your child is naturally energetic does not mean that he will never learn to be calm. Temperament is not fate, nor is it an excuse for misbehavior. Knowing your preschooler's temperament does not mean you should give up trying to improve his behavior.

One helpful outcome of the study of children's temperament is the emergence of a number of excellent children's books that tell stories about the value of different temperaments. These storybooks emphasize the uniqueness of being who you are and give your children the opportunity to recognize and appreciate their own temperament. They are great at bedtime! (See the appendix for books about being different.)

4

How Self-Esteem Affects Behavior

Simply stated, your self-esteem is your attitude or belief about yourself. Children who believe in themselves expect success from life. They feel good about themselves. They are confident, and they can take constructive criticism. Children with strong self-esteem are better learners, and more able to control their behavior. I have never worked with a child who was feeling worthwhile and misbehaving at the same time.

When children have poor self-esteem, they have difficulty learning, feel insecure, and lack persistence. They are oversensitive to what others think and often blame others when things go wrong. These children see the world as a place to fear. They feel unworthy, have little self-confidence, and do not have faith in themselves. Since they see themselves as failures, they often expect failure and behave accordingly—that is, they simply stop trying. For children who feel insecure, the surest way to avoid failure and embarrassment is to avoid participation; nothing ventured, nothing failed. Not trying makes more sense than trying hard and then failing anyway. Then the child can say, "Well, I didn't even try," which is better than saying, "I tried hard but failed."

Your child's future is contained within her self-esteem. In large part, this is because children believe in reasons for their successes and failures. Over time, your child will internalize these causes, and they will become part of her view of herself.

Children with strong self-esteem see their efforts and abilities as the cause of their triumphs and accomplishments. These children see failure as a temporary setback or challenge that can motivate them to put forth more effort to overcome their disappointment. On the other hand, children with poor self-esteem see success as the result of chance or destiny. This weakens their confidence and reduces effort: "It does not matter how hard I try. It's just luck." This can create hopelessness.

Your goal as a person should be to strive for healthier self-esteem. Your goal as a parent is to promote healthy self-esteem in your children. What follows are some basic beliefs and strategies that help your children feel good about themselves and what they do. Incorporate these into your style of parenting, and you will encourage strong, positive self-esteem in your children.

Feeling Good About Me

Give your preschooler love, respect, and acceptance, and he will develop healthy self-esteem. Support and encourage your preschooler, and he will gain confidence. For example, you are teaching your child how to ride a bike. He falls. If you say, "That's not how to do it. I've explained this once already. Pay attention this time," you are only reducing his self-esteem. A more productive comment would be, "Good try. You are doing better each time. I know you can do it." This reaction shows confidence in your child's abilities. It persuades your child to believe in himself.

When thinking about helping your child to learn to trust himself and be determined, you might remember the classic story of the Little Engine That Could—"I think I can, I think I can." When you believe you can do something, it will be easier to do.

Validate Your Children

Tell your preschooler that you love her, and do so regularly. Tell your child that you are happy he is in your family. You are proud to be his parent. Greet your child with warm words and a hug every morning when she awakens. Let her know she is special. Preschoolers need love and reassurance.

Accept, value, and love your children just the way they are. This does not mean that you have to love their misbehavior, but that you love your preschooler regardless of his misbehavior. When she misbehaves, you could say, "I love you. I do not like what you did." This message gives your child a feeling of security, since her misbehavior, which clearly you do not like, does not change your feelings about her.

Show your preschooler that he is an important person by treating him with dignity and respect. We often don't think about the messages we convey when our child has done something displeasing; think of the case of the spilled milk, for example. Suppose you invited your pastor to dinner. During dinner, he spills a glass of milk. How would you react? No doubt you would say something like: "Accidents will happen. Don't worry, it happens all the time. Here, I'll get it. Let me clean it up." Do you remember what you said the last time your child spilled a glass of milk? Was it something like this: "Not again! I told you to be more careful. You are so clumsy. You've ruined the tablecloth"?

Be a Good Helper

One day I asked Alyssa what she liked best about preschool. Her reply may surprise you: her favorite thing was being the teacher's helper. Preschoolers love to be helpers. When you ask your child's aid, state your requests in helpful terms. Don't say, "Pick up your toys." Say, "I need your help. Let's pick up these toys." Don't say, "Put your dirty clothes in the laundry." Say, "When you put your clothes in the laundry basket, it really helps me. Thank you." Preschoolers are more willing to do things if they feel they are being helpful.

Asking for your preschooler's help is one way to make her feel competent. Another way to build competence is to give your preschooler choices about what to eat and what to wear. This makes them feel important. When you give children choices, limit their options; two is usually enough. "Here are two outfits for school tomorrow. Which one do you want to wear?" If you are concerned about sending your child to school in an outfit that does not match, have your child choose the top, and you choose the bottoms.

Recognize your preschooler's contributions to the family. When your child helps match socks or feeds the cat, let him know that his help is appreciated. If your child makes a suggestion, give it value: "That is a very good idea. Thank you." Appeal to his innate desire to be responsible: "I think you are old enough now to pick up your dirty clothes and put them in the laundry basket."

Keep in mind that you should not do things for your preschooler that she can do for herself. Being overprotective can cause children to feel insecure or lazy. They will learn to depend on you to do things for them, which is the exact opposite of your goal—raising an independent and confident child.

Foster Compassion

Preschoolers feel good about themselves when they help others feel good. Teach your children to contribute to the well-being of others. Model compassion, kindness, and concern. Volunteer in the community and help others who are less fortunate. Even if your children are too young to accompany you, explain what you are doing and how your actions are helping others.

Many parents have their children collect outgrown clothing or forgotten toys to give to a children's shelter. Caring for pets teaches compassion and responsibility. Help friends in need or send cards to friends who are sick.

Learn Something New

Preschoolers gain confidence and build self-esteem by learning new skills and by trying new things. When preschoolers learn something new or accomplish a new skill, they feel successful and optimistic, which encourages them to be more determined and put in more effort. These in turn create another success—success gives birth to more success.

Unfortunately, many preschoolers are afraid to try something new. This is normal. Often they are reluctant because they are afraid they will fail. They will tell you, "I can't do it." You can encourage preschoolers to try new things without getting into arguments and power struggles. Recognize that the fear is real. Do not ask your preschooler to explain why he is afraid or reluctant to try something new. Instead, acknowledge your child's fear or apprehension: "Going down a slide can be a little scary. That's okay." Provide encouragement and support: "I think you can do it. Here, let me help you." Use examples from your childhood: "I was a little scared the first time my dad helped me go down a big slide." This gives your preschooler reassurance. You were afraid, and you survived.

Practice in private. Parents sometimes forget that preschoolers can be embarrassed in front of other children. Try going to the park alone to practice going down the slide. This could turn out to be great one-on-one time.

Nothing is more self-esteem-enhancing than working hard to accomplish a skill or task that is difficult. When five-year-old Elizabeth becomes frustrated while trying to print her name, her mother acknowledges that the task is not easy: "Your name has a lot of difficult letters. Go slowly. Just think about one letter at a time." Nurture persistence. Persistence is a gift for a lifetime: it teaches your child to pursue her goals. Be encouraging as your child attempts to complete a task by saying, "Keep trying and you will get it," or, "Working hard will pay off." Remember to offer congratulations when she achieves her goal: "Way to go. You stuck with it. You got it!"

Acknowledge Limitations

As important as it is for your preschooler to believe in his abilities, it is also crucial that he accept his weaknesses along with his strengths. Children with poor self-esteem only pay attention to their weaknesses. Since they dwell on their shortcomings, their positive qualities are overlooked. Explain that everyone has strong qualities and weak qualities. Even children with strong self-esteem need to learn this. Use yourself as an example.

Luke became upset one day when he was at T-ball practice because he could not hit as well as the other children. When he got home, his dad explained that each person has things he does well and things he does not do well. Using himself as an example, his father explained that when he was Luke's age, he was often disappointed. He wanted to be stronger, more coordinated, and more athletic. Sharing this kind of experience teaches your child that it is normal to feel disappointed. Be careful: don't fall into the trap of assuming that your weaknesses will become your child's. For example, do not say, "I was never good in math. You won't be either." This will set your child up for failure.

Accept Disappointments

There are few events more heartbreaking to a parent than watching her young child experience an intense disappointment. Preschoolers are so easily hurt, whether it is because his best friend did not play with him today or because she did not get invited to a birthday party. And yet at this age, disappointment is as common as bruised knees.

Recognize and empathize with your child's sadness and disappointment: "I see that you are very sad. That's okay. I would be sad, too. I am sorry this happened." Offer hope: "You will be sad for a while, but then you will feel better." Teach your preschoolers to accept and overcome disappointments. Explain that disappointments are part of life, and that we all have them. Help your children experience their disappointments without feeling that the results are tragic. Your child's self-esteem is enhanced each time he overcomes a disappointment or challenge.

Children are often disappointed or hurt by unkind words from other children. Natalie was upset because her friend Stacey called her a "bad girl." Here is how Natalie's mother helps her through the situation:

Mother: "Was that a nice thing to say or a mean thing to say?"

Natalie: "Mean."

Mother: "Do you think you are a bad girl?"

Natalie: "No."

Mother: "I agree. You are not a bad girl. You are a very good girl. Sometimes even friends say mean things sometimes."

By asking questions and summarizing Natalie's answers, her mother is teaching Natalie how to think through her feelings and accept disappointments.

Build Trust

There are two kinds of trust: relationship trust and environmental trust. Relationship trust is emotional, while environmental trust has to do with the safety and structure in a child's life.

Teaching your child relationship trust begins with your ongoing relationship with your child and involves a number of factors. Consistent parent behavior provides predictability, and it teaches children what you expect from them and what they can expect from you. Model trust for your child by keeping your promises. Children learn to be trustworthy by trusting in you.

Listen to your preschooler and help her sort through feelings that are new or confusing. Be fair. Give reasons why your child has to do certain things. When your child understands, she will be more trusting. Share stories about yourself. Preschoolers love hearing about things that have happened to you, especially the mistakes you made growing up. Spend time together. There is no substitute. Time builds relationships.

Establishing an environment your child trusts is very important. Preschoolers want to feel safe and protected, and they need security and predictability. Routines and schedules provide structure and help preschoolers anticipate events that will happen next. (For more on routines, see chapter 11.) Give your preschooler opportunities to be trustworthy. This will show him that you believe in his capabilities.

Beware False Praise

There is no doubt that praise, encouragement, and emotional support build confidence and enhance self-esteem development, *if the praise, encouragement, and support are genuine and deserved.* Verbal reinforcement for good behavior and self-control is a powerful motivator, but don't overdo it. Some parents compliment their preschoolers so many times in a day that the words become meaningless. Eventually, the children will not believe or trust what you say at all. Use praise and encouragement carefully, making sure it is sincere and specific. Praise the correct behavior or accomplishment, not the child. "You did a fine job picking up your toys. Good for you," is better than, "You are such a wonderful boy for picking up your toys." This implies a double message. Is your child not wonderful when his toys are all over the floor?

Be Careful When You Laugh

Three-year-old Mark always carried his stuffed animal, Big Bird, wherever he went. It was his best friend and comfort. One day Mark and his mom walked into a shop where a kindly lady looked at Mark and gave him a big smile. Mark was used to this. Then the lady said, "My, what a cute chicken," obviously referring to the big yellow bird tucked beneath Mark's arm. Mark looked up at the lady intently and exclaimed, "I am not a chicken, I am a boy!" Mom and the lady began to laugh out loud at Mark's clever remark. And then to everyone's astonishment, Mark began to cry. Why? He did not get the humor. Mark believed the lady called him a cute chicken. He simply corrected her, explaining that he was a boy. He did not understand that his remark was quite clever, coming from such a little person. It was funny to the adults but confusing to Mark, and it hurt his feelings to be laughed at when he was not expecting it.

It is hard to hold back laughter, but sometimes it is necessary. This is especially true when your child is doing something he should not do, but in a way that makes you laugh. When your child misbehaves and you laugh, he will think that what he is doing is cute and pleasing, and he will want to do it again.

Sometimes your laughter can make small problems bigger. A father told me about a situation where his four-year-old son, Andrew, began to get angry and argue with him. The dad said that his son was cute about the way he was trying to argue, and he began to laugh. His son then went into a tantrum and began screaming, "Why are you laughing?" Once again, this child was confused and hurt by his father's laughter.

Although these situations are sometimes unavoidable, be aware that they can and do hurt developing emotions and self-esteem. When the event is over, and your child is calmed down, discuss what happened. "Mark, what you said was so cute and clever that we laughed. We did not mean to hurt your feelings, and we are sorry if we did." Honesty and an explanation are always good strategies. "I am sorry that I laughed at you, Andrew. I did not mean to upset you. I am sorry." But don't forget, also, that humor and laughter should be an integral part of every parent-child relationship. Parents and children should have plenty of fun and laughs together. Humor builds a healthy family climate.

5

How Motivation Affects Behavior

 There are two kinds of motivation: internal and external. Think about why you get up and go to work each day. You get personal satisfaction from your work—internal. You also get paid—external. Most of us do not drive 100 miles an hour. We know it is unsafe—internal. We do not want to go to jail—external. Internal and external motivation work together to produce a responsible person.

All preschoolers are motivated to please their parents, teachers, and other adults. Preschoolers are motivated to play and have fun, to learn and experience new adventures in life. Despite this, they don't always behave well, and that's where discipline comes in.

Discipline is teaching preschoolers to make good decisions. It is an internal process that you cannot do for your children. You cannot control the way they think, and therefore you cannot control how they behave. Fortunately, you can influence the way they think and behave by using external motivation to influence and develop your children's internal motivation.

Strategies That Increase Motivation and Encourage Better Behavior

Spotlight Success and Accomplishments

Success creates good feelings and builds internal motivation. When your boss commends your work, you feel successful and continue to work hard. You can recognize good behavior and decisions to make your preschooler feel successful and boost his internal motivation. Success motivates preschoolers to continue to do the right thing. When you compliment your child for picking up his toys, he will feel good inside—he will feel successful. If you say, "Thanks for being a good helper. You did a very good job," he will be more motivated to be helpful in the future.

Some preschoolers believe they cannot be successful. This false belief usually comes from repeated failures. Sometimes it is the result of high expectations. Correct this problem by spotlighting the positive. Point out strengths. Show your child where he has made progress. Encourage him to believe in himself. This will help your child feel successful. Once success gets started, it continues.

Parents have a tendency to focus or dwell on negative behaviors. We tell our children what they are doing wrong. Misbehaviors get our attention. Many parents believe that being critical of mistakes is one way to focus their child on putting forth more effort. This is not true. Being critical deflates self-esteem. Focus on what your children do well.

A child who misbehaves frequently lacks the internal motivation to cooperate; instead, his internal motivation drives him to misbehave—to obtain negative attention or control. Use external motivation to redirect your preschooler's internal motivation. Use praise and encouragement, and charts and checklists or other external incentives, to create a good feeling in your preschooler, which in turn will build his self-esteem. This will get internal motivation going in the right direction. Use language that aims at self-reward and builds self-esteem. "I see that you are sharing with your brother. Good for you. I knew you could do it. I am very proud of you. I hope you are pleased with yourself." As your preschooler experiences good behavior and good feelings, he will be more motivated to behave in the future.

Create Interest and Eagerness

Make your preschooler's life fun and interesting. Preschoolers love to have fun, to play, and surprises. You can improve your child's behavior by playing games. Pat taught Katie how to make her bed by using role reversal. Katie played the mom, and Mom played the child. As a result, Katie was always eager to make her bed because she liked pretending she was the mother, and it had become a fun-filled activity.

Interest creates motivation. Suppose your three-year-old has difficulty listening to you read stories. Figure out what he likes to do and then get storybooks with lots of colorful pictures about that subject. If he likes dinosaurs, read books about dinosaurs. By reading books about dinosaurs, you will increase your preschooler's internal motivation to listen to the story, and make story time meaningful and fun. (The questionnaire at the end of this chapter will help you discover and stay in touch with your child's interests.)

Take One Step at a Time

Many parents make the mistake of giving preschoolers a task that is too complicated, and the child refuses to do it. Divide complex tasks into small sequential steps and teach the steps one at a time. Expect progress, not perfection. Develop expectations that build on success. This strategy is called *shaping* or *sequencing*. Consider this example:

Maria would like to teach Ben table manners. Table manners includes many behaviors: chewing with your mouth closed, swallowing your food before you talk, using silverware properly, using a napkin, passing food around the table, saying "Please pass the . . . ," "Please," and "Thank you." If Maria tries to teach all of these things at the same time, both she and Ben will be frustrated and fail. There are too many things for Ben to learn. Sequence the behaviors, and then teach them one at a time. You may need to work on one behavior for several days or weeks. Once it is learned, add the second, and then the third, and so on. The small sequence of steps improves the probability of success. Placing all the manners on Ben at once would have been unreasonable, and Ben would probably resist. Shaping takes time, but it is a good method of teaching because it encourages effort.

Use shaping to improve behavior gradually. Suppose your preschooler dawdles. He takes ten minutes to pick up his toys when it should take two or three. Set a timer and play "Beat the Clock." Begin with a time of five or six minutes. This is still an improvement over ten minutes. Recognize him for completing the job within a five-minute time limit, since a time limit of three minutes may cause failure. Once your child has accomplished the task numerous times within the five minutes, challenge him to see if he can do it faster and set the clock for three minutes.

If you want to teach your children to pick up after themselves, rather than doing it faster, you might try this strategy a mother shared with me. She bought her children a plastic grocery cart and taught them to push the basket around the house during cleanup time to pick up all the toys. This was creative and proactive!

When teaching new skills, reinforce improvements or steps in the right direction. Do not insist on perfect performance on your child's first attempt. Just because you have taught your five-year-old how to make his bed, do not expect him to do the job as well as you. He will be happy with a lumpy bedspread, and will steadily improve with your guidance and encouragement.

At times you may need incentives stronger than praise and encouragement. Incentives can be an allowance, toys, or privileges. Make an agreement with your child; for example, "Be a good listener this week, and we will do something special on Saturday." Children like working toward a goal. If you are asking your preschooler to do something for several days to earn a special incentive, be sure to use a chart or checklist to show your preschooler that he is making progress. (For more on charts and checklists, see chapter 11.) Do not set the standards too high; you do not want to create so much pressure that your child feels overwhelmed and unmotivated as a result. Don't ask your daughter to behave perfectly for a month and promise to take her to a movie if she does—that is expecting too much.

Whenever you use incentives such as rewards or privileges, always accompany the incentive with verbal encouragement. Always remind your preschooler that the reason to behave and work hard is to feel good about yourself. That is always more important than the actual incentive. Say, for example,

"Kevin, you have been a very good listener this week. Thank you. You have earned your prize. Tomorrow we are going to a movie. I hope you are proud of yourself. I'm glad you earned the movie, but being a good listener is even more important than the movie."

Family Climate

A pleasant family climate builds internal motivation and self-esteem. It develops in families where members speak politely to each other and discipline is positive. Everyone feels a sense of togetherness and cooperation. Structure is balanced with flexibility. Everyone is encouraged to pursue his or her own interests. The family has fun together. When the climate is warm and accepting, children learn your values and goals. Children are willing to accept guidance and punishment because they see that you are acting out of love and concern. If a problem occurs, children rebound more quickly. A pleasant family climate helps preschoolers feel secure and safe; children like everything in the family to run smoothly.

Unpleasant family climates develop in families where there is anger and criticism. The rules and structure are rigid—there is no room for flexibility. Everyone becomes defensive when something goes wrong. The parents see more bad than good, and as a result, the children are always bickering with each other.

Family climate begins with parents who are good models. Teach your preschoolers to thank people who are nice to them and to apologize to those they hurt. Teach them to be kindhearted, to comfort others who are not doing well. The best way to teach these qualities is by living them yourself.

Pleasant climate can be disrupted by a negative situation, such as an argument between two children. If your preschoolers have a conflict, help them reach a settlement; then redirect their energy. You may need to stay with them for a while to ensure better feelings toward each other. Try taking them for a walk or reading them a story. Whatever you do, it should be something pleasant.

Family climate can fluctuate. Some days are pleasant, others are not; this is normal. Your goal is to have more good days than bad days. If one parent promotes a pleasant climate and the other does not, the children will adjust. Don't be critical of your spouse, which may create more unpleasantness; stay positive, and it may rub off. Make your time with the children pleasant. Some pleasant climate is better than none.

One important aspect of pleasant family climate is humor. When everyone is feeling down, a little humor helps turn things around. Humor can also redirect misbehavior. This works especially well with preschoolers. Create some inside jokes with your child; for example, "Is that your Grinch face? What happened? What turned your smile face into a Grinch face?" If your child is familiar with the story of Snow White, you might make comparisons with Grumpy and Happy.

Have fun with your children. When Anthony was about fifteen, someone asked him what he remembered most about his childhood. "Playing monster" was his immediate answer. I would be the monster and chase him and Leah, or they would chase me. Playing monster did not cost any money, yet that is the thing he remembered most. All the expensive gifts were forgotten.

One type of humor that should be avoided with preschoolers is sarcasm. While older children and adults can appreciate sarcasm, preschoolers do not yet have the abstract reasoning capacity to understand the meaning behind such humor. They are too literal to understand that the person speaking actually means the opposite of what their words imply. A preschooler does not have the ability to decipher when "That's really bad" actually means "That is very good."

• YOUR TURN •

Strategies to Improve Family Climate

Make it a priority.

Spend one-on-one time with children.

Emphasize success.

Accent cooperation.

Speak in a pleasant tone of voice.

Practice giving compliments to each other.

Be helpful to each other.

Use manners.

Plan family activities.

Have dinner together.

Go to church together.

Read stories aloud.

Tell favorite family stories.

Write stories, make books.

Take pictures, make photo albums.

Develop shared hobbies—collect rocks, plant a garden.

Do drawings or arts and crafts.

Visit relatives.

Encourage humor and fun.

Tell jokes—read joke books.

Play board games—have fun!

Be a little silly—play monster!

Play "I Spy."

Enjoy music.

Listen to each other's favorite songs.

Sing and dance.

Make musical instruments, play songs.

Change the pace.

Go for a walk, hike, or bike ride.

Go to the park.

Go out for lunch, dinner, or dessert!

Go to the zoo or museum.

Go on a "Mystery Ride."

What You Can Do

Parents can do a lot of things to create and maintain a pleasant climate in their family. Try making a list of what those activities might be. Keep in mind that you will always have more fun when you plan activities together. The previous page has some ideas to get you started. (There is another list of activities in chapter 10.)

Write your own ideas here:

_____

_____

_____

_____

_____

_____

Test Your Knowledge About Your Preschooler's Interests

Knowing your preschooler's interests helps you become more proactive because you are able to create motivating activities. Think about your preschooler and then answer each question below as though your child were answering the question. You might want to add your own questions as well. When you are finished, read these questions to your preschooler and compare your answers to his. Many parents have told me that their children made a questionnaire for them. If you like, you can complete a questionnaire with each of your children. You may also repeat the activity every few months. Have fun.

Child's Name _____ **Date** _____

My favorite color is _____

My favorite book is _____

My favorite game is _____

My favorite movie is _____

My favorite TV show is _____

My favorite toy is _____

My favorite song is_____

My favorite fruit is_____

My favorite food for breakfast is _____

My favorite food for supper is _____

Other kids think I am _____

What I like best about Mommy is_____

What I like best about Daddy is _____

What I like best about me is _____   _____

When I grow up, I want to _____

I like people who _____

I like to learn about _____

I want to go to _____

6

How Preschoolers Learn

Educators and psychologists have been intrigued by how children learn for most of the twentieth century. Even though we have significantly greater insights and understanding now than we did a hundred years ago, we still have a lot to find out about how children learn. One thing we do know for sure: the best way to discover how preschoolers learn is to sit back and watch. Watching your preschooler's face as she figures out something for the first time, or puts two ideas together to create a third, is as exciting as it gets. I have always found this to be one of the most fascinating and rewarding aspects of parenting. This chapter presents some of the ways preschoolers acquire knowledge about themselves and the world around them. As you read, I would invite you to think about your children and some of the concepts and skills they have learned and how they have learned them.

Learning Through Imitation

Regardless of your educational attainment or profession, the most complex thing you ever learned was language. Yet about 90 percent of your functional language was acquired by your fifth birthday, probably before you started kindergarten. How did you learn language? We all learned through modeling—one of our most powerful learning tools. Preschoolers are adept at learning by modeling: watching, listening, and then imitating. A preschooler's brain is like a sponge, soaking up every drop of information in its path, and his ability to model is astonishing.

Preschoolers learn how to interact with people by modeling, including how to play, take turns, pretend, share, and be a good friend. They also learn attitudes, values, personal preferences, and some habits by modeling, as well as how to identify and manage their emotions. In fact, preschoolers learn much of their behavior by observing and imitating the behavior of the people around them.

You have a direct impact on your preschooler's learning. As a parent, you are your child's first and most influential teacher, so think carefully about your own behavior. What you say and do in front of your preschooler shapes his thinking and behavior, because like it or not, you are his most important model.

Many parents are confused about what being a good model means, thinking they have to be perfect all the time. Parenting is challenging enough without trying to do it perfectly! Trying to be a perfect parent will only add stress to your life. Being a good model means you need to be responsible, even when your children catch you misbehaving.

When Anthony was five, he and I went Christmas shopping one Saturday afternoon. We left the house in great holiday spirits, singing along with the Christmas music on the radio. As we approached the mall, the first thing I noticed was the number of cars in the parking lot. We drove around for several minutes looking for a place to park. I am not blessed with patience in these situations, and I found myself getting frustrated and angry. Anthony was oblivious. He was still singing. I was not.

Finally I spotted a car backing out of a parking place. I drove up and put on my signal, indicating my intent. As the car backed out, another car sneaked ahead of me from the other direction. That was all I needed. I got so angry, I rolled my window down and yelled something obscene at the driver. We exchanged a few angry looks, and then I continued my search for another parking place. I didn't have the courage to look at my son. He stopped singing. His silence indicated to me that he knew something had happened.

About twenty minutes later, after I had finally parked and cooled off, Anthony and I were walking in the mall. We were both in good spirits and were discussing what presents to buy. Without warning, he looked up and asked, "By the way, Dad, what is an a——h—— anyway?"

It felt like I had been hit with a ton of bricks. I can still close my eyes and see the curiosity on his pudgy face. He had heard me use bad language, and he remembered exactly what I said. I was embarrassed and shocked.

I explained that he had asked an important question. I asked him to walk with me over to a bench where we could sit face to face. Whenever you have important topics to discuss with your preschooler, sit or squat down so that you are at his level. Make eye contact. This lets your child know that the ensuing conversation is special and important. Do not stand over your child or talk down. This conveys that you are bigger, more powerful, dominating, or imposing, rather than an equal communicator.

I explained that what I had said was not a nice word, and I was wrong for saying it. I admitted that I had been angry and frustrated because I could not find a parking place. I added that I hoped he would not use the word as I had. It was a moment of truth for me. "Anthony, that was a bad word," I said. "I am sorry that I used that word in front of you. I apologize. I was in a hurry and could not find a place to park. I got upset. But I want you to know that even when you are upset, you should not use bad words. I hope you do not use that word, even though I did. I was wrong, and I am sorry."

You can be a good example to your children 95 percent of the time—yet it is 100 percent certain that your children will catch you when you mess up. When children catch parents misbehaving, many parents get defensive. "Never mind what that word means. Don't ever let me hear you say it." This response is wrong because it closes communication. It tells your child that you can say bad words but he cannot. Without a proper explanation, such unknown words will pique your preschooler's curiosity and end up at the top of his vocabulary list. The first thing your child will do when he gets to preschool the next day is start asking all his classmates what the word means. Try explaining that to your child's teacher!

It is always better for you and your child if you admit your mistake and take responsibility for your own behavior. Do not get defensive when your child catches you misbehaving; instead take advantage of this situation, which offers a teachable moment. Turn your discomfort into a valuable learning opportunity. When I was caught using a bad word, I explained that I was wrong, I had made a mistake. I took responsibility for my anger and didn't try to blame the person who took the parking place. I admitted my error, and I apologized. In so doing, I showed my son that parents make mistakes, that I am human, not perfect. More importantly, I impressed upon him that when I make a mistake, I admit it. I take responsibility. I apologize. I try to do better next time.

These are invaluable qualities to model for your children. Why? You want your preschooler to know that no matter what he does, he can come and talk to you about it, and that talking to your parents about issues and problems in your life is always a good idea. You also want him to understand that mistakes are okay—you make mistakes too:

> "You know your dad is not perfect. I make mistakes, and I am not always right. But I have learned to talk about things I do wrong or things that bother me. Talking to you is good for me. When things upset you or make you sad, I hope you know that you can always talk to me or Mom."

It is essential that you teach this lesson while your children are preschoolers, so that when they are adolescents, it is easier for them to do. Preschoolers learn from everything you do. Look at the chart below and see how easy it is to teach your child habits you may not intend.

WHAT YOU DO	WHAT YOUR CHILD LEARNS
You argue, yell, or call people names.	I can be rude.
You get angry with your children.	I can get angry with my parents, siblings, and friends.
You have an emotional outburst.	I can have temper tantrums.
You belittle or shame your children.	I can be critical of others and myself.
You tell the teacher that your child missed school because he was ill, when in fact you went shopping.	I can lie.

WHAT YOU DO	WHAT YOUR CHILD LEARNS
You snack on candy between meals.	I can eat candy between meals.
You watch TV several hours each day.	I can watch TV for hours.
You yell something obscene at someone who takes your parking place.	I can be verbally offensive.

Before thinking that you have condemned you child to a life of bad habits, keep in mind there is an easy way to teach good habits:

WHAT YOU DO	WHAT YOUR CHILD LEARNS
You apologize for using bad language.	I can apologize.
You speak in a calm voice instead of an angry one.	I can use a calm voice.
You take responsibility for your anger.	I can take responsibility for my anger.
You show self-control in challenging situation.	I can stay calm when provoked.
You use polite language.	I can use polite language.
You are kind to others.	I can be kind to others.
You try something new.	I want to try something new.
You share your things.	I can share my things.
You play fair.	I can play fair.

WHAT YOU DO	WHAT YOUR CHILD LEARNS
You read books to your children.	I like reading books.
You eat healthy foods and exercise.	I want to eat healthy and exercise.
You behave responsibly.	I want to behave responsibly.

Children learn by modeling every waking moment. You cannot turn it off. You cannot tell your children, "I feel like misbehaving a little, please don't model me today." If your child's behavior concerns you, look closely at your own behavior. Children learn what they live. When they live with responsible parents, they become responsible children. They will grow up to be responsible parents to your grandchildren. You have an obligation to be the best model that you can be. Your children do as you do. Always!

Learning Through Experimentation

Another way that preschoolers learn is by experiencing things in their surroundings. Preschoolers explore everything they can touch, see, hear, smell, taste, and do! They experiment as they explore. A preschooler's life is filled with trial and error and "what-ifs." What happens if I do this? What happens if I say, for example, "poopyhead"?

As they explore, experiment, and discover their world, their surroundings shape and guide their learning. Your preschooler's environment includes you and other family members, playmates, people in the neighborhood, classmates, teachers, the playground, TV, movies, books, music, and so on. All of these are the ingredients of your preschooler's world.

Learning by experimentation is different than learning through imitation. When a child touches a hot plate, he learns that hot objects hurt his fingers. The child learns about hot plates through his experience, not by any kind of modeling.

And yet experimentation is the way preschoolers learn some behaviors. For example, your preschooler may wonder, "What happens if I have a tantrum? If I get what I want, then tantrums must work. I will use them again!" This is exactly how many bright children reason. The lesson for parents to learn is not to reward or give in to tantrums and other forms of misbehavior experiments, such as whining, teasing, or arguing. Teach your preschooler that correct behavior is rewarded and encouraged. When you do that, your child's reasoning will follow these lines: "What happens when I ask for something using a polite voice? Using a polite voice works. I will use a polite voice often!"

Many preschooler behaviors are the result of their natural need to test limits and figure out how the world around them operates—specifically, how you will react. Teach your children what behaviors are worthwhile by encouraging them and which are not by not giving in.

Learning Through Integration

As a preschooler's brain develops, it creates new connections based on learning and experience. Preschoolers combine what they have learned through modeling with what they have learned through experimentation and exploration to create new information—in short, they start to figure things out for themselves. At about age three, children begin to use acquired learning to create generalizations. This new level of understanding is then transferred and utilized in new situations and used to solve new problems. Take the case of Marisa:

> One day when Marisa was four, she had a sobering insight while she was watching *Barney & Friends*.
>
> "Hey, wait a minute!" she announced with a puzzled stare. "There is something wrong here."
>
> "What?" her dad asked.
>
> "Dad, Barney is not real."
>
> "What?" he repeated.
>
> "Barney is a dinosaur, and my teacher says that dinosaurs are not alive anymore."
>
> "You are right. Barney is part of our imagination. He is pretend. You did a good job of thinking."

Marisa smiled because she realized that she had figured out something very important—all by herself. She took two separate pieces of information and put them together to create a new idea—Barney is not real. What an accomplishment! Many generalizations are less obvious; for example, preschoolers connect facial expressions to feelings and then try the expressions out on others. They observe how tone of voice and inflections improve the meaning of words. This is a remarkable developmental period. Every day is rich with insights for your preschooler and for you. Preschooler parents take great pride in sharing stories with their friends: "You won't believe what she figured out this week!"

This is also a time for increased parental responsibility. Begin by becoming more aware of what your children are learning and how they behave. Pay attention to what they do and listen to what they say. Guide their discovery. Point out things they do well in order to encourage and give them positive feedback; tell them they are on the right track. Facilitate new learning or prepare for a difficult situation by reviewing previous experiences that were successful. For example:

> **Dad:** "I know that sharing your toys with Shane is not easy, Luke. But I know you can do it. Remember last week when Julie was visiting? Remember what a great job you did? You and Julie shared your toys with no problems. You are good at sharing. I know you can be a good friend and share your toys with Shane when he comes over. When he gets here, let me know if you need my help."

Teach your preschoolers to solve problems by talking through the situation with them. Ask questions about alternatives in order to help them draw from previous experiences. Ask your child to think about ways to solve the problem. If your child seems stumped, make a tentative suggestion. Let's continue with the example of sharing.

> **Luke:** "But Dad, Shane is mean. I share with him. He won't share with me. He wants everything that I want."
>
> **Dad:** "Does that hurt your feelings?"
>
> **Luke:** "Yes."

Dad: "Do you get angry?"

Luke: "Yes."

Dad: "I can understand that. I might get angry too. Have you tried taking turns?"

Luke: "Sometimes."

Dad: "Here is an idea. Let Shane pick a toy first. Then after a few minutes, you can take turns. Try it and see what happens. Let me know if you need my help."

Luke: "Okay. I'll try."

Dad: "Thank you. I know you can work this out. I know you can be a good friend and share. Even if Shane does not cooperate, I want you to behave and have good manners. I know you can make the right choice."

It is always best to end with encouragement and a reminder of how you expect your child to behave. Having said this, don't expect total maturity from your preschooler. Every child has limits, even with exemplary pep talks from parents. All playmates are not raised equally. If you know from your previous play dates that Shane can be uncooperative, then you need to monitor their play time closely. Give both children ample encouragement for sharing and taking turns. Also remember that most young children have a few toys that they treasure above all. Your child may have difficulty sharing these toys because they are so special. To avoid a problem situation about these toys, put them away, perhaps in your bedroom closet, when other children come to play.

Learning Through Fantasy and Make-Believe

Adults use fantasy as a way of escaping the real world, while preschoolers use fantasy as a way of understanding the real world. Preschoolers use fantasy and pretend play to become absorbed and connected to a reality that they are hoping to be part of someday. We call it "make-believe" because pretending helps make it believable. They pretend to be Mommy, Daddy, Grandma, teacher, and doctor because these are the adults they know and want to be like. Pretending to be an adult gives preschoolers a feeling of competence and power; they feel grown up. They want to do what bigger people do. Preschoolers play house and school because that is what the adults in their lives do. They pretend to read books or write letters to Grandma. They pretend to use the computer and the phone. They want to control what happens in their lives just like you do (so they think!).

Preschoolers learn to make sense of things they don't fully understand through fantasy and pretending. They use blocks to create cities, castles, cars, and spaceships. They use little plastic people to have picnics and parties.

Children love to pretend they have power. That is why so many preschoolers pretend to be superheroes. Dressing up like Pocahontas or Superman carries them into a fantasyland that is rich in creativity and free of responsibilities, rules, and expectations. It feels good to be powerful. Children believe that no one tells superheroes what to do: "Everyone idolizes them," they think, "and that is what I want to be." This kind of pretending allows children to feel powerful, and because superheroes are not afraid of anything, they can also help children gain confidence and confront their fears without worry. If your child has trouble sleeping, she might ease her fears by telling herself, "Wonder Woman is not afraid of the dark."

Unfortunately, many of the superheroes your child will want to imitate display aggressive behaviors and solve problems by using violence. Let your children have fun but teach them that violence is not the way to solve problems. Set limits and establish guidelines. Jim and Kathy, who are the parents of three sons, established a no-gun rule. The boys loved pretending to be pirates, police officers, Power Rangers, and Ninja Turtles, but Jim and Kathy did not allow the boys to "pretend shoot" anyone.

By becoming someone else in play, young children discover who they are, what they like, and what their differences are. Dressing up and becoming a character also provides young children with a common story to explore, which promotes creative thinking and lays the groundwork for independence, social skill development, and self-esteem.

Learning Through Stories

Preschoolers are capable of learning great lessons by listening to stories, whether true or fantasy. Reading to your child is a valuable activity that encourages bonding and provides special shared moments between the two of you, while developing a lifelong love of reading. When you read to your preschool child, you stimulate cognitive and language skills. Books expand your child's world by providing information and an understanding of things she has not directly experienced. The closeness of cuddling up to read and talk provides a sense of safety and security, which is one of the reasons why it can be an important part of a bedtime routine.

By reading stories about other children who share similar circumstances, you help your child explore his own thoughts, feelings, and fears. When you use stories to instruct, your child can learn how to predict the rewards of making good choices and the consequences of bad choices. Reading to your preschooler can help you teach your child how to behave.

The goal of reading with preschoolers is not to teach them to read but rather to show them that books and stories are fun. Nurture a love of reading in your child, and you and it will impact his success at school by inspiring a desire to learn and gain meaning from words. Although there is no right or wrong way to read to your preschooler, you can do many things while you are reading to optimize what your child learns, as well as encourage him to share his thoughts, feelings, and concerns.

Start by cuddling your preschooler on your lap or sitting in a rocking chair, if you have one. Let him hold the book and turn the pages. If your child has difficulty sitting still and paying attention, start with short books and gradually increase the length. Allow a squirmy child to hold a toy or eat a snack while you read. For special occasions, get a flashlight and read under a tent made out of a chair and an old blanket.

Before you read a new book with your preschooler, page through it and look at the pictures. Talk about what the theme of the book might be. Pictures are important because they help young children attend to the story and grasp its meaning. Ask your child to relate the topic of the story to her own experiences. "Have you ever gone on a hike in the forest?" "Did Mommy read a book about zoo animals before?" If you are reading about a place, get out a map and show your child where it is located. How far is it from where you live or have traveled on vacation? Is it near Grandma and Grandpa?

Read with expression. Take turns acting out parts of the story that are exciting. Use your voice to exaggerate features of the characters. Ask your child to predict what happens next before you turn the page: "What do think will happen next?" If he is unsure, turn the page and look at the pictures for a clue. This will help your child learn cause and effect and how to predict consequences. After you have read a story, ask him to identify who, what, where, when, why, or how. Develop your child's sequencing skills by asking him to tell you what happened at the beginning, middle, and end of the story. Encourage your child to ask questions and provide the opportunity for him to develop answers to his own questions by giving him time to think. Be aware that this will be challenging for three- and some young four-year-olds, but easier for five- and six-year-olds. Once your preschooler is familiar with a story, omit key words so your child can fill in as you pause. Your child will learn to use the context of the story as a clue to figure out what the missing word should be. Books with lots of repetition are particularly good for this technique. Be aware, however, that most bright preschoolers will call you on it when you don't read the story the same way every time! Always allow plenty of time to reread the story if your child wants. Read books with content that your child already understands, as well as challenging books that your child can understand and enjoy with your assistance. Follow up on what you have read by doing activities from the storybook. For example, if you read about a girl who bakes cookies or flies a kite, make a batch of cookies the next day or go to the park this weekend and pretend to be the girl flying the kite.

You will also want to read books that help your child develop emotionally and socially. If your child experiences a trauma or loss, find a book that will help your child understand the emotions he may be feeling. There are books about death, fears, going to the doctor, starting a new school, making friends, bullies, having a new baby, and so forth. You can help your child adjust or prepare for events such as these by reading stories about children who have already been through it. These kinds of books are particularly helpful in allowing your child to recognize his feelings and encouraging him to express them to you. A word of caution before you begin: If you use a children's book to help your child with a challenging behavior or situation, *be sure to read the book in its entirety, before you read it with your child,* to ensure that its content is appropriate.

Make sure to choose a quiet place where you can talk about the story and how it relates to your child's experiences. While you are reading, stop and ask your child how he thinks the character in the story feels right now. Your child's reactions may provide insight into how he feels. Here are some sample questions you might ask:

"How do you think that little girl feels?"

"Have you ever felt that way?"

"What do you think the girl should do?"

"What would you do?"

"What can her mommy do to help?"

"What can I do?"

Encourage your preschooler to talk about her feelings, but do not pressure her to share. Remember that most preschoolers do not have a large vocabulary of emotionally expressive words. Children who do not want to talk may want to draw a picture. It can also be helpful if you and your child make up a different ending to the story. Feel free to change the words or names of the characters in the story to improve your child's understanding. Sometimes making up your own story to go with the pictures works best.

You will find an appendix at the end of this book that lists children's stories. Arranged by topic, they address common concerns that parents may encounter with their preschooler. Reading about other children who are apprehensive about going to school for the first time or visiting the doctor or dentist will help your child know what to expect. The more your child understands, the less anxious he will be.

Libraries with children's sections often have topic lists of books to help you match your child's current interests or concerns. If your child is already enrolled in a preschool program, ask if the school has a resource library for parents or a storybook library for preschoolers. Follow your child's changing interests. If he sees something on television that fascinates him or if he asks a question about something he heard at school, take his lead. No matter what the topic, you can find out more about it in a book, magazine, or newspaper. You can fan the sparks of curiosity and create more interest in reading and learning.

Books are great gifts. When you plan a vacation, check out books from the library about the upcoming trip. Going to the ocean? Borrow books about seashells, boats, swimming, and building sandcastles. Going camping? Try books about plants, forest animals, rocks, butterflies, fishing, and campfires. Vacation books help children anticipate activities and plan what they might want to do when you arrive. They are great for keeping children busy on the drive to your vacation spot. Books can also become part of special occasions. Holiday and special event books can help your child learn about traditions. Place books in your family room for all major holidays and be sure to have selections that relate to your family's culture and religious beliefs. Bring holiday books out about a week or two before the holiday and put them away a day or two after. (Christmas or Hanukkah may last longer!) You may want to add a book or two to the holiday library. Each year, your children will look forward to getting out the holiday books.

PART III

Better Behavior

Principles

7

Quick Start Strategies

The concept of parenting style was introduced in chapter 1. Your parenting style could best be described as your personality as a parent, because it is in fact related to your personality. Your parenting style touches all aspects of your relationships with your children. It consists of all your parenting beliefs and strategies. It influences the way you interact with, communicate with, and discipline your children. And it affects the way you react or respond to their behavior, especially their misbehavior, because it reflects your level of emotional self-control.

The purpose of this chapter is to introduce you to some fundamental beliefs and strategies that can be incorporated quickly into your parenting style. Practice these ideas, and both you and you preschooler will be on a course of improved behavior.

Belief #1: Discipline Is a Teaching Process

The word *discipline* derives its meaning from the Latin *disciplinare*, "to teach." Many parents confuse discipline and punishment. Discipline is an ongoing teaching process. It is management through guidance. It is a blend of firmness and reasoning and needs to be developmental. You need to consider your preschooler's language, his level of comprehension, his individual temperament, and the context of the situation. This requires time, tolerance, energy, commitment, and on most days, creative thinking.

Discipline includes everything we do as parents to understand, teach, guide, and nurture our children.

When your preschooler picks up his dishes and brings them to the kitchen and you thank him, you are using discipline. By saying, "Thank you for helping me clear the table," you are teaching him to be helpful. If you say, "You did a good job sharing your dolls with your friend," you are teaching sharing. Or if you say, "I like the way you use your words. You did not whine. You were very polite," you are helping your child learn how to communicate with words rather than whining.

Successful parents understand that discipline is a teaching process; it is everything we do to teach our children to think for themselves and make good choices. There are hundreds of discipline techniques and strategies. Punishment is one technique. While it is useful and necessary in some situations, most parents use it more than necessary, often because they are frustrated and angry. You will learn more about how and when to use punishment in chapter 12.

Preschoolers require discipline as much as they need love and affection. It not only guides their behavior but also teaches them values, how to think, and how to make choices. Discipline teaches preschoolers how to predict outcomes and the concept of cause and effect. It shows preschoolers that there are limits in our society and rules that we all live by. For example, every child would like to be first in a game, but we have to take turns. Understanding this helps preschoolers learn to get along with and respect others, and eventually it leads to self-respect. Discipline also helps protect preschoolers from dangerous situations. When you tell your child, "Hold my hand when we cross the street," you are keeping him out of harm's way.

The foundation of discipline is a solid parent-child relationship, which must include affection, support, trust, and limits. A strong relationship gives children a sense of stability—in their world, in their family, in you, and in themselves. This gives children a sense of worth. They feel important. A strong relationship means you will love your preschooler no matter how he behaves. Tell him you love him, but you do not like what he did. Explain why he needs to behave. Let him know that it is your job to help him learn to behave. It is his job to make good choices. This gives your preschooler a reason to behave—to please you and to feel good about himself—and it allows you to have more positive interactions and fewer negative interactions with your preschooler.

Belief #2: Teach What You Expect

Preschoolers need to know that you expect them to behave and what that means. Expectations guide your preschooler's decision making, so you need to communicate precisely and simply what your child should or should not do. Preschoolers need to know the rules so they understand how you want them to behave.

Many parents do not give their children clear and specific expectations. We assume that since we understand what our children should do, they should understand it too. Teach your preschooler what the rules mean rather than simply announcing the rules. This is a very common mistake; if your child doesn't understand why he should do something, he is likely to disobey.

Belief #3: Teach Self-Control

Your primary goal is to teach your preschooler self-control, to control his own behavior, to be responsible for his actions. This confuses many parents. Many parents believe that discipline means they must control their preschooler's behavior. This notion is incorrect. If you believe that your role is to control your children, think about your parenting style. Does this idea come from how you were raised? Clearly there are times when you need to control your preschooler's behavior, but even in these situations, your goal is to teach your preschooler self-control. When you teach your preschooler that he has the power to control himself, you will build his confidence and self-esteem. Not only will his behavior improve, he will feel more competent about making decisions, and he will develop stronger self-respect.

Belief #4: Teach Right from Wrong

Each of us has that little voice inside our heads that reminds us of right and wrong. We call this voice our conscience. It keeps us from misbehaving. Our conscience is a collection of our values, morals, and ethics. Conscience begins to emerge during the preschool years and develops with parental supervision. Small children rely on the voice of their parents to guide them between right and wrong. With practice, experience, and consistent guidance, children gradually begin to internalize this voice. The parent's guiding voice becomes the little voice inside the child's head that reminds him of right and wrong. Then when a child is tempted to misbehave, the voice encourages him to do the right thing.

Through consistent structure and teaching, preschoolers begin to internalize the attitudes and expectations of their parents. These attitudes and expectations guide their behavior. Teach your preschooler that his behavior is his choice by saying things such as, "It is up to you to behave." Provide your preschooler with opportunities to make choices. Teach him to evaluate the outcomes of each behavior: Follow the rules, and the consequences are favorable. Do not follow the rules, and the consequences are unfavorable. This is how preschoolers learn to make choices about their behavior and develop responsibility.

These four beliefs, along with others you already have, are the foundation for good behavior. They provide a framework that helps guide your thinking about discipline. By practicing the strategies that follow, you will be able to incorporate these beliefs into your style of parenting and be ready for most situations.

Strategy 1: Accentuate the Positive

Successful discipline includes strategies for building and reinforcing correct behaviors and attitudes. Some positive behaviors occur naturally as part of a preschooler's normal development. Use encouragement to strengthen and refine these behaviors. Other desired behaviors are not part of a preschooler's normal development, and need to be taught. For example, preschoolers are naturally possessive of their belongings and need to learn how to share. They are self-centered and must be taught how to play and socialize with others. Preschoolers are impatient, so you must show them how to wait and take turns. They are self-absorbed and need to learn to be sensitive to the feelings of others. Preschoolers are not born polite, so you have to educate them about manners.

Model these qualities, and your preschooler will learn from your example. Recognize good behavior when it occurs. Catch children being good. Teach your preschooler to recognize when he has done the right thing. Teach him to associate behaving correctly with feeling proud of himself. (For more detail see chapter 10, "How to Build Positive Behaviors and Attitudes.")

Strategy 2: Keep Rules Simple

Use simple language and ask your child to repeat the rule. Then check for understanding and give an example of how to follow the rule. You even may want to role-play how to follow the rule.

Four-year-old Alan plays too loudly, often yelling instead of talking. Marsha wants to teach him to learn to speak more quietly. Many parents would manage this problem with criticism: "Alan, you are yelling again, be quiet." This may remind Alan to be quiet for a few minutes, but it is not a long-term solution because it does not teach the correct behavior. Instead, Marsha has decided to create a rule that is stated in positive words: "Use a soft voice." (Alternatives could be "Use an inside voice," or "Use a quiet voice."). Let's see how Marsha teaches Alan this rule.

"Alan, let's talk about voices. Sometimes voices are loud [she raises her voice], sometimes voices are soft [she lowers her voice]. Let's practice. Let me hear a loud voice. You try it."

Alan smiles and shouts, "This is loud."

"Good. Now let me hear a soft voice," replies Mom.

Alan whispers, "This is soft."

"Great."

"When you are playing, please use a soft voice."

Then, when Alan uses a soft voice, Marsha needs to recognize him. "Alan, that was using a soft voice. Good job."

It is helpful to develop rules with your preschooler. If your child helps make the rules, he will be more likely to obey the rules. Choose a time when your child is behaving well; otherwise he will think the rules are a result of his misbehavior. Sit at a table with your child. Start by explaining why rules are important. Here is an example.

"We need to have some rules so you and I know when you are doing a good job."

Then ask questions that help your child think of rules: "Do you think it is important to be a good listener?"

"Yes."

"What would be a good rule about listening?"

"Always listen to your mother."

You may accept this answer or you may help refine it: "That's a good rule. But we need to be a good listener when Dad and Grandma talk to us, too. How about this rule? Be a good listener."

"Yes. That's a good one, Mom."

"Let's play a game about being a good listener. You go into the other room. I will call your name. When I do, you answer, 'Here I am, Mom!'"

"Okay."

This strategy is helpful, but it by no means guarantees that your child will always listen. Rehearse the rule often. (Be sure to read the section "How to Teach 'Good Listening' Skills" in chapter 2.)

Have a few well-developed rules and expectations. State the rules in positive terms. Here are some examples:

Be a good listener.

Do what you are asked.

Be a good friend.

Take turns when playing.

Use a big-girl (boy) voice.

Use an inside voice.

Cartoons after breakfast.

Storybooks after bath.

(There is an extensive discussion of expectations, rules, and behavior in chapter 12, "Use Rules to Provide Guidance.")

Strategy 3: Be Proactive

Hundreds of personal qualities, skills, and strategies are required for successful parenting. When it pertains to discipline, you can take all of the skills and strategies and divide them into two categories: *reactive—*

knowing how to manage misbehavior that is happening right now; and *proactive*—knowing how to prevent misbehavior from happening in the first place. Remember Smokey the Bear's philosophy? It is easier to prevent forest fires than put them out. That is being proactive.

In order to be proactive, you will have to plan. Many discipline problems can be avoided if you spend a little time thinking and planning ahead. By doing so, you make use of the only advantage you have over your children: experience.

Create routines for your child; these will provide consistency and predictability. A simple routine after school helps children unwind. Regular mealtimes and bedtime schedules are also important. When routines are the same every day, preschoolers are more able to concentrate on what to do next, which encourages them to figure out what to do on their own so that you have to spend less time reminding them. This strategy requires self-discipline on your part as well. You may need to prepare dinner ahead of time to solve some suppertime problems. You will have to create a structured bedtime routine to get the children to bed on time. You may need to get your child's clothes ready at night to avoid the morning fashion crisis.

Being proactive also means giving preschoolers choices, keeping them engaged, and allowing them to participate. Giving preschoolers choices empowers them with confidence and can minimize resistance. Lori solved a recurring problem by thinking about the situation from her three-year-old son Samuel's point of view. Samuel loves to have pancakes for breakfast, but Lori doesn't have time to fix pancakes every day. She used to ask, "Do you want cereal today?" Samuel's reply to this question typically was, "No, pancakes!" Now, she offers him two choices: "Would you like cereal or a bagel today?" This allows Samuel to feel he is getting what he wants, even when he can't have pancakes.

Initially, being proactive means anticipating problems. You know the places where your children typically misbehave, whether it is the supermarket, church, or Grandma's house. If you suspect there might be a problem, talk with your children before you leave. Tell them what you expect from them and what they can expect from you. You might say, "I really need your cooperation when we go shopping. You did a very good job last week. I know you can do a good job again today."

Strategy 4: Use Distraction

Mom and three-year-old Julie are having lunch at a restaurant with Grandma. While they are waiting for their food, Julie reaches for the sugar canister and turns it upside down. Julie smiles with pride at Grandma as the sugar spills onto the table. Grandma smiles in return. Mom goes into action. She reaches for the backpack and pulls out some crayons and a piece of paper. Mom places the paper in front of Julie and hands her a crayon. "May I have the sugar, please?" Mom asks Julie as she takes it away. Julie begins to scream, grabbing for the sugar. "I am sorry, Julie. The sugar is for coffee, not for playing." Mom puts the sugar on a table behind them, removing it from view. "Let's draw a picture for Grandma. What can you draw? Would you like Julie to draw a picture for you, Grandma?" Mom has distracted Julie from the sugar and avoided a possible tantrum.

Distraction is a quick and powerful intervention strategy, and it is as easy to use as it sounds. It is the strategy of choice for infants, toddlers, and preschoolers, and it is the first strategy you should use when your child begins to whine or demand something he cannot have or do. Distraction means to divert your child's attention from what he wants to something he can have. It means substituting an appropriate object or activity for one that your child wants that is not appropriate.

Distraction is another way of being proactive. When you go out, bring along a "bag of tricks" that is immediately accessible and contains a variety of small toys, books, or paper and crayons. When your preschooler wants an inappropriate object, such as your steak knife, hand him something else, like a spoon. If he wants your hammer, hand him a toy hammer, explaining, "This hammer is for Daddy, and this one is for you." If your daughter wants your scissors, hand her a pair of children's safety scissors, telling her, "These are Mommy's scissors, and here are your scissors."

You may not always have a toy hammer or safety scissors at your disposal. Use whatever you have that is quick and handy. Choose items that will capture your child's attention and hold his interest for a while and keep him engaged and busy. Think ahead, however; if your child always wants your hammer, buy a toy hammer the next time you see one. If your daughter wants to use your vacuum cleaner, buy a toy vacuum cleaner or a small, handheld vacuum that she can use alongside you when you vacuum. If your child wants your cell phone, give him a play phone or an old nonworking cell phone (it looks real).

Although toys and other objects work well as distractions, there may be times when you need to use an activity. Four-year-old Troy wants to play soccer with his older brother and his teammates. Even though the older boys let Troy play for a few minutes during warm-ups, it is now game time, and Troy needs to leave the field. Troy begins to cry and scream. Dad takes an extra soccer ball. "Hey, Troy, let's you and I go play over here." Troy smiles through his tears. Note that Dad's involvement is part of the distraction; Dad does not simply hand a ball to Troy and say, "Go play over there." Whenever you use an activity distraction, be part of the activity, at least for the first few minutes. This will help assure that your preschooler is engaged in the new activity and no longer fretting about not getting his way.

Take a book along when you expect to wait to see a doctor or be served at a restaurant or at the bank. Books will help your child wait patiently because he will be engaged in the story. When the weather keeps your preschooler inside, use a book to take him to other places using his imagination. You might read a book about camping and then make a tent using chairs and a blanket.

Strategy 5: Redirect Misbehaviors

Redirecting has two parts: correcting an inappropriate behavior and then teaching the correct behavior. Explain to your child why her actions are not acceptable; then explain what to do instead, giving her an example of the correct behavior.

Four-year-old Hanna has just pushed her friend Amy off the swing in her backyard. Hanna climbs onto the swing, while Amy sits on the ground, crying. Hanna's mother intervenes, using a firm but calm tone of voice: "Hanna, that was not being a good friend. We do not push. Look at Amy crying. She is sad because you pushed her off the swing. Please tell Amy you are sorry for pushing her and hurting her feelings." She encourages Hanna to apologize. Then she explains the correct behavior: "Did you want to use the swing? If you did, you need to use your words. You could say, 'Let's take turns, Amy.' "

Redirection works well when your child is trying to make you give in, by such methods as whining, nagging, pleading, or throwing a tantrum. If your preschooler misbehaves frequently, it means that he has not learned appropriate methods of getting what he wants. Think about the purpose behind your preschooler's misbehavior. What does your preschooler hope to gain by whining or nagging? Then show him an appropriate alternative that will enable him to earn what he seeks through correct behavior. If he seeks attention, show him how to get your attention without misbehaving. For example, Matthew whines a great deal. His father might say, "Matthew, I will not listen to whining. If you want me to read you a story, you need to stop whining. Please go sit for a minute. Then come back and ask me in a polite voice." In this way he teaches Matthew that there are acceptable ways of getting what he wants, and how to correct his behavior. This takes time, commitment, and planning.

Redirection is a powerful technique that works as long as you do not give in. Do not reward unacceptable behavior. If you do, your child will not be easily redirected, because he knows that he can get what he wants on his own terms.

Redirecting is not always easy, especially when the misbehavior is rewarding to your child in other ways. If you become angry when your child whines, your anger may be rewarding because it gives him control. So even if you do not give in, the whining may persist. You will not be redirecting your child's misbehavior successfully because you are still allowing him to control you emotionally.

Strategy 6: Anticipate Transitions

A transition is a change. When preschoolers need to move from one activity to another, they have to make a mental as well as a physical transition. They may need to change from a mental state of excitement to a mental state of calm and quiet, or they may need to change from a physical state of high activity and arousal to a physical state of being still. They need to stop being engaged in one activity and begin another activity. This is difficult for many preschoolers, especially when they are doing something fun and they have to stop. Behavior problems often occur during transitions.

Transitions occur many times a day during the life of a preschooler. Successful preschool parents anticipate transitions and plan to make them as smooth as possible. Develop a transition strategy that begins with a time warning. Then remind him of the sequence of events involved in the transition.

Susie loves going to the playground, and her mother knows from previous experiences that Susie does not like to leave the park when it is time to go. Susie will whine and plead to be allowed to stay longer. Sometime she will have a tantrum. Her mother decides to be proactive, so before leaving home, she explains how she expects Susie to behave when it is time to leave.

"Susie, would you like to go to the park?"

"Yes."

"We can go for thirty minutes. I will tell you when you have five minutes left to play. You need to come when I call you. And you need to be ready to leave without crying or teasing. Can you do this?"

It is also helpful to end the explanation by giving your preschooler something to anticipate. When you have to leave someplace fun, talk about something exciting to do on the way home or at home. Do not emphasize leaving. For example, Susie's mother tells her, "If you do a good job when it is time to leave, we will have a snack and some juice when we get home from the park, and you can watch TV until supper."

The five-minute warning is crucial. That is what sets up the transition so that it will go smoothly. It gives your preschooler time to think about changing from one activity to another. It is often helpful to focus your child on doing what she likes best for the last five minutes.

"Susie, come here, please."

"What, Mom?"

"You are doing great. I see you are really having fun. We need to leave in five minutes. What was your favorite thing to do here today?"

"Go down the slide."

"You have time to do that two or three more times. Maybe that is what you should do before we leave."

Sondra has two children, four and two. She explains her use of time warnings: "One thing that has worked for me in almost every situation is giving a five-minute warning before a change of activity. In some situations, I use a two- or one-minute warning. When we are at the playground, I let them know that in five minutes we are going to have to go home. Before bed, I let them know that in two minutes it will be cleanup time. It works well. We still get major arguments from time to time, but they occur at the five-minute warning, which still gives me time to work things out before we really need to get moving. This keeps my temper down and helps them feel like they have time to wind their activity down before I arbitrarily make them drop what they're doing to follow my schedule."

Strategy 7: Negotiate and Compromise

Negotiation and compromise skills teach preschoolers to solve problems through communication and agreement rather than hitting or name-calling. Negotiating gives preschoolers a productive way to express their feelings. It reduces negative behaviors by providing a positive way to get their needs and wants met. Solving disagreements begins by encouraging preschoolers to listen to the other person. This teaches preschoolers to see things from the other person's perspective.

Preschool children often need help identifying their feelings with words. You may need to provide the words for young children: "I can see that you are upset. Are you frustrated because you want the doll stroller and Jamie is using it?" You can help preschoolers learn conflict resolution skills by asking questions that lead to good choices: "How could the two of you share the blocks?" You can also provide suggestions to get them thinking about alternatives: "If you both want to play doctor, how could you do it together?"

Here are some other guiding questions that you can use to help your preschooler think through situations. Your goal is to help your preschooler develop his own alternatives to work through concerns and problems.

"What could you do differently?"
"Could you have done something else?"
"How did you feel?"
"How did your friend feel?"

Compromise and negotiation let preschoolers have more control over their world and foster cooperation. Five-year-old Steven is playing a computer game. His mother tells him he can play for one more minute, and then he will need to get ready for bed. Steven can start to tease and whine to put off his bedtime and get his way. However, he knows how to negotiate a compromise. He says to Mom, "Can I please finish this game first, Mom? I promise I will go right to bed." Mom agrees because Steven asked politely and did not fuss.

Teaching these skills is beneficial not only during your child's pre-school years; they become essential as he grows older and reaches adolescence.

Strategy 8: Do Not Make Excuses

Some parents make excuses when their children misbehave: "He is just tired." "She has had a long day." "He has not eaten." "She always acts this way when he is around." By making excuses, however, we can teach our children to misbehave.

When you make excuses, you are implying that your child is not capable of behaving and that he does not have to be responsible for his behavior. You are teaching him that misbehavior is justified as long as you can come up with a good reason. Making excuses will come back to haunt you; all you are doing is giving your children reasons to misbehave in the future. They will use these excuses to argue and avoid responsibility.

We are tempted to bribe children into behaving because there is a temporary payoff. We like quick solutions. Bribery teaches children to be more argumentative and oppositional. Bribery encourages more misbehavior. Do not reward unacceptable behavior. Do not give in to demands, whining, or teasing. Stop the payoff permanently. Be consistent and patient. Do not make excuses. When a child misbehaves, deal with it—always. Excuses give children reasons to misbehave.

Strategy 9: Avoid Guilt Control

Controlling a child's misbehavior with guilt, ridicule, or humiliation is ineffective because it damages the child's self-esteem. Each indignity chisels away at a child's self-worth and confidence and creates strong feelings of embarrassment. When a child is humiliated, it can do permanent harm to his moral character. A child who is frequently shamed or humiliated may begin to think he is inferior and incapable of self-control. Common examples of shame and humiliation are:

You will never have any friends if you act that way.

That was a stupid thing to do.

That is a dumb question.

What's wrong with you?

Why are you so selfish?

No matter what I do for you, it is not enough.

Any parent can fall into a negative pattern occasionally. Even if guilt or humiliation seems to work, it doesn't. You may think you are stopping your child's misbehavior, but he stops because he wants to avoid the embarrassment. Some parents believe that a little guilt or embarrassment is okay. An occasional bit of embarrassment may be motivating for older children, but it is never a good idea for preschoolers. Their self-esteem is too fragile at this age. You do not want your preschooler to behave to avoid embarrassment, but rather because it is the right thing to do.

Avoid using sarcasm or any comments that impinge on self-esteem development. You want your children to accumulate as much self-esteem as possible before they crash into adolescence. Adolescence is a time of great personal insecurity. Most teenagers do everything possible to fit in, to be the same as everyone else, and to avoid embarrassment. Strong self-esteem gives your teenagers the confidence they need to navigate the perils of adolescence and resist the influence of negative peer pressure. The time to prepare your children for adolescence is when they are four.

8

You and Your Preschooler
Learn from Each Other

You now have an appreciation for several of the developmental factors that significantly affect preschoolers' behavior, some insight into how children learn, and some fundamental beliefs and strategies to help you get started. Now let's take a closer look at how behavior is learned. Preschoolers learn many of their behaviors from their experiences interacting with other people—primarily you, the parents. Young children are like sponges; they take in good behaviors such as being polite, sharing, and being kind to other just as easily as they do less desirable ones, such as whining, not listening, screaming, or arguing. Many behaviors begin as experiments; preschoolers like to test their behavior on the world around them to see the result: "What happens when I whine?" The resulting outcome or response from the parent is then integrated into the preschooler's pattern of behavior: "If whining gets me what I want, I'll use it again. If it doesn't, I may try it again just to be sure, or I may try something else and see what happens." If all this sounds calculating, it is. A preschooler's brain is busy calculating nearly every minute she is awake.

Parents learn from these experiences and interactions as well. We continue to use responses that work, and abandon those that do not. Or at least, that is how it is supposed to work. Consider this common situation.

As soon as four-year-old Rebecca walks into a grocery store, she begins to whine and plead for a cookie. Her mother, Marilyn, says, "No, not today." Rebecca sulks and makes a face. She pouts and says, "I want a cookie." A few minutes later, Rebecca shouts at her mother, "Why can't I have a cookie?" "Not now. Maybe later. Please behave." Rebecca's shouts escalate into a demand, "I want a cookie right now, Mommy." Marilyn holds her ground. "No. Stop it, or you will get a spanking when we get home." Rebecca begins screaming. Marilyn is getting frustrated. Rebecca begins kicking the cart. Then she starts taking things out and throwing them on the floor. Rebecca is having a tantrum. People are beginning to stare. The more she screams, the more Marilyn wants to hide. She can take no more. She gives in. She buys Rebecca a cookie.

What did Rebecca learn from this interaction with her mother? She learned that whining, demanding, and tantrums work. If you whine and have a tantrum you get what you want. Rebecca has learned that no does not mean no; it means escalate and try harder. No means whine again and again, and get more demanding each time. When your behavior becomes unbearable, Mom will change her no to yes. It's like magic! No becomes yes! Rebecca has learned that her mother does not mean what she says. If I have a tantrum, she thinks, I can persuade Mom to change her mind.

Marilyn has taught Rebecca to be stubborn and demanding. She didn't do it on purpose, but inadvertently taught Rebecca that whining and screaming pays off. If you scream and yell loud enough and long enough, you can get a cookie or whatever else you want. Have a tantrum—get a cookie. Have a tantrum—get your way.

What has Marilyn learned from this exasperating experience? You may be thinking that she has learned nothing, but she has. She has learned that she can get a few minutes of peace and quiet and stop the embarrassment if she buys a cookie. Probably, it will cost less than 50 cents, and it's much cheaper than therapy. It's a small price to pay for all it does: halting a full-blown tantrum and all the screaming that accompanies it; stopping the embarrassment and maybe even the feelings that she is a bad parent; giving her a few minutes of peace and quiet to finish her shopping.

All of Marilyn's other attempts at redirecting Rebecca's behavior were futile. She could only achieve peace with a cookie. Why did her positive efforts not work? Because Rebecca has learned from previous experience that whining and tantrums work. A pattern has been established, and it is likely it will happen again.

There are parents who live every day of their lives this way. They believe that giving in to demands is the only way to stop the whining or tantrum. This is a big mistake. Reward a child's tantrum once, and you will be teaching your child to have more tantrums in the future. Give in to your child's shouted demands once, and you will be listening to shouted demands again and again.

I refer to this as the first parent trap. It usually begins when our children are about two. Armed with little language expression, toddlers often use whining as a way of communicating their needs and getting what they want. Yet when they grow older and acquire language, they continue to whine because it is a pattern they have mastered, and it works. Here is the trap. Parents have a tendency to rationalize giving in to whining in young children. It's just a cookie, we justify. But here is the trap: the cookie is not the problem, it is the pattern that you are establishing: whine and win. (There is more about whining in chapter 17.)

What can you do if you are already trapped in this dilemma? It is difficult to manage outbursts in public if your preschooler still has outbursts at home. When you are in a public place, the misbehavior is more aggravating because it is so embarrassing. You have a lower threshold and tend to give in to whining more easily. So work on the home behavior first. Get that under control, and it will be easier to teach correct behavior when you go out. In the meantime, do not take your preschooler into public places unless you absolutely have no other choice. It is better to get a baby-sitter or go shopping when the other parent is home than to risk repeated outbursts in public that not only lead to your child's winning but also put you in a more vulnerable position. Leave your child at home until the outbursts at home have diminished and your child is being more cooperative.

Marilyn's plan to change Rebecca's supermarket behavior took time, but it was successful. She began by not taking Rebecca on long shopping trips. Meanwhile, she worked for several weeks on reducing tantrums at home. Once Marilyn felt more confident about not giving in to whining and tantrums, she began taking Rebecca on short trips to the local convenience store, for practice. Before they left the house, Marilyn would explain how she wanted Rebecca to behave. She would emphasize that she needed Rebecca's help. Preschoolers like being helpers. Marilyn would explain where they were going and what they were going to buy. She would show Rebecca the shopping list, with three or four items on the list. Since most preschoolers don't read, Marilyn asked Rebecca to help her draw pictures and find cutouts from magazines to create the list.

Here is how Marilyn can explain her expectations for Rebecca's behavior:

Marilyn: "Rebecca, I am going shopping this morning. Would you like to come with me?"

Rebecca: "Okay, Mommy."

Marilyn: "Remember the rule. No whining. You have been doing very well lately. That is why I would like you to come with me this morning. I know you will not whine."

Rebecca: "Yes, Mommy."

Marilyn: "You can be my helper. Here is the grocery list. We need to get bread, milk, and eggs. When we find each item, you can cross it off the list. Would you like to add anything to the list?"

Rebecca: "I want some cupcakes."

Marilyn: "If you don't whine, and you are a good helper and a good listener, you can buy two cupcakes before we leave, one for you and one for Daddy. But you have to be a good helper first. We need to buy the bread, milk, and eggs first, before we buy your cupcakes. I know you can do it."

Rebecca: "I can do it."

Once they got to the store, Marilyn would let Rebecca hold the list while they shopped. This gave Rebecca ownership in shopping as well as something to do. It also allowed her to have something to control. As they gathered each item, Rebecca would cross the item off the list. If Rebecca did a good job, she could choose the cupcakes.

While they were shopping, Marilyn was generous with encouragement, telling Rebecca, "You are doing a good job of keeping track of the list. Thank you." "You are waiting nicely. Thank you, Rebecca." "I appreciate your help." After two weeks of practice and a few minor setbacks, the plan seemed to be working.

As Marilyn and Rebecca became more familiar with the rules of shopping, they took their plan back to the supermarket. Marilyn began with quick trips and short lists. This strategy eased the transition from the convenience store to the supermarket. Gradually, she was able to extend her shopping time. Rebecca had learned how to behave. So had Marilyn.

Another situation many preschool parents face is not listening. Remember that sometimes, preschool age children do not listen because they are engaged so deeply in an activity that their brain blocks out any distractions. On the other hand, children may start to deliberately ignore their parents' requests.

Tommy is an active five-year-old who is obedient most of the time. A few times each day, however, Tommy becomes too energetic and loud. He crashes his toys together and tosses them around the room. These behaviors annoy his father, Ron, who always begins by calmly and politely asking, "Please play quietly, Tommy." But Tommy continues to play loudly. Ron becomes irritated by the noise and raises his voice. "You are getting wound up. Please quiet down, or you will have to put your toys away!" Tommy responds, "Okay, Daddy." Tommy stops being loud for about five minutes. Then he starts again. Now Ron becomes angry and starts yelling: "If you do not get quiet right now, I am getting out the paddle!" This time, Tommy becomes quiet and remains so for the next hour.

What have Ron and Tommy learned from each other? Tommy has learned that he does not have to do what Dad asks the first time; he does not have to listen when Dad raises his voice the first time either. Dad threatens to take away his toys, but he never does. Tommy has learned that he does not have to listen until Dad starts yelling about the paddle. Then he is serious.

Here is what Ron might say about this situation: "Tommy never listens when I ask him to do something. He just ignores me. The only time he listens is when I am angry. Then he knows he needs to stop or else." This statement is partly true, but Dad is also part of the problem. If Ron would admit this, his analysis of the situation would expand: "One thing I have learned is that my threats do not work; only when I get angry and start talking about the paddle do I get results. Calm and polite requests are ineffective. I have to change the way I am handling this. I have to figure out how to get Tommy to listen without always having to threaten punishment."

This is an important insight. Ron realizes that the way in which he reacts to Tommy is part of the reason that Tommy does not listen. Many parents do not like to admit this. It is easier to justify misbehavior as a phase or to say, "Five-year-olds always have to be told six times!" Many parents cannot face the idea that they might be doing something wrong. In most situations, both you and your children need a behavior change.

There is another valuable lesson in this example. Whenever you use punishment to correct misbehavior, without using a positive approach to build proper behavior, you will get a recycling pattern of the misbehavior. Ron threatens Tommy a few times. Tommy doesn't obey. Ron becomes angry and gets out the paddle. Tommy becomes quiet. *For a while!* But sooner or later, Tommy will start up again. It may be in twenty minutes or an hour or two, but his misbehavior will return. Why? Because next time he may get away with it for a little longer than last time. Tommy gets loud. Ron threatens. Tommy doesn't obey. Ron gets angry. The cycle continues.

Ron needs to be consistent by doing what he says he is going to do. He needs to follow through the first time he asks Tommy to be more quiet. He needs to respond to Tommy's refusal to play more quietly with a consequence, actually taking away the toys for a few minutes, as he promised.

Ron may also need to be more involved with Tommy's playing behavior. When a child plays too loudly, one good way to teach quiet play behavior is to play with your child and model the correct behavior. This is how children learn. Tommy will gradually play more quietly because he sees that his father is playing quietly.

You and your children also learn from each other when things go well. Let's take a look at how Margaret teaches her three-year-old daughter, Terry, how to get ready for bed. Together, Margaret and Terry create a chart with pictures of the things Terry needs to complete to get ready for bed. They include things like brushing her teeth, putting away toys, and getting into pajamas. The chart is posted in Terry's bedroom. Margaret rehearses the activities with Terry each night. Because this strategy is positive, Margaret has found no need to nag or argue with Terry about getting ready for bed. Terry is learning what is expected, and she enjoys spending quiet time with her mother before going to sleep.

What have Margaret and Terry learned from this arrangement? They have learned to cooperate. Margaret has found a way to get Terry to bed. Terry has found a way to earn time with Mom. Charts and checklists are helpful teaching tools. Children learn what you expect from them, and what they can expect from you. (For more about charts, see chapter 11.)

What's the Payoff?

Each of these examples demonstrates that parents and children learn from each other. Although these three situations are very different, the principles are the same. The principle at work here is that of the pay-off—we often do things to get what we want. Let's examine the behaviors and the payoffs in each example.

Rebecca's misbehavior was a tantrum. Her payoffs were the cookie and winning, and power and control over Mom. Marilyn's behaviors were giving in and buying the cookie. Marilyn's payoffs were a few minutes of peace and no further embarrassment. They each got what they wanted. What's wrong? The method! Rebecca got what she wanted by screaming in public. Marilyn got what she wanted by giving her authority and control to her child.

Tommy's misbehavior was not playing too loudly, but rather deliberately ignoring Ron's requests. Tommy's payoff was having his way a little longer. At first, Ron's behavior was to threaten and do nothing. Once he was angry, Ron's behavior was to get the paddle. His payoff was that Tommy finally became quiet. While the paddle seems immediately effective, it isn't in the long run. Tommy is not learning to be quiet. He is not learning to cooperate. He is learning only that he has to become quiet when Dad brings out the paddle. If Tommy is like most children, he will become noisy again. Dad will go through his threats again. The cycle may never end.

Think about what your preschooler hopes to gain by misbehaving— a treat, more time doing what he wants to do, attention, asserting his independence or control over you. If your preschooler misbehaves often, it means that he has not learned appropriate ways of getting what he wants. Teach him to redirect his behavior. Give him an appropriate alternative that will enable him to get what he wants. Do not reward unacceptable behavior.

When Marilyn stopped giving in to Rebecca's shouted demands, she taught her daughter how to get what she wanted through proper behavior. Rebecca helps with the shopping, stays calm, has a little patience, and earns a little treat. Both mother and child still get a payoff, but it is achieved in a positive manner, and Marilyn, not Rebecca, has remained in charge of the situation. If Ron teaches Tommy to play quietly, both Ron and Tommy get the payoff they want. Ron has a quieter child, and Tommy gets to play longer because he plays quietly.

As a parent, you can create positive payoffs by taking the time to explain your expectations to your child, just as Margaret did with Terry. Margaret took the time to be proactive by planning a bedtime routine. Then she implemented the plan by spending quality time with Terry, taking the time to teach her what is expected. Terry learns how to get ready for bed. Her payoff is more time with Mom and a good feeling about herself. Margaret's payoff is her ability to put Terry to bed without fuss and seeing her daughter learn to be responsible and develop good self-esteem.

How Some Preschoolers Learn Misbehavior

"Please pick up your toys, Paul."

"I don't feel like it now."

"Paul, please be a good listener."

"No. I don't want to."

"It's time now, Paul, please."

"I don't want to."

"Pick up your toys, and you can have a cookie."

"I want three cookies."

"Okay."

This parent is offering a reward to a child who is not listening, not obeying, and not picking up his toys. *A bribe is reward for misbehavior.* A bribe is an attempt to coax a misbehaving child into good behavior. Bribery makes children oppositional and increases stubbornness and resistance.

When Rebecca had a tantrum in the supermarket, Marilyn bribed her into being quiet by giving her the cookie she demanded. Although Rebecca did become quiet, Marilyn may get a tantrum whenever Rebecca wants something she can't have. This is how misbehavior patterns develop. Many reasonable and well-meaning parents have unintentionally taught their children to misbehave. Marilyn never intended to encourage Rebecca to have tantrums.

Some parents begin rewarding unacceptable behavior while their children are quite young. Consider the parent who uses a treat to comfort an unhappy child. The treat will probably coax the child into a better mood. The youngster may learn that one way to get a treat is to act unhappy. Unhappiness is rewarded. The child associates unhappiness with food. Whenever something unpleasant occurs, food will make the hurt go away.

Extinction

What do you do if you are already trapped in a pattern of giving in or bribing? Use extinction, a strategy in which you do not reward misbehavior, and as a result it happens less frequently. If whining no longer works, your preschooler will have less reason to whine. Extinction means that Marilyn must stop giving Rebecca a cookie when she has a tantrum. She must stop, no matter how embarrassing her tantrum becomes. This may sound simple, but it is not easy. If you have a stubborn, persistent child, this strategy will be work.

Extinction works better when you combine it with redirection (see chapter 7). Don't give in to the whining, but redirect your preschooler to the correct behavior. When Rebecca begins to whine and plead for a cookie, Marilyn redirects her by saying, "Sorry, not when you whine. Please ask in a big-girl voice." If Rebecca continues to whine, Marilyn will continue to ignore the whining and offer reminders or suggestions for the proper behavior: "You know how to ask for a cookie. Mommy, may I have a cookie, please?" This redirection shows how to give your preschooler the correct words to use.

With parental determination, consistency, and ample redirection, tantrums and demands that are not rewarded will eventually disappear. The key word is *eventually*—behavior change takes time, and in many cases tantrums will get worse before they get better. This increase is called an "extinction burst." Consider the child's point of view: "I usually get what I want by having a tantrum. Now Mom is ignoring my tantrums. I'll get her attention this time. I'll show her a tantrum she will never forget." The more a child has been rewarded, the more the misbehavior will resist extinction.

Once you decide to stop giving in, you must do so forever. Never give in again. Let's look at Marilyn and Rebecca to see why this is so crucial. Marilyn decides that she will not give in to Rebecca's tantrum. She will not buy her the cookie she demands. Off they go to the supermarket. By aisle 3, Rebecca is having a tantrum. Marilyn hangs in there. Rebecca is yelling, screaming, and kicking. The situation has never been this bad. In aisle 5, Rebecca is having a meltdown. Marilyn's determination is weakening. The crowd of astonished shoppers is getting larger, and the embarrassment is becoming too much to bear. Finally, Marilyn's will crumbles. She gives in and buys the cookie. Marilyn has just taught Rebecca to have bigger tantrums and be more persistent. If you start to use extinction and then give in, you will make the misbehavior worse. If you give in to bigger tantrums and demands, you will be rewarding bigger tantrums and demands. You will get longer and louder tantrums in the future.

Be consistent. Follow through. Once you say it, stick to it, even when you are tired and do not feel like being consistent, and even when you have had a long, miserable day. If you do not think you can outlast an extinction burst, then do not start. Wait until you have the courage and the energy. You will need support from your spouse. It is important to work together to emphasize the point to your preschooler that you both mean business. If your spouse will not cooperate, be consistent anyway. It will take a little longer for your efforts to show results. Your child will learn that you mean what you say. She will behave better for you. She will behave as always for your spouse.

Be patient. Most parents fail because they lack patience. You must be more persistent than your child. If you give in, you lose. You must control yourself. Do not yell or lose your temper. That will only make matters worse. Your ultimate reward will be well-behaved children.

If you have a bad day, put it behind you. If you give in, do not dwell on it. If you are short on patience, regain your balance. Being patient and consistent is not easy. If you slip back into old habits, do not criticize yourself. Start fresh. Think of the future.

While extinction weakens misbehaviors, it also weakens good behaviors that are not recognized. When positive behaviors are ignored, they may be replaced by misbehavior: "Why be good? It's not worth it." Use positive feedback when your preschoolers are behaving. Do not ignore good behavior. Focus on what your children are doing right. Catch your children being good.

9

Being Consistent Is Seldom Easy, but It Is Always Worth It

One evening, when Leah was three years old, we went out for dinner. Leah knew that after dinner, we often had dessert. Leah ordered her usual—a cheeseburger, fries, and a small milk with one straw. For some reason, Leah was more interested in looking around the restaurant than eating. We gave her the familiar reminders. With each reminder, she took another nibble of her burger or sip of her milk, but she was not eating very well. Meanwhile, the rest of us were nearly finished.

Realizing that she was not hungry, I wanted to be reasonable. I cut the remainder of her burger in half. "You have to eat this half of your burger before it's time for dessert. If you do not eat it, you will not get ice cream." Leah smiled and agreed but continued to look around and not eat. Soon the time of reckoning was upon us. It was time to order dessert.

We thought about buying her some ice cream anyway. Although she had not eaten, she was polite and well behaved. We thought about the scene she would create when she realized she was not getting any ice cream. We thought about how embarrassed we would be. Many parents think this way. This is how we justify giving in, especially in public, but we knew we could not give in to these thoughts. Our only alternative was to follow through on the deal I had made with Leah: If you do not finish the half of your hamburger, you do not have dessert. Consistency is more important than a few tears and some embarrassment. After a few more minutes, I told Leah we were leaving. She asked if she could have her ice cream now. I said, "No, you did not finish your dinner." "I'll eat it now, Daddy," she pleaded. Then she saw three ice-cream cones, not four. We softly explained that we had finished our dinners. That's why we each had ice cream.

As I carried my screaming daughter under my arm past a crowded dining room of families, I felt dreadful. I wondered what everyone was thinking. I wanted to explain, "It's okay, I'm just being consistent."

Leah cried and pleaded all the way home. She said she would eat her dinner if we would only give her another chance. It was the first time in my life I did not enjoy eating ice cream. I wanted to roll down my window and toss it out. We love Leah. Watching her cry was excruciating.

Think about the future. Sometimes saying no and being consistent is not easy. It can hurt. It would have been much easier to give in and buy the ice cream, but we knew it was more important to be consistent, even though being consistent is sometimes painful. We wanted Leah to learn that her parents mean what they say, even if it means some temporary unpleasantness. You have to eat your dinner if you want dessert. If you do not finish your dinner, you will not keep the rest of us from having dessert. You have to do what you are asked, even in a public place. When we followed through with Leah, we were thinking about the future more than the present. We wanted Leah to know that she had to eat her dinner this time and every time.

What Happens If You Give In a Little

Parents often ask what to do about their child's not listening or whining or some other misbehavior. At some point I will always talk about consistency and how important it is not to give in to such behaviors. I am always amazed how many parents respond, "Well, I don't give in that much." For most preschoolers, it doesn't take that much.

The hardest part about being consistent is being consistent all the time. Being consistent 90 percent of the time is not enough for most children. If you give in even once in a while, they win once in a while. This teaches preschoolers to be opportunists. They learn to be persistent in a negative way; every once in a while it works, so it is worth the chance. If preschoolers whine and tease and even occasionally get their way, they win. They learn that whining and teasing work.

I am not sure that any parent can be 100 percent consistent with every possible misbehavior. But if you are working on specific behavior problems with your preschooler, please be consistent with these. If you tell your preschooler that he needs to listen the first time, then be consistent. If you say no whining, then be consistent. (See strategy 2, "Narrow the List," later in this chapter.)

The Difference Between Threats and Warnings

Have you ever been in a waiting room where there were parents and preschoolers? A parent threatens, "If you do not sit down, I will put you in the car." The child sits for a minute or two and then starts jumping around again. Mom threatens again. The child sits a few minutes and then gets up. Mom threatens again. The cycle goes on.

A threat is an *intention* to take action, or to punish. Threats are just words. Many parents threaten because they do not know how to redirect misbehavior. Some parents threaten because they are afraid to use punishment. They worry that if they take action, their preschooler will retaliate with more offensive misbehavior. Some parents threaten because they are too lazy to follow through. Whatever the reason, threats often make a child's misbehavior worse.

Threats often arise when a parent is angry and frustrated. We often threaten action when we are angry that we would never consider when we are calm and rational. We say things because we do not know what else to say or do.

Lois, for example, screamed at her four-year-old, "Do that again, and I'll take your dog back to the pet store!" Lois was angry at the time and admitted she would never say this when she was calm. Nor would she ever take her son's dog back to the store—but it was too late, her anger had already left its mark. Instead of setting a boundary, the threat built a wall. Instead of promoting cooperation, the threat created fear, anger, and resistance in her child. It took Lois several days of soothing to rebuild their relationship and reassure her child that she would not return his dog.

Threats teach your children not to believe what you say. Children know that threats are not always enforced. How do they know? You have not followed through in the past. Threatening is a magnified form of inconsistency.

Warnings are different, and can be effective if you use them sparingly and with plenty of judgment. The difference between a threat and a warning is found not in what the parent says, or even in the parent's tone of voice, but in what the child hears. If you are a parent who has a history of following through when you ask your child to do something, your child will hear a warning. He will probably stop, because he knows you will take action. If you are a parent who says, "Stop that. Please stop. How many times do I have to tell you to stop?" your child will hear your words as a threat and not stop until he knows you are serious, which unfortunately for many parents means when they become angry and punish.

Melody brought four-year-old David to our house for a birthday party. Midway through the party, David began to act up. Melody warned him to stop. He did not. Melody told him that they would leave the party. He continued to misbehave. She picked him up and headed for the car. He cried and pleaded to stay. They left and did not return. The party was over for David. Even though Melody also had to leave, she followed through. David has been good at parties ever since.

Only parents who have a reputation for following through can use warnings successfully. If you have consistently followed through with what you say, your preschooler will hear a warning. Your child has learned that when you say stop, you mean stop now. If you have been inconsistent, your preschooler will only hear a threat when you say stop. Your preschooler has learned that it takes several threats before he actually has to stop.

A warning with redirection works best. Most preschoolers will need warnings because they are still learning what is proper behavior. Use a warning when your preschooler may not know that he is behaving inappropriately. For example, preschoolers have a tendency to get loud and disruptive when they play. Say, "Children, your voices are too loud. Please play more quietly. Use a soft voice."

Another type of warning that can be used effectively is a time warning. These are very helpful for parents and children, since they help preschoolers make the transition from one activity to another. Here are some examples:

"We can read for ten more minutes, then it will be time to turn off
the light."

"Dinner will be ready in five minutes. Please finish your picture."

"You can play until the timer goes off. I'll set it for five minutes."

Time warnings let your preschooler know ahead of time that something is expected of him very soon. When it comes time to make a transition, it is less of a surprise, and preschoolers are generally more
cooperative. For some reason children love timers; use them to your advantage, whether it is the timer on the oven, a bell timer, or an egg
timer. Not only do timers make these transition periods more fun for
your children, they also help teach them about time itself.

"Five More Minutes," "Maybe," and "We'll See"

Many parents are afraid to set limits. The reasons some parents do not
say no range from wanting to avoid an argument, to embarrassment or
guilt if their child has a tantrum, to worry of being disliked by their
children, and to being lazy and not wanting to take firm action. These
parents tend to use stalling statements: "Five more minutes," "Maybe,"
and "We'll see."

"It's time to go home."
"Can't we stay a little while longer?"
"Okay, five more minutes."

"Can we have some ice cream after supper?"
"Maybe."

"Can we go to the park tomorrow, Dad?"
"We'll see."

Stalling statements delay the inevitable. It is okay to use delays as
long as your preschoolers know that "Maybe" sometimes means yes and
sometimes means no. Your preschoolers must realize that "We'll see"
sometimes means yes and sometimes means no. Your preschoolers must
understand that "five more minutes" means five more minutes, not ten
more minutes.

How do you teach your children that "Maybe" sometimes means no? Every now and then, follow a "maybe" with a "no." "I know I said maybe. I have thought about it. The answer is no." You may find that your children do not like hearing this. That's all right, they will live. As always, be consistent. It will be worth it in the long run.

Using stalling statements occasionally is harmless. Use them too often and your children will whine and plead and beg, hoping you will give in. Use them carefully.

What Consistency Means to Your Preschoolers

If you want self-disciplined children, you need to be consistent. You need to mean what you say and follow through. You can significantly improve your preschooler's behavior by being more positive and more consistent. Consistency is the most important element in your relationship with your child, yet it is the most frequently omitted. If you change one thing about the way you discipline your children, be more consistent.

Karen was not a strong disciplinarian. Her three-year-old son, Eric, behaved any way he pleased. Eric would throw his toys and refuse to pick them up. He argued about everything from eating his dinner to going to bed. Eric was in charge. Karen didn't want to take him anywhere because she was embarrassed by his behavior. He called the shots. He manipulated his mother by whining and throwing tantrums. Eric always got his way because Karen always gave in. Karen was afraid to enroll Eric in preschool because she worried that she would be embarrassed by his behavior.

After Karen attended one of my parenting workshops, she began to understand the need to regain control at home by being consistent and following through. She developed a plan and began setting expectations and consequences. She stopped giving in to Eric's shouted demands. She began to look for and recognize cooperative behaviors. She made a strong personal commitment to be consistent and positive. Gradually, Karen saw improvement. As Eric improved at home, Karen began taking him to the park, the movie theater, and the library. She even enrolled him in preschool. Karen's hard work paid off. By the time she enrolled him in preschool, Eric was able to follow the classroom rules with a little help from his teachers.

Consistency means you follow through and manage misbehavior exactly the same way every time it occurs. This is especially true when working with persistent misbehaviors. Once you tell your daughter,

"Use a big-girl voice, please do not whine," be consistent. Do not give in to whining. Some parents rationalize: "A little whining is okay." "It's not that big a problem." "I'm too tired to deal with this now." You are fooling yourself. How big must the problem be for you to act? Will you be less tired tomorrow?

When misbehavior occurs, deal with it now. If you let it slide, you will pay the price in the future. Do not let friends, neighbors, or grandparents influence your commitment to be consistent. They might say, "Let it go this time." "He is only three." "How often do we get to see him?" "He's okay. He's just a little excited." You are the parent. You do what is best for your children. Let other people raise their own children. You be consistent.

Preschoolers learn to make decisions by predicting the outcome of their actions. They must be able to see the relationship between cause and effect, how they behave and what happens to them: If I choose this behavior, then this consequence will happen. Your preschoolers must be able to predict your reaction to their behavior. They need to know how you behave. They need to know the consequences. Children will learn this cause-and-effect relationship more quickly when you behave consistently.

These lessons can be taught by any adult who cares for your children. Listen to Fiona describing her baby-sitter: "My baby-sitter knows that discipline is important. She has firm expectations, and she enforces them consistently. She has a better reputation with my children for follow-through. My children listen to her." While Fiona isn't behaving as consistently as her baby-sitter, she understands the key issue: her children find the baby-sitter's words more credible than their mother's because of how consistent each woman is with them.

How to Be More Consistent

You know the rule now: You cannot be consistent some of the time, you must be consistent all of the time. Consistency is not always easy—it is exhausting, it drains your energy, and it weakens your spirit—but it is always worth it. Think of the future. Do not let little problems grow. Deal with misbehavior immediately. Do not be afraid to say no. Talk with your spouse about discipline, even if you are divorced. Plan to manage misbehaviors consistently. Here are eight strategies that will help you be more consistent.

Strategy 1: Parents Unite

Becky was three. Her mother and father were sitting on the couch. Becky asked Mom for some yogurt. Mom said, "No, it is too close to dinner." Without a moment's hesitation, Becky turned to Dad and asked him for some yogurt. Children learn to manipulate at a young age: if one parent says no, try the other.

Consistency is important between parent and child. It is also important between parent and parent. If Dad is too easy and Mom is too strict, your preschoolers will learn to manipulate. This results in disaster. Preschoolers will learn which parent to ask for what things. When you want a treat, another cartoon, or to stay up past your bedtime, ask Dad. He usually gives in on these matters. When you want a new toy, or to have a friend come over to play, ask Mom. She's easier than Dad.

Agree on the house rules and expectations. Agree on what your preschoolers can and cannot do. Agree on things that relate to discipline. If you disagree, that's fine, but disagree behind closed doors. Work things out when your children are not around. Even if you do not agree, present a united front to your children. Compromise if you must. If you disagree in front of your children, you will be teaching them where you are vulnerable. Then you will hear statements such as, "Well, Dad said I could have some chocolate cake," or "Mom said I could go play."

Talk with your spouse about discipline. Explore each other's feelings and beliefs. Review your ideas periodically. That way, whichever parent is around, behavior will be handled consistently. Preschoolers learn that you are working together. They will not be tempted to play one of you against the other.

When unplanned situations occur, it is permissible to say, "I'll have to talk with Daddy about this. You will have to wait." Do not confuse this suggestion with "Wait until your father gets home." Do not depend on one parent to make all the decisions about discipline. Only special problems need to be discussed. Day-to-day discipline must be handled immediately. If Mom depends on Dad to be the heavy, the children will seldom listen to Mom. Mom must take charge of her time with the children.

Strategy 2: Narrow the List

It is easy for most parents to make a long list of their preschooler's misbehaviors they want to correct, but long lists are overwhelming and exasperating; they don't help because you cannot keep up with them all.

Choose your battles. Focus on one or two priority behaviors at a time. A priority behavior is a behavior that you are going to manage with special diligence and awareness. For example, if you want your preschoolers to cooperate with each other, cooperation is the priority behavior. Catch your preschoolers cooperating and recognize them for it. This will teach your preschoolers that you value cooperation. A priority behavior can also be a misbehavior. Many preschoolers develop misbehavior patterns, displaying the same misbehavior repeatedly. Common misbehaviors for this age group are whining, nagging, and disobeying. Your preschooler may exhibit several misbehavior patterns. Attempting to work on all of them at once would be impossible for you and confusing for your child. Choose one or two patterns as priority behaviors, and be aware of these misbehaviors at all times. Never give in. Do not reward them. Be consistent. This will not be easy; at times you will be tired and will not want to follow through. If you do not, however, you will pay for it later.

Remember to watch for positive behaviors while you are consistent with misbehaviors. Suppose your preschooler's priority misbehavior is having tantrums. Be consistent; never reward any tantrum, and at the same time reinforce your preschooler's good behavior: "I'm glad to see that you did not cry when I told you that you could not have a candy bar. I really appreciate that. Thank you."

It is important to identify one or two priority behaviors and focus your energy on them. Be consistent and diligent with the priority behaviors you have selected, and your children will learn them more quickly. And as a bonus, when you are consistent with priority behaviors, it will have a positive effect on all other behaviors. Your preschoolers will generalize what they learn from one situation to another. It is like having a two-for-one sale on good behavior—be consistent with priority behaviors, and get improvement in other behaviors free. How could you refuse such a deal?

Strategy 3: Remind Yourself

Tangible reminders help you be more consistent. Write little notes to yourself: "Do not give in to tantrums." "Catch your preschoolers playing quietly." Put a sign on your bathroom mirror: "Look for cooperation." Put a sign on the refrigerator: "Stay calm. Do not argue." Notes and signs help you remember to be consistent and remind you to focus on priority behaviors. Charts and checklists are excellent visual, tangible reminders. (See chapter 11.)

Strategy 4: Practice Patience

The fourth strategy that you need to be more consistent is really a quality—patience. Parents want quick changes, but preschoolers do not change misbehavior patterns easily. Misbehaviors that your child has mastered take time to relearn. Just because you have decided to read this book and be consistent, your preschooler's misbehavior will not change overnight. You will have to be patient.

Patience is difficult. You want immediate results for your energy and commitment, but think about things from your child's point of view. If you have been using threats and warnings before taking action, your child has learned that this is how you behave. Now you have changed: you are consistent. You are following through. Your child will be confused and resist change. It took time and energy to change your behavior; your child is no different. Be patient.

Strategy 5: Choose a Good Time to Start

If you are going to initiate a new plan or start a new discipline technique with your children, choose a good time to begin. An experienced mom gave me this idea. She was a tax accountant and she explained that she had learned never to start anything new during tax season, when she was working sixty-plus hours per week. She recognized that this period was not a good time to make any new resolutions, start a diet, change a bad habit, or try to enforce a new behavior with her children.

Do not try to initiate change of troublesome behaviors when you or your child will be in stressful or unusual circumstances. For example, do not try to start a new routine just before Christmas vacation or the annual visit from grandparents or when your child is starting a new school. Choose a time that is more stable and predictable for everyone. This will give you the time and structure that you need to be consistent.

Strategy 6: Be Sensitive to the Time of Day

Three periods of time each day are associated with increases in misbehavior. The morning routine is often difficult because of the pressure to be out the door and off to work and school. This extra pressure makes parents and children feel tense and urgent; tempers flare, and reason and calm abandon us. Prepare for this each day. Awaken everyone twenty minutes earlier to ensure enough time to get ready. Take the time to have breakfast together and have fun. Relax. Model calmness. This teaches preschoolers to get their moods ready for the day.

Research has shown that the most difficult time of day for parents and children is the time between after school and dinner, when parents are tired, and children want to release energy that has been stored all day in school. This is also a time, these studies have concluded, when everyone's blood sugar is low, which makes us irritable. It may be helpful for you and the preschoolers to have a snack. It also helps to have a plan for the children. Keep them engaged in fun activities—the few minutes that you spend designing distractions will buy you more time for yourself.

Bedtime is also a problem for some children. Do not teach your pre-schooler that going to bed is a punishment that comes at the end of each day. Going to bed is a time to relax and get comfortable. Have a bedtime routine: bath, snack, story, hug, and kiss. Use a chart or check-list to teach children to regulate their own bedtime routine. Do not use going to bed early as a punishment.

Strategy 7: Expect Challenge
Preschoolers will test you. No matter how carefully you plan or how strongly committed you are, your children will resist change. Preschoolers often respond well to new discipline techniques at first, but after a while they drift back to their previous patterns, and misbehaviors increase. When this happens, do not despair. This is normal. Once you realize that occasional testing of limits will occur, you will be less frustrated and disappointed. Knowing this helps you be more consistent during these periods.

Strategy 8: Make the Commitment
The eighth strategy that helps you be more consistent is the awareness that consistency is one of the most important factors in successful parenting. Consistency teaches preschoolers what to expect. It teaches children how to predict the consequences of their actions. Once a preschooler can predict the outcome of his behavior, he will make better choices, which is the key to developing responsibility.

Understanding the importance of consistency will make you more consistent. Consistency is important when teaching positive behaviors. The more consistently you use positive feedback, the more quickly your preschooler will learn appropriate behaviors. This is especially true when you are trying to teach new behaviors. Every time you find your preschoolers playing nicely, thank them for being cooperative. When you see your son making an effort to pick up his toys, mention how proud you feel. Explain how he is growing up and becoming responsible. He is helping the whole family.

Consistency is important when you use punishment. Once you tell your child that misbehavior will be punished, always follow through. If you slip up or only use punishment when you feel like it, you will make the problem worse by teaching your child that you do not mean what you say. Your preschooler will learn to be persistent in a negative way, and that sooner or later he will get away with misbehaving.

Consistency is an expression of love and caring. When you behave consistently, your children will have better self-discipline. They will see that they are important to you: "I know my parents care about me, because they put in the energy and time to make sure that I behave." When you behave consistently, you are telling your children that you will do whatever it takes. That's your job.

Inconsistency causes preschoolers to be unsure of themselves. It makes children feel unimportant, insecure, and confused. This confusion compels children to manipulate, tease, or take advantage of unclear situations. Once your children learn that you mean what you say and you are consistent, they will take you more seriously. They will think more carefully about all their behaviors and decisions. Thinking is what you want.

Inconsistency teaches children that you do not mean what you say. Once your child learns this, he will try to get away with other disobedience: "If I don't have to pick up my toys, maybe I don't have to brush my teeth either." This creates a cycle where children become increasingly persistent in a negative way. Consistency breaks this cycle.

A certain amount of misbehavior is normal in all children. When you respond to misbehavior consistently, the misbehavior will decrease. When you respond to misbehavior inconsistently, the misbehavior will increase. Consistency is most important, yet it can be extremely difficult. So remember to reward yourself after you have persisted through a difficult situation!

PART IV

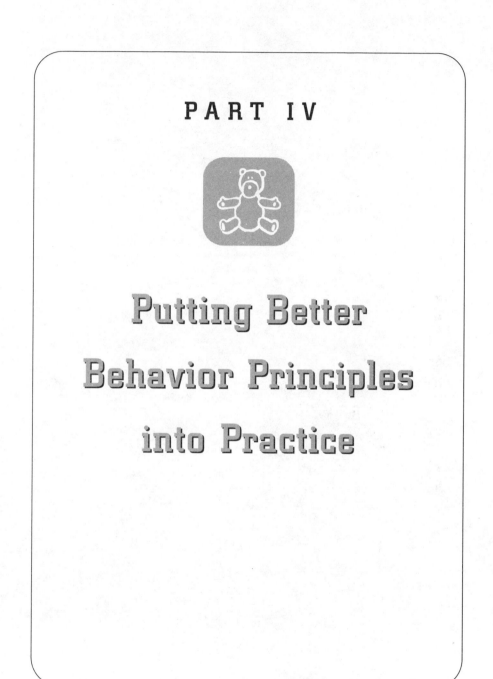

Putting Better Behavior Principles into Practice

10

How to Build Positive Behaviors and Attitudes

 Four-year-old Tiffany runs up to her mother. "I picked up all my toys. My room is clean, Mommy. Come and see." Mom inspects the room and smiles. "Great job, Tiffany. You should be proud of yourself. Your room looks very neat." Tiffany's mom is using positive feedback. She is looking for good decisions. She is pointing out the things her daughter is doing well. She is shining a spotlight on Tiffany's good behavior.

Use Positive Feedback

When you recognize your preschooler's good behavior, you are giving your child positive feedback. Positive feedback is a payoff for good behavior. It means using words or words and incentives to encourage proper behavior, positive attitudes, and good decision making. This is the most powerful tool you have to improve your preschooler's behavior and self-esteem. Positive feedback lets your preschoolers know they are doing the right thing.

This is not a new method, and you no doubt already know that positive feedback is important, yet parents often forget to use it, which is a mistake. If you desire better behavior from your preschooler, increasing your awareness and use of positive feedback is fundamental.

I have been convinced of the power of positive feedback for the past thirty years. During that time I have worked as a teacher, school psychologist, and administrator in school programs for behavior-disordered children. These programs provided special services for children who were unable to function in a regular school program because of disruptive behavior. Many of these children were seriously emotionally disturbed, some were delinquent, and many were undisciplined. Regardless of their problems, nearly every child made improvements within the first few weeks. People who knew these children's history were amazed. How did they improve their behavior so quickly? The first thing the staff did was stop looking for negative behavior and look instead for positive behavior. Once these students realized that they could behave, and that it felt good to behave, it was easy for them to learn how.

A mother recently explained how she taught the concept of positive feedback to some college students who were doing an internship at her son's day-care center. Every day when she picked up her son, the college students would tell her all the things her son had done wrong. Each day, she would ask, "Tell me something good he did." After several days, the students began to look for positive behaviors to report. Soon the youngster was behaving more appropriately, as were the college students.

You can use positive feedback in two ways: to focus on correct behaviors and attitudes in your preschooler, or to help eliminate or weaken some types of misbehavior. This second technique is called *replacement* and is discussed in the next section.

Using positive feedback to strengthen a desired behavior is easy. Simply look for good behavior. When it occurs, reinforce it with a few words of praise or encouragement, a hug, or a privilege. For example, you would like your children to share with each other. When your child shares something, you can reinforce him by saying, "I like the way you are sharing." "I see you have decided to share your toys this morning. That's a good decision." "I am proud of the way you are sharing the TV. That shows you are growing up. Good for you!"

Positive feedback is simple to use. The difficult part is remembering to look for the good behavior. Often we only see the misbehavior in our children and take good behavior for granted. Be proactive. Strengthen good behavior by telling your children you appreciate it. Focus on the positive aspects of your children's behavior. It takes practice, but if the only change you make is to increase your use of positive feedback, your children will start making better decisions.

Teach Replacement Behaviors

You can also use positive feedback to eliminate or weaken many types of misbehavior, including patterns of misbehavior. Replacement is a long-term, proactive strategy, and it takes time. It does not work for misbehavior that is staring you in the face. (When your preschooler is misbehaving, stay calm and do not give in to his demands. Try using redirection and a firm warning. These techniques are discussed in other sections of this book.)

Here is how to use the replacement technique. First, determine the misbehavior pattern you want to address. Common misbehavior patterns among preschoolers are not listening, arguing, whining, not sharing, screaming, and having tantrums. Next, determine the opposite behavior. What is the correct behavior that you want to see? This opposite, correct behavior is the replacement; it replaces the original misbehavior. Next, look for the replacement behavior. When it occurs, give your preschooler a healthy dose of positive feedback. Let's take a look at how this technique works:

Four-year-old Nathan argues with and teases his three-year-old sister, Ashley. The opposite of this misbehavior occurs when Nathan is playing nicely and cooperating with Ashley. When Nathan's mother sees him playing nicely with his sister, she reinforces the correct behavior by saying, "You are helping your sister draw. Good for you." Playing cooperatively will eventually *replace* arguing and teasing. He will learn a more acceptable way of playing, and the arguing and teasing will occur less often.

Replacement is the most powerful and effective technique you have to eliminate misbehavior and build positive behaviors in your preschooler. In fact, replacement is the misbehavior strategy used by most preschool teachers. They know that using positive feedback strengthens the opposite behavior and causes the original misbehavior to decrease.

Most parents see the value in using positive feedback, yet there are some parents who resist the use of positive feedback and incentives. If you share this concern, think about how children are motivated. Many preschoolers are self-motivated to be well behaved and cooperative. These children are internally motivated to please you and do the right thing simply because you request it. They know how to make good choices, and they are motivated to do so. This is not the case with all preschoolers, however; many preschoolers are only motivated to do what they want and could care less about what you request or expect. Positive feedback gives resistant children a reason to make better choices. It gives them a motivation boost because it builds self-esteem. Positive feedback encourages children to be more self-motivated to behave correctly and make better decisions.

Aim for Self-Reward

Positive feedback can include tangible incentives. Some parents use stickers, charts, tokens, points, and even money. Be careful about using tangible incentives; while they work well, they can give a preschooler the wrong idea. When tangible incentives are overused, a child may become motivated to earn "things" but forget about the real reward—the self-reward of making good choices and having a good attitude and proper behavior.

The strongest form of positive feedback is verbal encouragement, words that recognize your preschooler for his correct behavior. Let your preschooler know he is making good choices when he listens, shares, uses manners, obeys, and cooperates. Even more important, however, is to make sure your verbal encouragement teaches your preschooler to value himself: "You made the right choice because you knew it was the correct thing to do." It is okay for preschoolers to behave and work hard to please their parents. It is better when they behave and work hard for themselves.

Good: "You were a good listener. Thank you."

Better: "You were a good listener. Thank you. I hope you feel proud of yourself."

The second statement creates a sense of success and self-value. It is aimed at building self-esteem. Whenever you reward your preschooler with an incentive, such as a sticker on a chart, be sure to add a verbal reminder that teaches your preschooler that he has done the right thing: "Thanks for picking up all your toys. You earned another sticker on your chart for being a good helper. You really did a good job. Thanks for making the right choice. I knew you could do it. I hope you feel happy about yourself."

Misbehavior After Rewards

Many parents ask why children often misbehave shortly after being complimented. This dilemma occurs because children have the mistaken belief that once they get their reward, they are free to do what they want. To handle this behavior, first and most important, use external reinforcement to build internal motivation. Your child only behaves to get something; once he gets it, he has little internal motivation to continue. The truth is that if he can behave in order to earn a reward, he can behave once he has received the reward. So it is very important that you aim for self-reward. Second, explain that when he earns a reward and then misbehaves, you feel discouraged or unhappy. Tell him that you will take away the reward if he begins to misbehave. Then don't be afraid to do it! This will let him know you are consistent, and he needs to make a better choice.

Preschoolers Believe What You Tell Them

Several years ago, there was a popular T-shirt for toddlers that read, "Here Comes Trouble." When you put a T-shirt like this on a child, you are encouraging your child to think of himself as a troublemaker. Even though many adults passing by may laugh or make a cute comment, there is no humor here. The reality is that most preschoolers act the way you expect them to act. If you tell your son that he is noisy, he will live up to that expectation. If you tell your son that he knows how to play quietly, he will live up to that expectation.

Sadly, many parents convey messages that they are not even conscious of. Listen to what Linda says to her energetic daughter:

"Brianna, stop being so hyper. Can't you ever play quietly? I do not understand why you have to run through the house all the time. Look at your toys. What a mess you made. What's wrong with you?"

What is Linda saying to Brianna? You are hyper. That's why you are so loud and messy. You will always be this way. That is what I expect from you. I am giving up hope of any improvement. When you use words such as *hyper, loud, messy, selfish, lazy, bad,* or *mean* to describe your preschooler, you plant the idea that your child is hyper or mean, and that is how she will always be. Your preschooler will then begin to think of herself as being this way, and soon she will be acting hyper or messy all the time. Listen to Linda when she addresses the situation differently:

> "You know, Brianna, this is not like you. You are a quieter child than this. I know you can play more softly. I have seen you keep your toys where they should be. I know you have pride in yourself. I'm sure you can do better. Don't you think so, too?"

Here is what Linda is saying now: You are a quiet child. You can play softly. You can take care of your toys. I trust you. I have confidence in you. You can do better. Do it for your own sake. Your preschooler will not make radical changes overnight, but you will be planting a healthier seed in her mind. Your child will gradually be quieter and less messy.

Many preschoolers need extra encouragement, especially children with shy temperaments, children with poor self-esteem, and children who lack persistence and determination. Encouragement gives children a boost of motivation. It helps them through difficult situations, helps them face fears and withstand stress, solve problems and feel successful. Encouragement provides support, trust, and belief.

Tell your child that you love and value her. Accept your child for who she is, not for what she does. Show trust and confidence in your child's abilities and decisions. Recognize effort and improvement. Preschoolers act the way you expect them to act. If you focus on positive qualities, you will build stronger positive qualities.

Have you seen the poster that pictures a child looking rather discouraged? The caption reads, "When I mess up, no one forgets. When I do well, no one sees." Don't turn your preschooler into this poster child. Positive feedback is easy to use, but we often forget. Retrain yourself to look for the positive qualities in your children.

HOW TO USE VERBAL REINFORCEMENT AND ENCOURAGEMENT

HOW TO SHOW TRUST

"I like the way you made a good choice."

"Knowing you, I am sure you will do a good job."

"I am sure you can be a good friend."

"I am sure you will do your best."

"I think you can do it."

"I am sure you can make a good choice. Come and get me if you need my help."

"I want to know what you like."

HOW TO SHOW THE IMPORTANCE OF HARD WORK

"If you practice, you will get better."

"Do your best."

"It looks like you really tried your best."

HOW TO POINT OUT STRENGTHS AND IMPROVEMENTS

"You worked hard at . . ."

"Look at how well you are doing."

"You are getting good."

"What a good try."

"You have really improved in . . ."

HOW TO TEACH CHILDREN TO LEARN FROM MISTAKES

"So you made a mistake, how can you fix it?"

"If you are not happy, what can you do?"

HOW TO ENCOURAGE RESPONSIBILITY

"It's up to you."

"If you want to."

"You can choose that for yourself."

"Your choice will be fine with me."

How to Use Activities and Incentives as Reinforcement and Encouragement

Wise parents connect special events to good behavior. We were visiting a friend's home a few summers ago. She had invited several children and parents over to swim. The afternoon was lovely, and all the children were behaving well. While we were there, our friend brought out a large box of Popsicles and began handing them out to children and parents. They were delicious and refreshing. The children were excited.

As we were leaving, she commented on how well the afternoon went. I smiled and said, "The kids were great. Too bad you gave away the Popsicles." She stopped and looked at me with astonishment. I smiled again. "I never give away Popsicles." Then I paused, "Without telling the kids what a great job they are doing." Now she smiled. She knew exactly what I meant. Connect special events to good behavior. "You are playing so well together, we decided to have a special treat. Who would like a Popsicle?"

You can be more specific: "You have all been polite to each other. That's something that makes Mom and I feel fantastic. When we feel good, we feel like doing something special."

Many parents worry about using food as reward. It can be a problem. Instead of stuffing sweets in your preschooler's mouths whenever they are well behaved, choose special activities. There are many ways to make the connection between having a good day and special events: going out for dinner, going to a movie, or even going for a Sunday-afternoon drive. What about days when behavior has not been so good? Do not get out the Popsicles on bad days.

Do not give special activities away. Preschool teachers who are good disciplinarians use this idea instinctively. These teachers make statements such as, "Katie, you worked hard on your art project this morning. Please ring the cleanup bell." "Sean, you really shared with Dillon during free time. Please help me hand out the snack." "Luke, you have been a good friend to your classmates. I'd like you to stay at the end of the line and shut the lights off when we go to the playground." This clever teacher made a privilege out of being last in line.

Activity incentives are things children want to do; for example, playing games, having a friend come over to play, going to a movie, or renting a video. Use activity incentives this way: first you work, and then you play. Pick up your toys before you go outside to play. Finish your breakfast before you watch television. Do not get trapped by promises, like, "I'll eat after cartoons."

Always add an encouraging comment when your preschooler earns an incentive: "You picked up your toys. You did it. Now you can play a game on the computer. Good for you." Emphasize that your child should feel good about himself, not the computer game. Enhance activities by becoming involved. For a child, playing a game is fun, but playing a game with a parent is more fun.

In addition to activity incentives, you can use tangible incentives such as snacks, stickers, toys, dolls, games, and prizes. Always accompany tangible incentives with words of thanks and encouragement: "Here's your game, Sue. You did a great job on your chart this week. Good for you." Make sure you do not mislead your children into thinking that the only reason to behave is to get something. This is a trap. Incentives are fun and motivating, but remember to aim for self-reward; make your child understand that he should do the right thing because it is the right thing. It makes you feel good. It makes you proud of yourself.

Special privilege activities include staying up late or going to a children's theme restaurant for dinner. Connect privileges to good behavior—but be careful. Do not dangle every little activity in front of your child's nose, as that will give him the wrong idea. You do not want him to think he has to be perfect. Children resent this and develop a poor attitude about working toward goals. Allow some fun activities to happen routinely and naturally. You also do not want preschoolers to think that every time they behave, you have to come up with a special reward. Children need to learn that good behavior is important because it is the right thing to do.

What follows is a list of incentives that was developed with the help of more than two thousand parents during a two-year period. Whenever I taught a class for parents of preschoolers, I would have parents write down examples of incentives that worked with their children, and I include these here. Use this list to create a menu of incentives. (This menu can be used with charts and checklists, which are discussed in the next chapter.)

A LIST OF INCENTIVES FOR PRESCHOOLERS

AFFECTION/APPROVAL

Hugs and kisses	Smiles
Eye contact	Nods and winks
Thumbs-up	Okay sign
High five	Happy dance

VERBAL

Praise and encouragement	"Good job."
"Awesome."	Compliments
"I like the way you . . ."	Complimenting your child in front of others
Thank-you notes in the lunch box	Thank-you notes through the mail

TANGIBLE

Treats/ice cream	Stickers/sticker books/happy faces
Stars/points on a chart	Mystery jar with awards inside
Painting/drawing/ supplies	Snacks
Children's magazines	Activity books

TANGIBLE

New clothes	Camera/photo album
Balloons	

ACTIVITIES

One-on-one time with a parent	Back rubs
Brother's Day/ Sister's Day	A special day with a parent
Roughhousing with a parent	Surprises
Finger-painting	Drawing
Playing with shaving cream in the tub	Having lunch at preschool
Books/reading or writing a story	Working on models, building kits
Gardening	Playing games/board games/ puzzles
Magic tricks	Going for a walk
Going on a bike ride	Going on a mystery ride
Watching television together	Renting a movie
Making popcorn	Having a friend come to play
Making a blanket tent	Singing songs/playing music
Kite flying	Going swimming
Going to the movies	Going to the zoo/park/library
Going out to eat	Allowing child to choose the restaurant

ACTIVITIES

Having a pizza delivered	Bubble baths/toys in tub
Brushing hair	Helping prepare a meal
Baking cookies	Playing computer games
Having a friend over for lunch/dinner	Going out with a friend for lunch/dinner
Choosing an activity for the family	Making playdough
Using a calculator (not to calculate, just to play!)	Tic-tac-toe
Staying up late on weekends	Visiting a fire station
Dressing up in parent's clothes	Playing with costumes
Using play tools	Making a movie

•YOUR TURN•

While giving positive feedback and reinforcement are easy to do, we often forget to do it. Try the following exercises to start practicing right now.

1 Kayla does not like to share her toys with her friends. Today, Kayla announces that she has selected a few toys to share with her friends who are coming over to play after lunch. How would you recognize this good decision?

_____

_____

_____

Positive feedback encourages your children to make good decisions. When Kayla selected some toys to share with her friends, she made a mature decision. It would be easy to miss what Kayla is doing and say, "It's about time you learned how to share." This would be a mistake. Do not let Kayla's effort go unnoticed. "Kayla, I am glad to see you decided to share some of your toys. Your friends will be happy, too."

2 Devin whines about everything that his mom asks him to do. In most cases, his mother gives in, and Devin wins. How would you use positive feedback to help neutralize Devin's constant whining?

_____

_____

_____

Even children like Devin sometimes do what they are asked without whining; his mother needs to look for cooperation. "Devin, thanks for helping me fold the laundry. I appreciate your help. I am really glad that you didn't whine about it. Did you feel like a good helper because you didn't whine?" By calling attention to the times when Devin does not whine, his mother is emphasizing his good behavior. By using this replacement strategy, she is encouraging more cooperation from Devin in the future.

3 Make a list of the positive behaviors that your preschooler demonstrates that you need to recognize with positive feedback. What words could you use to provide verbal reinforcement and aim for self-reward?

_____

_____

_____

_____

_____

_____

4 Make of a list of your preschooler's misbehavior patterns. For each misbehavior, write down one or two replacement behaviors that you need to recognize with positive feedback. What words could you use to provide verbal reinforcement and aim for self-reward?

_____

_____

_____

_____

_____

_____

11

Use Charts and Checklists
to Teach Accountability

Preschoolers love using charts and checklists. You can see the excitement in their eyes when they earn stickers and smiley faces. Charts and checklists display the behaviors you expect from your preschoolers. They motivate preschoolers to remember the rules and be accountable. Because they give immediate, positive feedback about accomplishments, charts and checklists create feelings of success and internal motivation, which build self-esteem in your child.

Charts and checklists help you as well by increasing the number of positive interactions between you and your child. They encourage you to focus on specific, positive, important behaviors and attitudes and are tangible, visual reminders to be consistent with the goals you have for your children. They enable you to be proactive and plan. They give both parents the same tool, which not only improves communications between parents but also increase positive feedback and consistency, promoting a positive family climate and encouraging everyone to work together. Charts and checklists provide a record so you can evaluate progress, showing what behaviors are improving and which need more work.

How Charts Work

Charts focus on positive behaviors and attitudes. Begin by identifying the behaviors you want to improve. Choose one or two behaviors, and then list each behavior on the chart. When your child does what is expected, put a sticker or smiley face in the box on the chart. Many parents have their child put the sticker he has earned on the chart, which encourages the youngster to feel proud of himself for his accomplishment. At the end of the day, add up the number of smiley faces. Points, check marks, or stamps work equally well.

Stickers are enough to satisfy and motivate most preschoolers. They do not need other incentives. However, sometimes, a persistent behavior problem may need stronger incentives. Develop a plan where you exchange stickers or smiley faces for an incentive. Each smiley face could be worth a minute or two of extra story, game, or playtime before going to bed.

Some children like working for an incentive each day plus a bonus incentive for having a good week. So each smiley face could be worth special time at the end of the day, *and* at the end of each week. Having a friend over for a special activity might cost ten smiley faces, for example. This strategy works for five-, six-, and possibly some older four-year-olds. Most children who are younger than five, however, cannot understand the concept of waiting for a bonus on the weekend. Younger preschoolers prefer their fun or prizes at the end of each day.

If your child is able to wait for a bonus on the weekend, you may want to provide him with a menu of incentives. Each incentive requires or "costs" a certain number of stickers. In order to rent a movie, your child might need to have earned seven stickers throughout the week, and making popcorn requires five more stickers. This technique encourages preschoolers to earn as many stickers as they can. Maintain high interest and motivation by changing the incentives every week, or adding new items to the menu.

Be flexible, but be sure to set up the rules in advance. Include a section for bonus points on the chart. Anytime your child does something extra that is especially helpful, polite, or makes a special effort, add a smiley face. Preschoolers respond favorably to this technique.

Developing Your Child's Chart

Select behaviors that increase the chance of success. Do not load the chart with too many troublesome behaviors, or your child will perceive the chart as impossible. Choose some behaviors that are easy and fun. You can also change the behaviors. You may have a list of eight or more behaviors. Rotate two or three behaviors each week to keep things interesting.

Develop charts with your preschoolers. When words are too hard, draw pictures. Participation causes preschoolers to have ownership in the chart. Let them draw designs and color the chart. Even more important, encourage them to suggest some of the behaviors and incentives. Help them decide where to post the chart—on the refrigerator, in the bedroom, in the bathroom. Involvement creates interest and motivation.

Develop charts for a week at a time. Some parents only use charts during the busy workweek, while others use the chart seven days a week to provide a high level of consistency. Do what works for you. You can use a laminated tag board with an erasable marker so that the chart can be reused each week. Or you may want to draw a grid on a sheet of paper and make several photocopies. If you create the chart on a computer, you can make changes and print a new version each week. If you need ideas of how to get started, use the charts in this chapter as examples.

A Simple Behavior Chart

Here is a simple behavior chart that encourages two behaviors: "Use my words," and "Be a good listener." Each time Jasmin is caught using her words or being a good listener, she earns a sticker on her chart. When she earns ten stickers for using her words, she and Mother will bake cookies. When she earns ten stickers for being a good listener, she and Mother will have a tea party. Jasmin's chart has a bonus section in the form of flowers at the bottom of the page. She gets to color one of the flowers whenever her mother catches Jasmin making a really good choice about her behavior. When she gets five flowers colored, she can invite her friend over to play.

Always accompany an incentive with verbal recognition. It is important to earn an incentive, but it is more important to develop a sense of responsibility. As always, aim for self-reward: "You had a great week. I'm glad Nick can come over to play today. I hope you feel proud of yourself. You earned it by being a good listener." You can use a chart to improve a child's attitude. For example, Doris wanted her son Craig to talk politely to his sister. Each time Craig was polite to his sister, Doris put a smiley face on his chart and told him she appreciated his politeness.

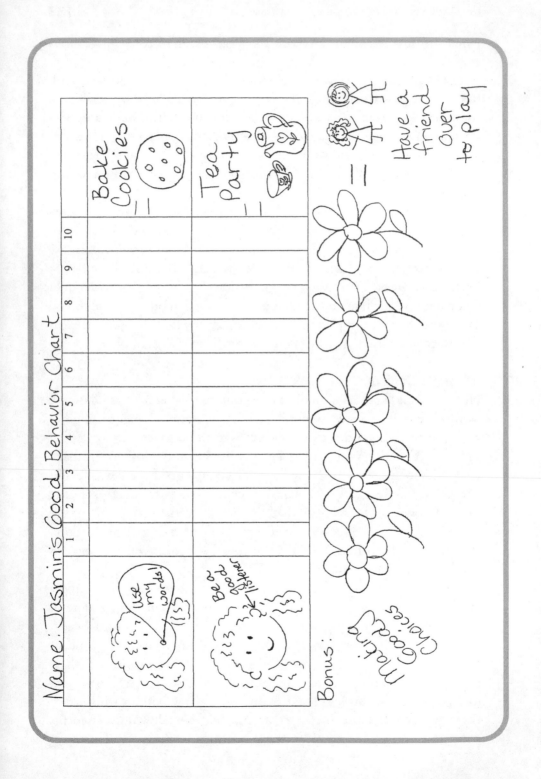

Name: Jasmin's Good Behavior Chart

	1	2	3	4	5	6	7	8	9	10	
Use my words!											Bake Cookies =
Be a good listener											Tea Party =

Bonus: Making Good Choices

= Have a friend over to play

Charts help older preschoolers to work for goals. Five- and six-year-olds begin to understand how to save money. Six-year-old Monica wanted a new dress for her doll. Mom and Monica created a chart that listed jobs Monica could do around the house. Beneath the list, her mother drew twenty pictures of quarters. Each time Monica completed a task on the chart, Mom would tape a quarter onto the chart. (You can use real quarters or play money.) When all twenty quarters were on the chart, Monica and mom went shopping for a new dress. By seeing the twenty quarters on the chart, Monica was able to see her progress.

What if the dress costs more than $5? Buy the dress anyway. You need to stick to the agreement you made, and the important thing here is to teach your child how to plan for goals, not earn every penny she needs to buy things she wants. If it takes too long to reach a goal or if the goal requires too many quarters or stickers, your child will become discouraged, not motivated. With items that are expensive, have your child earn money for part of the cost only. Even contributing some of the money gives preschoolers a sense of accomplishment and pride, and it also gives them more ownership and more respect for the cost of things.

Charts can sometimes be used to improve or redirect inappropriate behavior. They can help turn around poor days. Here is how this strategy works. Alex's chart has an item for "good listening." He has been doing well for the past three days. However, today he is having some difficulty being a good listener. Mother uses the success of the past three days to redirect him to think about being a better listener.

"Alex, come here, please. I want you to see something. Look at your chart. Look how well you have been listening. You have earned twelve stickers in the last three days. Look how you have improved. All these stickers show you can do it. Remember how proud you have been for the past few days. I know you can be a good listener. I know you can make a better decision."

Here is the wrong way: "I don't know why you can't behave for more than three days. This chart is supposed to make you behave."

When your child is doing well, a chart shows progress. This creates feelings of success and increases motivation. When your child is not doing well, a chart will show the exact behaviors he needs to improve. You and your child can concentrate on the behaviors that need work.

How Checklists Work

Checklists are very similar to charts. A checklist is like a "to-do" list. Use a checklist whenever you ask your preschooler to do a task that has several parts, such as morning routine, bedtime routine, or picking up her bedroom. Strategies for managing these situations are explained in more detail, with examples of checklists, in chapter 17.

A checklist promotes success, since it breaks a complex set of behaviors into bite-size pieces; as a result, the task does not look so overwhelming to your child. A checklist may or may not earn other incentives. Some parents do not think it is wise to use incentives to teach children household duties, while other parents do use incentives. Use what works for your children. On page 137 is a checklist for daily jobs.

Checklists can be particularly useful with preschoolers because they teach them about sequence and how to get things done. We do jobs to keep order in our lives. It is best to teach these responsibilities to children when they are young.

Charts and checklists give your preschooler a motivational boost. They are tangible reminders of the expectations between you and your children. They help you focus on goals and keep a record of your preschooler's progress, evaluating which behaviors need further work. Most important is that charts and checklists help your preschooler feel successful by emphasizing achievements. Even if progress is slower than you would like, they show you where the gains are occurring, giving you and your child incentive to go on, which helps you be patient.

Name: _____

Daily Jobs	Monday	Tuesday	Wednesday	Thursday	Friday	Saturday	Sunday	Total
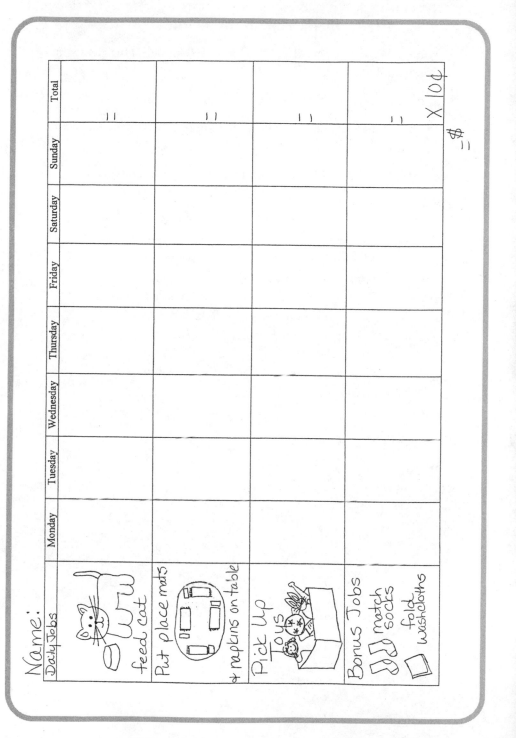 feed cat								=
Put place mats 4 napkins on table								=
Pick Up Toys								=
Bonus Jobs match socks fold washcloths								=

X 10¢

$ =

Chart-Making Guidelines

Create the charts or checklists with your preschooler. This gives your preschooler ownership.

Do not overload the chart with troublesome behaviors.

Maintain a high level of interest by changing priority behaviors occasionally.

Provide your child with a menu of incentives. For example:

KAYLA'S MENU OF INCENTIVES

Making cookies	10 points
Going to the park	15 points
Renting a movie	10 points
Going out for lunch	20 points
Buying a computer game	30 points
Going to the zoo	15 points
Ordering a pizza	20 points

12

Use Rules to Provide Guidance

 Three-year-old Jessica is demanding a new toy from the display at the supermarket. Four-year-old Tommy is pouting for another story before bedtime. Five-year-old Becky is crying because she wants a treat before dinner. Preschoolers repeatedly challenge the limits parents establish. It is easy to become frustrated and discouraged about enforcing rules. In spite of the difficulty, rules are essential and ultimately make discipline easier.

Preschoolers need rules as much as they need love and affection. Rules provide structure and guidance. They teach preschoolers what you expect—good attitude and correct behavior; in short, how you want them to behave. Children need rules to prepare them for the world, for even when they enter preschool, they will have to learn to follow rules. Rules such as taking turns, not interrupting, sharing and being polite, saying please and thank you, help children socialize and get along with other children. Learning to wash their hands before eating teaches routine. Rules also teach safety: "Please hold my hand in the parking lot. There are lots of cars here."

Since parents want their children to do what they are asked, a good rule is, Do what you are asked when you are asked to do it. Therefore, rules and requests go hand in hand. When you ask your preschooler to come inside, the request is for him to come into the house; the rule is that he needs to do it now. Rules and requests are expectations that guide children's decision making.

Rules and requests must be *specific*. They are specific when they communicate precisely what your preschooler should or should not do. Most parents do not give their preschoolers clear and specific requests. If you say, "Go clean up your room," you are being vague. From your preschooler's point of view, "Clean your room" is unclear. She thinks, I use a toothbrush to clean my teeth, a washcloth to clean my face. What do I use to clean my room? A specific request would be: "Jill, it is time to clean up your room. Please put your toys away. Then put your dirty clothes in the laundry basket."

There are a few cautions here. Be specific when you ask your preschooler to do something, but do not give more than one or two instructions at a time. Younger children may only be able to remember one instruction at a time. As their ability to attend and remember develops, increase the number of instructions to two or three. When your preschooler remembers and completes your requests, compliment her for being a good listener.

Anytime you ask your preschooler to do something, the results will always be more positive if you participate. When your preschooler goes into her room and sees three days' worth of toys and clothes spread all over the place, the job will look insurmountable. Help her clean up, modeling the proper attitude to keep her engaged in the job.

With requests and jobs that recur on a regular basis, such as cleaning up bedrooms, it may be helpful to post a checklist in your preschooler's room. Use pictures to indicate the instructions:

All toys in the toy box.

All dirty clothes in the laundry basket.

Be specific, but remember that preschoolers are literal. Roseanne and her husband had friends over for dinner. During the meal, her daughter was talking with a mouthful of food. "Please don't talk with food in your mouth," Roseanne reminded. Her daughter immediately spit out her food and finished her sentence.

Rules and requests must also be *reasonable*. Do not expect your three-year-old to sit at the dinner table for thirty minutes. Ten minutes is more reasonable. Do not expect your four-year-old to sit in church for an hour. Have activities handy to keep him busy and happy. Most children want to do what their parents ask of them. If they do not, you may be asking too much. Pay attention to your child and adjust your expectations to fit his behavior, and you will both feel more successful. Have a set of rules that cover the basics: safety, cooperation, listening the first time, following directions, and personal responsibilities or chores. Create rules for morning and evening routines.

Consequences Enforce Rules

Consequences teach preschoolers how to make decisions. Good decisions result in positive consequences, while poor decisions result in negative consequences. Consequences teach preschoolers that there is a relationship between cause and effect in the world: This is what happens when I choose this behavior. When you explain the consequences of a particular behavior, they must be specific and reasonable. A consequence is specific when your preschooler knows exactly what is going to happen, and understands that if she chooses this action, this will be the result. Consequences are reasonable when they make sense.

Use rules and consequences to teach your preschoolers that having a good attitude and behaving correctly are their choice. Their choices determine the consequences, you do not. Behavior is a choice. Tell your preschoolers how you expect them to behave. Then follow through with positive feedback when they follow the rules. Follow through with a negative consequence when they do not follow the rules. Be consistent with this technique, and your children will make better decisions. They will choose correct behavior.

There is a little Picasso in every preschooler. Preschoolers love to draw. Many preschoolers love to draw on everything but paper: the walls, the floor, the chair, and so on. Here is a way to handle this situation using consequences. First, state the rule in terms of the correct behavior: "Only draw on paper." If your preschooler decides to be artistically creative on the wall, you remind him of the rule. Then have him clean the wall as best he can and take his crayons away for a while. Explain that these are the consequences of not following the rule: "You can draw on paper. When you draw on something else, you lose your crayons." How long you withhold the crayons takes judgment. For first offenders, five minutes may make the point. When you are ready to give the crayons back to your child, reiterate the rule: "Are your ready to use your crayons? Can you tell me the rule? I hope you remember the rule this time." For chronic offenders, you may need to withhold the crayons for thirty minutes or even up to a day or two. When you return the crayons, take time to talk about the rule. Have plenty of paper in a convenient place and always supervise at first. When your preschooler begins to draw on paper, reinforce him for doing the right thing: "I am glad to see you know how to draw on paper. Good for you."

Preschoolers learn well from natural consequences. If you misuse the crayons, you lose the crayons for a while. If you throw a toy, you lose the toy. If you refuse to eat dinner, you will not have dessert. Natural consequences teach responsibility and decision making because they permit children to learn from the real world.

Using Punishment with Preschoolers

Preschoolers need rules, limits, and boundaries to learn self-control, and that they cannot always do what they want to do. Situations will arise where preschoolers may need a negative consequence, or a punishment, to learn a lesson in self-control. How to punish preschoolers is a concern of most parents.

Punishment is a negative consequence. There are two reasons to use punishment: to teach your preschooler to obey rules and requests, and to teach your preschooler to learn right from wrong. Notice that the word *teach* appears in both reasons. The only reason you should use punishment is to teach better decision making.

A few words about misbehavior and punishment before going on. Remember that preschoolers can do many things that are irritating and annoying. Behaviors that are annoying or irritating should be handled with distraction or redirection (see chapter 7). Also remember that many behaviors are due to natural curiosity and should never be punished. Do not punish your preschooler in an attempt to teach him not to stick objects in the electrical wall outlets. Explain that doing this is very dangerous and could hurt him. Make sure to buy enough safety plugs to eliminate the hazard. Nor should you punish you daughter for wanting to play with your expensive crystal. Put it out of her view and reach. Better still, put it away for a few years. None of these behaviors are deliberate, intentional, willful misbehavior or misconduct, and you should not use punishment when dealing with them.

When used properly, punishment eliminates or reduces deliberate, intentional, or willful misbehavior. This is not easy, and it requires consistent follow-through. Too much punishment is harmful, as it creates unpleasant feelings and drains energy. Most parents believe that punishing misbehavior will stop their preschooler from repeating the misbehavior. Sometimes this is true; sometimes it is not. Let's listen to how a parent in one of my workshops explains how she punishes her daughter.

"How do you punish your child?"
"I start by yelling at her."
"How does she react to your yelling?"
"She usually ignores me."
"Then what?"
"I get angry. Sometimes I yell again."
"Does that get her to obey?"
"For a while, maybe."
"What do you try next?"
"Sometimes I spank her."
"How often do you have to spank her?"
"About three or four times a day."

Any punishment that is used this often is not working. The misbehavior is not getting better. Her daughter is not listening to the yelling, and she is not even trying to avoid the spankings. This parent is not communicating to her child, so even the punishments are having no impact on her daughter.

Good Punishments Are Seldom Used

As a parent, you must learn the golden rule: *A true punishment is one that is seldom used because it is seldom needed.* The goal of punishment is to reduce the need for more punishment. Punishment should decrease the misbehavior. If you punish your child five or six times a day for the same misbehavior, the punishment is not working. If you keep adding to the punishment and the misbehavior continues, the punishment is not working. It is not the punishment that is important; it is the misbehavior. A punishment must change the misbehavior. If it doesn't, try something else. You may think that yelling, threatening, scolding, and spanking are good punishments. While these may allow you to release your anger, they are not good punishments because they have little long-term effect on misbehavior. Anger and punishment do not mix.

Explain the Purpose for the Punishment

When you need to punish your preschooler, start by telling him the purpose of the punishment. When you explain punishment, you increase your child's understanding and cooperation. As part of the explanation, tell your child that you are not mad at him and that you love him: "I am upset that you drew on the coffee table. But I still love you." Then, explain that you are trying to help him learn better behavior, not to get even. Only explain it once; don't become caught in lengthy explanations and arguments.

> "I want you to learn that you cannot draw on anything but paper.
> You are going to lose your crayons because you made a poor choice.
> You drew on the table. I want you to learn so you will not do it again.
> Only draw on paper."

Do Not Punish When You Are Angry

When you punish in anger, you are actually doing two things at the same time. You are punishing, and you are reacting with anger. What if your child intended to get you angry? What if your child wanted to get even or retaliate because of something that happened earlier? Seeing you get angry is not a punishment, *it is a reward!* When you get angry at misbehavior, you are teaching your child how to have control over you emotionally and giving your child power over you. This is a payoff. The misbehavior is reinforced, not punished, and as a result, the misbehavior increases. The effects of the punishment are neutralized by the reward of getting you angry. Some children would trade a stern scolding for the power they receive when they succeed in getting you angry. The only way to break this cycle is to stop punishing with anger. If you find yourself getting angry, walk away. Dispense with your anger first, and then confront the misbehavior. Do not let your children push your buttons.

Another problem with punishing your child when you are angry is that you may overreact. Take the case of Seth, a student I worked with who was upset because he was grounded forever. When I spoke with his dad, he explained that the boy had lost some of his tools. He got so angry at his son, he grounded him for the rest of his life. He had overreacted. When you overreact because you are angry, you may say things that you do not mean. You cannot ground a child for life. Do not punish when you are angry; the only thing you will be teaching your children is that punishment is a form of revenge.

The purpose of punishment is to change misbehavior and teach better decision making. Punishment is most effective when it is predetermined and planned; it does not work well as an impulsive reaction. When you become angry, you are acting as a model for negative behavior. Instead of modeling self-control, you will be teaching your children to react impulsively.

Anger impedes our ability to be good teachers, and it interferes with our decision making. Yet managing our anger is often very difficult. Getting angry is one of the most common problems parents face, and it is the largest stumbling block in our relationship with our children. If you get angry easily, reducing the amount of anger you express to your children becomes your number-one priority. For strategies on doing so, see chapter 13, "Managing Your Anger."

Do Not Embarrass

Punishment should not embarrass, humiliate, or degrade preschoolers. When you embarrass your preschooler, it creates feelings of unworthiness, such as guilt or shame. Your child may fear he has done something to cause you to stop loving him. These feelings may cause him to think of you as mean or unfair. When this occurs, your child will not learn to make better decisions or to cooperate. Instead, he may strike back in anger, which can start a negative cycle. Never use statements like these:

That was stupid.

What a dumb thing to do.

What's wrong with you?

You are nothing but trouble.

How many times do I have to tell you that?

Do not punish your preschooler in front of other children. Take your child aside. Tell him what he has done and that he needs to stop, or tell him you will talk about it later, when the two of you are alone. Here is how you might approach the situation: "Nathan, come here, please. I want to talk with you privately." When Nathan arrives, you continue, "You are pushing. Please stop. Please be a good friend to Alex. Make a good choice, or we will leave the park."

Be Consistent

There are two rules for punishing consistently. Rule 1: Once you decide to punish a particular misbehavior, do so always. If you punish only when you feel like it, you will make the problem worse. Rule 2: Once you tell your preschooler that he is going to be punished, follow through. You must use punishment consistently, even after you have had a long, miserable day. You can never miss or let the misbehavior slide—not even once.

Be Reasonable—Short and Simple

Short and simple punishments are more effective than harsh punishments. Keep things in perspective and react appropriately to the size of the misbehavior. Do not restrict your daughter from desserts for a week because she did not finish her vegetables tonight. Instead, explain that tonight she cannot have dessert, and that you hope tomorrow she'll eat both her vegetables and dessert. When punishments are reasonable, children learn what behaviors are important. Mild punishments are usually more productive than harsh punishments.

When you use large punishments, such as losing TV privileges for a week, you teach your preschooler to obey rules and requests out of fear of being caught. He will not really learn right from wrong; rather he obeys because he is afraid not to obey. Some parents believe this is acceptable. It is not; when the threat of punishment is not present, your child has no internal reason to obey the rules. He will obey as long as he is fearful; as he grows older, he will fear you less and less and misbehave more and more.

Large punishments often create feelings of anger or revenge. When your preschooler feels angry, little learning takes place. When your preschooler believes that you have been unfair, he may retaliate with a tantrum or outburst. This can start a negative cycle. You punish; your child retaliates by misbehaving again. You punish again, perhaps a little more severely, just to make your point. Your child becomes angry and retaliates by misbehaving again.

When you use mild punishment along with an explanation of the reason for the rule, your preschooler will have a better understanding of and appreciation for what you are trying to teach. Not only is this the appropriate approach for a preschool child, but it creates a positive parent-child dynamic, which will be invaluable as he grows up.

Be Quick

Preschoolers have very short memories. Punishment should be administered as soon after the misbehavior as possible. The more immediate, the more effective the punishment will be. The only exception to this rule is when you are angry. In this situation, you might say, "I will talk to you about this in a few minutes, when I am not so angry."

Be Realistic

Dealing with chronic misbehavior can be frustrating. One such behavior that parents of preschoolers face is a child's refusal to pick up her toys. If your preschooler deliberately refuses to pick up toys, try this. Put all the toys that are left out in a box. Put the box in your closet. Do this every day. After a few days, most or all of the toys will be in your closet. When your preschooler begins asking where all his toys are, explain that because he was not taking care of them, you had to put them away:

> "Remember when I asked you to pick up your toys? You did not want to. I put your toys away. You were not taking care of your toys. Would you like to have a few toys to play with? Later today, when I ask you to pick up your toys, what will you do?"

When it is time to pick up these toys, remind him of the rule. Compliment him for picking up his toys. Gradually, he may earn the remainder of his toys back. Select consequences that fit the crime. A child who makes a mess cleans the mess. Children who fight and argue will be kept apart for a while. Consequences that are relevant to the misbehavior have more meaning to your child because they help teach a lesson.

Sometimes five- and six-year-olds can be trusted to choose their punishment, a technique that helps them learn more quickly. It shows them that you want to be fair while encouraging them to be mature and responsible.

> "Your behavior has been very good until now. I am going to trust you to choose your own punishment for this misbehavior. I know you will be fair and just. Let me know what you decide."

Be Positive First

With recurrent misbehaviors, punishment should only be used after you have tried several positive remedies. Most adults think of punishment first, thinking that you always treat misbehavior with a punishment. For example, your two children argue constantly. Too often, our first instinct is to threaten punishment: "If you do not stop fighting, you will both go to bed." Instead, point out the opposite behavior. Improve the misbehavior by using positive feedback to strengthen the replacement behavior, cooperation. The opposite of arguing is cooperating. Use encouragement and positive feedback when they are cooperating and sharing: "It's good to see you having fun. You should be proud of yourselves for the way you are sharing the computer." When you resort immediately to punishment, you trap yourself; neither you nor your children like how it feels. Avoid this trap by focusing on positive behavior.

You can be positive even when you use punishment. For example, Joshua and Elliot are playing a game when a disagreement occurs. You try to redirect: "You are doing a nice job playing that game. Please be pleasant." They continue to disagree, starting to call each other names. It is time for you to intervene. Go over and explain that you will have to take the game away because it is causing a problem. "I am sorry, but I have to put the game away. Name-calling is not allowed." Then get the two boys involved in a less competitive activity. "How about getting out the crayons and drawing paper? We have lots of new paper." After a while, ask if they want to try the game again, playing without calling names.

Adjusting our responses to our children's misbehavior is not easy, and it takes practice. Here are a few exercises to get you started.

1 Pam cannot understand why Steven will not behave. Pam wants to be more positive, but sometimes she forgets. Steven is a very active child. He gets into things he is not supposed to touch. Whenever Steven does not mind, Pam becomes upset and frustrated. Pam yells a lot. She spanks too. Nothing seems to work. What can you tell Pam about her behavior?

_____

_____

_____

_____

Pam needs to realize that her style of punishment is not working. Steven has become immune to the yelling and the spanking. His misbehavior is not improving. Pam needs to control herself. Getting frustrated and angry is only aggravating the situation; her anger may even be rewarding to Steven. Most of all, Pam must remember to be positive. The strongest tool she has is positive feedback.

2 Four-year-old Marie pulls her friend's hair when she does not get her way. How can her parents use a punishment for this misbehavior?

_____

_____

_____

_____

Although this type of misconduct is embarrassing and can easily get you angry, it is important to stay calm. Do not yell or scold, and do not pull her hair as a way of showing her how it hurts. Rather, an appropriate punishment would be to remove Marie from the situation for a minute or two. Then ask her if she is ready to play nicely with her friend. You could say, "It is okay to be upset, but it is not okay to pull hair. That hurts. If your friend has a toy you want to play with, you need to ask to take turns. That is being a good friend. Can you be a good friend?" As always, as a long-term strategy, look for the replacement behavior. When Marie does use her words instead of pulling hair, recognize her: "You asked to take turns. Good for you. That's being a good friend."

3 Six-year-old Rachel talks back to her parents. Her parents, Jan and Bill, want to try positive strategies to correct this misbehavior before using punishment. What positive strategies could they use?

_____

_____

_____

_____

Rachel's parents are wise to think of positive strategies first, before using punishment. With misbehavior such as talking back, punishment sometimes creates more resistance in children, thus creating more back talk. They need to look for situations when Rachel listens and cooperates without back talk or arguing. When Rachel does this, they could say, "I appreciate your listening. I really feel better when you do not talk back. It shows me and you that you can do it." This approach builds self-esteem.

When Rachel does begin to talk back, give her a reminder of the correct way to behave. For example:

Jan: "Rachel, it's time to pick up your toys."

Rachel: "No. I don't want to. I'm sick of picking up toys."

Jan: "Rachel, please think. Are you arguing? I understand how you feel. What do you need to do?"

Use a chart as a long-term positive strategy for Rachel. List such behaviors as listening the first time, doing what she is asked without arguing, or using a proper tone of voice.

Punishment works, but it is not easy to use. Positive feedback is much easier and more fun to use. It creates internal motivation in preschoolers, teaches self-discipline, and promotes a healthy and pleasant family climate. Successful parents emphasize the positive.

Positive feedback, extinction, and punishment are always in effect, whether you are conscious of them or not. The key to successful parenting is to be aware of these principles and use them to your advantage. Parents who are only interested in controlling misbehavior will punish. Parents who want children to be cooperative will balance positive feedback with extinction and redirection and use minimal punishment. If you emphasize the positive, you will need very little punishment.

The pages that follow will help you evaluate your own method of punishment and offer some strategies for changing your child's behavior. You may want to photocopy them so you can have them near at hand; reviewing them will help you to keep a positive focus.

TEN QUESTIONS TO ASK BEFORE YOU USE PUNISHMENT

1. Will this punishment teach my child better decision-making skills and self-control?

2. Does this punishment improve the misbehavior?

3. Does this punishment reduce the need for more punishment?

4. Am I angry right now?

5. Is this punishment part of a positive plan? Am I using it impulsively?

6. Am I getting even? Will this punishment humiliate or embarrass my child?

7. Am I being consistent?

8. Will I follow through immediately (except when I am angry)?

9. Is this punishment reasonable and fair?

10. Have I tried several positive remedies first?

HOW TO STRENGTHEN OR WEAKEN BEHAVIOR

To strengthen a good behavior:
Use positive feedback.
Example:

When your preschoolers behave, recognize them by thanking them.
When you see your preschoolers sharing, tell them that they
should be proud of themselves.

To reduce misbehavior:
1. Use positive feedback to strengthen the correct, replacement behavior.

Examples:

If you want to reduce the amount of arguing between two children,
call attention to the time when they are not arguing.

If your preschooler is not a good listener, attend to situations
when he does listen the first time.

2. Use extinction to eliminate any rewards for misbehavior.

Examples:

Do not give in to your preschooler's demands, such as whining, teasing, and tantrums.

Ignore your preschooler when he tries to get your attention in a negative way.

Use redirection: "I won't listen to the teasing. Please ask in a polite
voice."

3. Use punishment for deliberate misbehavior.

Examples:

A child who draws on the wall loses his crayons.

A child who refuses to pick up toys has her toys taken away for a
while.

A child who refuses to eat does not have dessert.

A COMPARISON BETWEEN POSITIVE FEEDBACK AND PUNISHMENT	
Positive feedback feels good to give and receive.	Punishment creates unpleasant feelings, often anger.
Positive feedback emphasizes good behavior. It teaches children to think.	Punishment draws attention to misbehavior.
Positive feedback increases motivation.	Punishment can have a negative effect on motivation.
Positive feedback creates feelings of success.	Punishment can cause children to feel like failures.
Positive feedback improves a child's self-esteem.	Punishment can have a negative impact on self-esteem.
Positive feedback gives children self-confidence.	Punishment weakens self-confidence.
Positive feedback teaches children to trust their decisions.	Punishment does not teach trust. It sometimes teaches fear.

Positive feedback motivates children to seek goals.	Punishment may cause children to feel despair: "Why try? I always get in trouble anyway."
Positive feedback develops responsibility: "When I make good decisions, I feel good."	Punishment often teaches children to avoid admitting responsibility for their actions.
Positive feedback promotes healthy family relationships.	Punishment may alienate family members.
Positive feedback encourages children to talk to their parents.	Punishment discourages children from talking to their parents.
Positive feedback teaches children to be positive with others.	Punishment that is aggressive teaches children to be aggressive toward others.
Positive feedback is easy to use effectively.	Punishment is difficult to use.

13

Managing Your Anger

In the last chapter, you learned that you should not punish when you are angry because you may say or do things you later regret and perhaps teach your children how to gain emotional control over you. Most parents know intellectually that anger gets in the way of thoughtful parenting, but in the heat of the moment they do not know how else to react. If you struggle with anger, you are not alone: getting angry is the one of most common parenting problems. Perhaps this should not surprise us, given that we live in a society that produces angry people, in part due to the pressures and urgency of modern life. Some experts report that one out of every five American adults has a problem with anger management. Eighty percent of us are angry when we drive.

Anger is an inborn emotion, and everyone gets angry occasionally. Allow yourself to feel angry; if you try to ignore or suppress these feelings, they often build up and come out as an overreaction. Showing your children that you are angry is not necessarily harmful, as long as you do not react with physical or verbal aggression. When you express anger constructively, it can help teach children what is unacceptable behavior.

Repetitive anger is a problem, however, especially if it is directed at your children. Anger impedes our judgment and causes us to react emotionally and impulsively, often with negative results. It does not teach children responsibility. Moreover, an angry parent can be frightening to young children and cause them to doubt their personal safety. If you are a parent who becomes angry often, getting control of your anger is the best thing you can do for yourself, and is crucial to your relationship with your children.

Model Anger Management

Being a good model for your children includes proper anger management. Your children will learn to manage their anger by watching the way you manage your own. A sobering thought for most of us is that anger habits are learned. The way you manage your anger is part of your parenting style and is sometimes affected by your temperament. Some parents suppress their anger, letting it simmer until it boils over and then exploding over a little misbehavior. This confuses children; they never know when you are going to go off. Some parents vent their anger by "blasting" every chance they get. This may seem to work sometimes, but the constant yelling only teaches children to stay out of your way. Children learn that yelling, screaming, and adult tantrums give them control. Neither of these styles teaches your children good anger management strategies.

Anger management has two basic components. First, identify the events or situations that provoke your anger and then avoid or reevaluate them, so your anger is not activated as frequently. Second, practice appropriate ways of expressing your anger, so the results are productive rather than destructive. While this explanation of anger management is accurate, it is oversimplified. This is not an easy task, and many individuals spend their entire lives learning to manage anger.

What provokes your anger? It is helpful to think of anger as a secondary emotion. Something happens that upsets you, and then you become angry. These activating events are called *triggers*. The most common triggers among parents are frustration and disappointment. We become frustrated when we have to repeat things over and over, and then we get angry. We become disappointed or hurt when our children disobey, defy, or talk back. Another trigger is fear. A preschooler does something unsafe, and we get angry.

We all have our own set of triggers, which are derived from our expectations. These expectations can get us into trouble if we are not realistic. If you expect that your preschooler will always behave perfectly, you will be frustrated and disappointed frequently, which may cause repetitive anger. If you understand that your preschoolers naturally misbehave at times, and you do not take it personally when they do but see it as part of your job to guide and correct them, you will be far less frustrated and disappointed, leading to much less anger in your relationship.

Parents who are successful anger managers have learned to handle anger in a way that helps rather than hinders. It can be helpful to verbalize your triggers: for example, "I am angry because you were arguing with me, and I was frustrated." You need to learn to acknowledge your anger and then use it to motivate yourself to find positive ways of correcting your child's behavior. Parents who manage their anger are aware of their triggers, planning ahead to avoid having these events become emotional button pushers. Parents who are good models apologize after they have expressed anger inappropriately: "I am sorry I got angry and yelled at you. I will try to do better next time. Everything is better when we work together."

Be Responsible

Take responsibility for your anger. Anger almost always comes from a faulty thought process; from the way you think about or internalize an outside event. Your preschooler disobeys; you internalize his behavior as frustration or disappointment and become angry. You have the expectation that your child should obey, and when he does not, you find the situation frustrating, leading to your anger. Yet you control your thoughts—so you control your anger. Anger is a choice. When you say, "That makes me angry," you are telling yourself a lie. It would be more accurate to say, "This happened, and I am choosing to be angry." Notice how the word *choosing* puts the responsibility on you.

I lived many years of my life believing that unsafe drivers, poorly planned freeways, dead car batteries, and uncapped toothpaste made me angry. Things happen that I don't like. Things happen that can be irritating. If *I let them*. I can choose to be angry or not angry. I like being not angry. I allow much less anger in my life than I did twenty years ago. You can make the same choice.

Many parents do not realize they have this choice. At a recent workshop, I was explaining this concept when a mother disagreed with me. She did not believe that she could control her anger; to her, anger was an automatic, irrepressible reaction. When I asked her to elaborate, she explained that when her four-year-old became defiant, she immediately became enraged. This occurred several times a day. She would yell and scream at the top of her lungs and get right in the youngster's face. Sometimes she would spank him. Sometimes her son would scream in return. Sometimes he would hit back. Sometimes he would run away crying. By the end of her story she was in tears, because she knew this was not working. Her son's behavior was not improving, and she was angry several times a day, yet she didn't believe she could change this cycle. You may feel caught in this trap. If you do, listen to what happened when we explored the situation more fully:

> "Who is around when you become so angry?
> "Usually just my son and me."
> "Do you ever get this angry in front of your husband?"
> "Not as much."
> "Do you ever get this angry in front of your mother-in-law?"
> "No, of course not."
> "Why not?"
> "It is humiliating. I don't want her to think I am a nut case."
> "Would you get this angry in front of your pastor?"
> "No."
> "Would you get this angry at your son if I were having dinner at your home?"
> "Probably not."
> "Why not?

She did not say anything for a moment. Then she began to smile. She had figured it out. I asked her to say what she was thinking.

"If I can control myself in front of my mother-in-law or my pastor or you, then I can do it all the time."

I interrupted. "Maybe not all the time, at first. But you said you could never control your anger. You said it was automatic. It is not. If you can control it in some situations, you can learn to have better control in all situations. But it will take practice."

This mother could manage her anger in some situations because she changed her expectations for herself. When she was in a situation where she knew it was important, she could do it. She did not want to look insane.

It is always important to manage your anger in front of your children. If you are like this mother and can selectively control your anger, pretend you have a guardian angel. This strategy is one I use, because I was raised to believe that we all have an angel whose job it is to protect us and help us get to heaven. So before you do something wrong, remember that your guardian angel is watching, even when your mother-in-law is not.

Some parents find it helpful to have a routine that defuses their anger. Use a delay strategy to weaken the effects of the trigger event. Count to twenty-five or practice deep breathing. Meditate. Think peaceful thoughts. Say a prayer for tolerance and forgiveness. Distract yourself. Listen to music. Find someone to watch the children for ten minutes and sit in your room or go for a walk. Think about the times that you were able to maintain your control in frustrating situations. Remember the times you were successful. Long-term anger management should also include plenty of sleep, good nutrition, and exercise.

If you do become angry, use it as a signal that you need to take action. Stay calm. Be brief and specific, using a calm but firm voice. Since preschoolers can only pay attention for a minute or two, focus on the important issue. Do not bring up the past. Do not moralize or lecture. Do not get angrier because your child's attention drifts elsewhere.

Do not feel guilty about getting angry. It is okay for your children to know that you have a boiling point, but it is not okay to let your anger get in the way of good discipline. Express anger constructively. Let it out slowly, and in small amounts. Tell your child what he did, how you feel, and why you feel that way: "When you fight like that, I get angry because you could get hurt or break something."

Avoid blaming your child for your anger. This will create guilt and resistance in your child. Do not say, "Can't you see I am on the phone? Stop interrupting me all the time!" Instead say, "I am on the phone. Please do not interrupt. I do not want to be angry." Do not make generalizations, such as, "Why do you always have to make such a mess?" This will cause your child to think she is always messy and disappointing to you. Stay centered on this incident—what needs to happen? Say, "It is time to clean up."

Do not take your child's anger personally, even when he is angry with you. When your child strikes out at you with anger, stay calm. Walk away if needed. This is not easy, but if you get angry in return, you are setting up a pattern of power and control, which may cause your preschooler to seek revenge by becoming even angrier. Do not let your emotions get the best of you. Deal with misbehaviors as they happen, which helps you vent without blame, and keeps you from saving up anger and then exploding. It is better for your mental health, and it is better for your children.

Most importantly, always separate your child from your child's behavior: "I love you. I will always love you. Nothing will ever change that. But what you did was not nice, and I am angry." This will reassure your child that even though his behavior may have caused you to feel angry, you still love him.

This chapter has been about parental anger and what you can do to manage it. Teaching your children how to manage their anger and aggression is discussed in chapter 18. The following lists give strategies for managing frustration, disappointment, and anger. Remember, learning to reduce the amount of anger in your life and learning how to express it constructively when it occurs are two of the best things you can do for your children.

TIPS TO KEEP FROM GETTING FRUSTRATED OR DISAPPOINTED WITH YOUR CHILDREN

1. Tell your children when you begin to feel frustrated, while you are still in control. Explain how they need to change or correct their behavior.

2. Keep children engaged. Have a variety of activities that hold their interest and keep them busy.

3. Allow your children to watch a movie while you get your work done or simply take a break.

4. Try to see the situation from your child's perspective. How is your child feeling right now?

5. Remember that all annoying and irritating behaviors are not misbehaviors. Your child may be tired, hungry, or ill.

6. Do not dwell on past problems. Start each day (or hour) fresh.

7. Choose your battles. Focus on behaviors that are most important and let the rest go. Your children will grow up fine.

8. Very young children may simply be trying to communicate. Encourage young children to "use their words" instead of whining.

9. Recognize children for correct behavior: "Thank you for using a quiet, polite voice."

10. Spend some time with other adults. Adult conversation is very therapeutic after a long day of two- or three-word sentences.

TIPS AND STRATEGIES FOR MANAGING YOUR ANGER

---

1. Be aware of your anger. What triggers it? How long does it last? Does anything positive or productive come from the way you express your anger?

2. Be aware of your children. They learn how to manage their anger and other emotions by watching and copying you. How do you want them to manage their anger?

3. What do you think about your anger? If you believe that you cannot manage your anger, you won't. If you believe that you can manage your anger, you will.

4. Develop ways to express anger constructively. Use a calm voice to express how you feel rather than yelling. It will have more impact.

5. Tell your children how their behavior makes you feel. Do not let anger build up. Deal with it as soon as possible: "I am beginning to become angry about this teasing. Please stop now."

6. Do not blame yourself when your children misbehave. It is not your fault. All children misbehave.

7. Do not feel guilty about losing your temper or getting angry. Recognize that it is part of your life. But make a commitment to change, for your benefit as well as your child's.

8. Apologize to others when you have expressed anger inappropriately: "I am sorry I lost my temper."

9. Have a specific plan for managing your anger. (See below.)

10. Keep a diary or logbook about your anger. Record what strategies work for you and use them when you start feeling angry.

11. Take a break from the children once in a while. Get a babysitter, go out with your spouse or a friend, and have fun. If you cannot get away, call a friend you have not spoken to for a while.

12. Reward yourself when you do manage your anger successfully. Put a dollar in a jar each time you survive an anger threat. Spend the money on yourself.

13. Look for specific reading material about anger management.

14. Know when to get help. If you are overwhelmed with parenting and find yourself getting angry every day, get professional help. Anger is a very common problem. There are anger management support groups everywhere.

• YOUR TURN •

What are your button pushers? Many parents have found it helpful to have a specific plan of action that helps them manage their anger when their children misbehave. Make a list of the misbehaviors that push your button and trigger your anger. Next, map out a plan that includes your immediate and long-term strategies. Here is an example:

Button pusher: Your two children argue.

Immediate plan (to defuse your anger):

    Take three deep breaths. Let them out slowly.

    Tell your children your feelings: "I feel angry when you argue."

    Separate the children.

Do not get drawn into their conflict.

Get them engaged in independent activities.

Long-term plan (to prevent the misbehavior and minimize your anger):

Do not save your anger until it erupts.

Spotlight the positive.

Focus on cooperation.

Look for times when they agree.

Use a chart to encourage your children to play cooperatively.

Write your plans here:

Button pusher:

_____

_____

_____

Immediate plan (to defuse your anger):

_____

_____

_____

_____

Long-term plan (to prevent the misbehavior and minimize your anger):

_____

_____

_____

_____

Alternatives to Spanking

"My daughter never listens to me."

"What do you do?"

"I ask her again, sometimes three or four times. She ignores me."

"Then what?"

"I get mad. I spank her. Even though I know it's wrong."

"What happens then?"

"She cries, and then I feel terrible. There must be something else I can do."

Most parents use spanking and other forms of punishment because they are angry or frustrated with their preschooler's misbehavior and do not know what else to do. There are several strategies that you should consider before you resort to punishment, and if you do use punishment, do not use spanking. You will need to assess each situation and ask yourself the following questions:

1 Can your child communicate with you about the situation? Some misbehavior may be due to a young child's inability to communicate and express his or her feelings. Decide if the misbehavior is intentional or simply reflects the child's inability to understand, express, or process language. When children are frustrated or feel hurt and cannot express these feelings, they often act out by whining or throwing tantrums. Focus on helping your child use language to express his feelings. Being able to communicate his emotions and have you understand them will calm your child down. Do not use spanking or punishment.

2 Is the misbehavior intentional, or may it be the result of something else? A child's needs and wants drive most misbehavior. Your child's intent is not always to be willful. Distinguish between misbehaviors that are deliberate and behaviors that result from other influences, such as fears, stress, fatigue, hunger, mood, time of day, type of activity, or peer influence. If you suspect that your preschooler is misbehaving because of other circumstances, eliminate or change the situation as best you can and divert your child's attention to positive, acceptable behavior. Do not use spanking or punishment.

3 Is your child's misbehavior the result of his temperament? If your preschooler has abundant energy and is overly active, do not punish him just for being too active. Punishment is for deliberate misconduct. Plan activities and routines that keep him busy and out of mischief. Channel his energy into more appropriate physical activity. Likewise, do not punish your persistent, argumentative child every time he is persistent and argumentative. Stay calm. Use reasoning to work through the problem. Excessive punishment will only create a more stubborn attitude.

4 Is your preschooler still learning self-control? Self-control needs to be learned and therefore needs to be taught. This is a normal part of your child's development. Use language and reasoning to teach your preschooler how to control his behavior. It may seem easier to control your preschooler's behavior with a spanking or other punishment rather than take the time and energy to teach him to control himself. This is a mistake. Your preschooler will someday be an adolescent and need to have self-control.

5 Have you taught replacement behaviors? As you learned in chapter 10, replacement is the most powerful technique you have to reduce misbehavior and build positive behaviors in your preschooler. Use positive feedback to strengthen the opposite, acceptable behavior. The original misbehavior will decline.

When misbehaviors are not deliberate and intentional, they need to be managed with proactive, positive techniques that promote self-control and good decision making. Remember that your goal as a parent is to teach decision making and personal responsibility. More than 90 percent of the parents who attend my workshops and who spank their children wish they didn't. The last sentence says a lot. Many parents want a better way of punishing their children. Parents want to manage their children's misbehavior without getting angry and without spanking.

What Happens When You Spank

A spanking usually stops a preschooler's misbehavior. When the misbehavior stops, the parent thinks the spanking works. A spanking can result in good behavior, just as a candy bar can buy peace and quiet in the supermarket. Using candy to quiet a tantrum is a temporary solution. You will be feeding your child a lot of candy to keep him quiet in the future. Spanking is also a temporary solution. You will be doing a lot of spanking.

A child who is spanked will usually settle down and behave. After a while, the child will act up again, and then the parent spanks again, because the spanking seemed to work the first time. The child is good for a while and then misbehaves again. The parent spanks again, and so on. This pattern snares many parents.

This cycle occurs because spanking provides external control of children rather than encouraging preschoolers to make responsible decisions. It does not promote internal decision making, it only teaches children to behave "or else." Not surprisingly, children who are frequently spanked do not learn self-control. An eight-year-old once told me that he could misbehave as long as he wanted; "My mom spanks me when I have to stop."

Problems can arise in families where one parent spanks and the other doesn't. When this pattern exists, children avoid the parent who spanks. This avoidance interferes with the development of a healthy parent-child relationship. Children see the parent who does not spank as weak and unable to manage them. The result is that the children continue to misbehave for the parent who does not spank while avoiding the parent who does. Both parents lose.

Spankings also have side effects. They are embarrassing, which causes children to get angry or think about retaliation. They seldom teach children to think about how they could have made a better decision. Spankings can affect a child's attitude. Children who are frequently spanked feel insecure. They do not trust themselves, thinking, "If I do the wrong thing, I will be hit." Many children who are spanked have poor self-esteem. Some children withdraw. Others become excitable, overactive, and aggressive.

The Impulsive Spanking

Many parents of preschool children spank impulsively. Whenever the child does something wrong, he receives a swat. The parent does not think much about it. Because these spankings are impulsive, they occur frequently. A mother once said, "I spank him and spank him and spank him, and he still will not listen." He is not listening because the spankings have become meaningless.

Impulsive spankings are commonly used with preschoolers. These parents are never too serious about the actual swat. They usually grab the child with one hand and swing with the other. The swat is almost automatic or reflexive. The preschooler hollers and then goes on playing.

Many parents use a technique called slap-the-toddler-on-the-hand. Young children like to experiment and touch things to see what happens. When they touch something they shouldn't, they get slapped. The problem with this is that slaps do not teach. Instead, you need to explain why an object should not be touched and remove the child or the object. When you slap, the only thing your child learns is how to slap.

The impulsive approach has no lasting effect on a child's misbehavior. After the child has been spanked on the butt a few dozen times, the swat becomes meaningless. For these parents, spanking is a continuous reaction. These parents do not know any alternative. They think, "That's the only way I can get her to behave." They believe they are doing the proper thing to be good parents.

Do children learn anything from the impulsive approach? Not really. They don't learn anything that will teach them to make better decisions. Far too often, the spanking depends on how the parent feels at that given moment. If you are short-tempered today, your children get spanked for every little thing they do. If you are feeling more tolerant, your children get away with murder. This inconsistency confuses children, who rightly wonder, "If I did this yesterday and it was okay, why am I getting a spanking today?" This inconsistency teaches children to be sneaky. It does not teach them right from wrong or how to make better decisions.

Children who are impulsively and frequently spanked believe that hitting is a normal part of life. So when another child does something they do not like, they hit. This becomes a problem with siblings, at school, and with playmates. When children hit each other, they get into trouble. This confuses children who don't understand why it is okay for adults to hit, but not children.

Many preschoolers who are frequently spanked believe that everything they do is wrong. This creates poor self-esteem and a lack of self-confidence. The goal of good discipline is to teach our children to make responsible decisions. Frequent spankings do not promote this; instead they teach children to behave because of fear. As a result, when the parent is not around to provide external control, the child has no control at all.

The impulsive approach is not an effective punishment because it perpetuates the need for spankings. Frequent spankings model negative behavior. They are reactive and never planned. Parents who use the impulsive approach seldom use positive remedies to change misbehavior; their children misbehave because their parents have not taken the time to teach them what they expect.

The Angry Spanking

Many parents use spanking when they are angry. This approach is the most common and the most harmful. When you become angry and spank your preschooler, a number of problems result. You teach your child how to push your buttons, and that his misbehavior has power over your self-control. Spanking in anger is an impulsive reaction. And because your anger is controlling you, you could become carried away and hurt your child. Even when you mask your anger and pretend to be calm when you spank, your child will still see that you are at your last resort and have no other options. Clever children will see this as having control over you.

When you spank in anger, you are often vengeful. You let your frustration build until it explodes. Then you retaliate with revenge, sometimes humiliating and embarrassing your child. Children learn they are a source of frustration to you. You also create intense negative emotions in yourself, your child, and the rest of the family. These negative emotions disrupt family climate, and can damage your child's self-esteem. Many children begin to fear their parents. They begin to mistrust their parents, which leads to a lack of self-trust.

Spanking in anger teaches children to strike out when they are angry. They learn that when they are angry, they do not have to exercise self-control, because that is exactly how you behave when you are angry. Most important of all, spanking in anger does not teach children how to make better decisions.

If your anger has you trapped in a pattern of spanking, make a commitment to stop. It will take plenty of self-control and rethinking, but it is a habit worth changing. Strategies for managing your anger were discussed in chapter 13. Try some of these and begin eliminating this pattern from your parenting.

The Question of Spanking and Safety Rules

At a recent workshop, a father asked, "What do I do when I have to teach my three-year-old not to do something right now? I do not want him to put something in the electrical outlet or walk around with scissors. Would a swat teach him not to do these unsafe behaviors?"

No. There are some experts who say that it is permissible to spank children to teach them safety rules. I do not agree. The reality is that small things and small holes intrigue small children. If you spank your child for attempting to put something in a wall outlet, he will probably stop, but the spanking will arouse his curiosity. It is similar to the apple in the Garden of Eden—once it was forbidden, it was all Adam and Eve could think about. Spanking your child will only make him think about the electrical outlet more: "What's the big attraction about this small hole in the wall?" Then he may try again when no one is around, which is a much greater danger.

Child safety is an essential component of parenting. Your job is to do everything possible to assure safety. Put plastic plugs in *all* the wall outlets in the house, not just the ones your child can see now—children grow and climb. All sharp objects need to be out of reach and out of sight. Drawers that hold unsafe items or cabinets with cleaning fluids or medicines need childproof safety locks. If you own a gun, it needs a trigger lock and should be in a gun safe. If you have a toddler, use childproof toilet lid locks. If your child is a runner, hold his hand or carry him in parking lots, anyplace there is traffic or when there is risk. You assure your children's safety by being proactive and physically protecting them.

You can raise happy, safe, and self-disciplined children without spanking. Spanking may be a good release for your anger or frustration, but it is a temporary solution that does not teach responsibility and can do more harm than good. There are a number of positive alternatives to spanking. Use communication to work through problems. Natural consequences and loss of privilege are effective strategies that teach better decision making. Stay calm. Be firm and consistent and emphasize correct behavior. If you need to use a punishment when your preschooler intentionally misbehaves, use time-out.

Correcting Misbehavior
with Time-Out

Have you ever watched parents of a new baby? Notice how excited they are about everything. They have so much anticipation about the future. Have you ever known a mother to smile at her baby and proudly exclaim, "I am really looking forward to the first time I have to put you in time-out"? No parent thinks about their beloved baby misbehaving or having tantrums. But as infants grow into toddlers and preschoolers, managing misbehavior becomes a necessity.

Preschoolers expect and need limits and rules. Rules provide security and predictability, but they need to be explained and consistently reinforced. Simply explaining and reinforcing rules does not always render ideal behavior, however, because there are times when preschoolers intentionally misbehave.

There are several techniques you can use to manage misbehavior. Time-out is one of these. A mild form of punishment, it is a consequence for deliberate misbehavior. One of the most harmful mistakes you can make is immediately using time-out without thinking through all of the other ways to manage misbehavior. Many other misbehavior strategies and techniques have been presented in previous sections of this book, including the previous chapter. The following chart is a brief review.

PRE-TIME-OUT CHECKLIST

Remember to consider these questions and alternatives before using time-out.

Can your child communicate with you about the situation? Some misbehavior may be due to your preschooler's inability to communicate and express his or her feelings. When children are frustrated or feel hurt and cannot express their feelings, they often act out their frustration or hurt with anger, whining, or tantrums. Talk with your preschooler about what may be troubling him.

Is the misbehavior intentional, or is it the result of other circumstances? Is your child afraid, stressed, fatigued, or hungry? If so, eliminate or change the situation as best you can and divert your child's attention to positive, acceptable behavior.

Is this behavior related to my child's temperament? Is your child's behavior due to a fear caused by shyness? Be reassuring and supportive.
Is the behavior due to a high energy level? Stay calm and be proactive. Channel your child's energy into appropriate physical activity.
Is the behavior due to persistence? Stay calm and do not argue. State your requests firmly and consistently.

Can my child control his behavior right now? Is your child emotionally out of control? Comfort your child, and then use language to teach your preschooler how to control his behavior.

Have I taught the replacement behavior consistently? Does your child know how to behave correctly in this situation? Use positive feedback to strengthen the opposite, acceptable behavior.

Preschool children often exhibit behaviors that are irritating, annoying, and sometimes defiant and disobedient. When these behaviors are not deliberate and intentional, they need to be managed with proactive, positive techniques that promote self-control and good decision making. When these behaviors are deliberate and intentional, you may choose to use time-out as a method of correcting and guiding your child to make better choices about his behavior.

Four-year-old Bernie was a bedtime procrastinator. In spite of his mother's positive strategies and bedtime routines, Bernie began screaming and having a tantrum as soon as his mom mentioned bed. Pajamas wrestling was followed by stalling tactics: "Can I have a drink of water?" "There is something wrong with my pillow." Bernie was not afraid of anything, he simply did not want to go to bed.

Bernie's mom used time-out to get her son to bed. If Bernie argued or began whining, she would give him a choice: go to bed or go to time-out. If Bernie refused to go to bed in any way, he would go to time-out. His mom was consistent. When Bernie argued or whined and did not change his behavior when given the opportunity, he went to time-out. Then once every minute, she would ask Bernie if he was ready to go to bed. After ten or fifteen minutes of sitting in time-out, he was ready to go to bed. In two weeks, the battles were over.

Time-out is effective. It eliminates the need for yelling, scolding, threatening, and spanking. It also prevents your children from pushing your buttons. Time-out means placing your preschooler in a boring place, away from the group, away from fun, for a minute or two. It means time. Time-out means time away from anything positive. Being denied activity is a kind of punishment. *Time-out means time to think of a good choice—time to think about correct behavior.*

Time-out works because it gives you a tool to back up what you say. It is a teaching technique and a mild punishment that you administer quickly and easily. Time-out works because preschoolers do not like it, and they will behave properly to avoid it.

In athletics, coaches call a time-out to rethink their strategy or to regroup their players into a more effective team. Time-out with preschoolers works the same way, giving your child a break to think about what he is doing wrong and how it needs to be corrected. It is time to regain self-control. It gives you (the coach) time to regain composure and build a strategy.

The time-out techniques used with preschoolers are slightly different than time-out techniques used with older children. This chapter will teach you how to use time-out with preschoolers between the ages of three and six. It will explain how to introduce time-out to your child and how to connect *making choices* with *time-out*. Not all children who have celebrated their third birthday, however, show the same level of maturity, understanding, and expression. Adjust the strategies to fit your child. Do what works—whatever improves your preschooler's behavior.

Since language development is critical during the preschool stage, it is a key element in the teaching process. Language guides learning. Using time-out with preschool children requires a verbal prompt or reminder in the form of a choice. Give your child an opportunity to change or correct his misbehavior. For example, "Please stop teasing your sister. If you do not stop, you will have to go to time-out. You decide. I hope you make a good choice and stop teasing. I know you can do it." Give one opportunity for self-correction, not several.

Use direct and explicit instructions with preschoolers. If you consistently explain the connection between your child's choice (behavior) and the consequence (time-out), your preschooler will eventually begin to understand the connection without your prompting: If I make this choice, this is the result. If I behave this way, this is what happens. Continue misbehaving, and I will have a time-out. Correct the misbehavior—make a good choice—and I avoid time-out. Because the preschool years are so developmental and formative, time-out requires a tremendous amount of guidance, instruction, and patience to be effective.

Here is an overview. The first step is to select the proper setting. Next, choose a misbehavior that you want to correct. Finally, explain time-out to your child. Describe the misbehavior that must stop. Explain that the misbehavior will result in time-out. You will need an egg timer or a timer that sounds a bell or a buzzer. An oven timer works fine, as long as your child can hear it from the time-out location. It may help to have two timers, one timer for your child to see and one for you. Explain that you have the official clock! Each of these steps is explained in detail later in this chapter.

I have been teaching the time-out technique in my workshops for more than twenty years. Years ago, most parents had never heard of using time-out. So after proper instruction and some discussion of how to avoid time-out's common mistakes, parents left the workshop armed with a new tool. Today, most parents have not only heard of time-out, they have tried it and failed. This means they have to make changes in the way they think about time-out, which is, of course, more difficult than starting correctly. There are eight common mistakes that trap parents and result in time-out being ineffective.

1 Do not use time-out impulsively. Use it with determination and planning. Your preschooler must understand when and how you will use time-out. If you use time-out for not listening, do not send your child to time-out for messing up the family room. Choose a more suitable consequence, such as picking up the toys in the family room.

2 Never use time-out as a surprise. Your preschooler will see this as unfair. Your preschooler needs to understand how time-out works in advance of its initial use.

3 Use time-out consistently. Once you have given your preschooler an opportunity to correct his misbehavior and he does not, follow through with time-out. Do not give in. Do not make excuses. If you do not follow through, even once, you will make the problem worse. You will be creating more work for yourself in the future.

4 Remain cool and calm when you use time-out. If you let your child push your buttons and get you angry, or if you yell and scream when you use time-out, it will not work. If your child succeeds in getting you upset, the time-out will be less effective.

5 Stay calm. This is crucial. If you feel a surge of anger, take a deep breath and count to ten or twenty, slowly. Walk away from the stress if there is someone else around to supervise the children. Then return to the situation. Interacting with your children when you are angry often has bad results.

6 Be prepared. When you first implement time-out, you will probably face resistance. Some children really work you over in the beginning, particularly if your preschooler is used to getting his own way. Please be assured that after the first few difficult episodes, time-out becomes easier for everyone. There will be a day when your child no longer becomes angry when sent to time-out. There may even be a day when you will not need time-out at all.

7 Use time-out as part of a total plan. If you use time-out to correct misbehavior and forget to reinforce good behavior, time-out will

not be effective. Time-out should be a small part of the plan. The larger part of the plan should emphasize the positive aspects of your preschooler's behavior. Focus 90 percent of your energy on positive behaviors and attitudes, and you will have little need for time-out. Recognize your preschooler's good behavior. If you take positive behavior for granted, improvements in your child's behavior will be minimal. Without emphasizing the positive, time-out by itself will not work. Instead, it will become just another form of correction that your preschooler learns to tolerate.

8 Do not use time-out as control. This is the most common and most legitimate argument against using time-out with preschoolers. Many parents become impatient and irritated with annoying and troublesome behaviors and immediately resort to time-out. This is wrong. Successful discipline is a teaching process. Successful discipline requires you to spend time teaching correct behavior—not just enforcing time-out.

Some parents disagree with using time-out with preschoolers, because time-out is a punishment. Using time-out is your decision. Discipline is built on beliefs. If you are not entirely comfortable with time-out, do not use it, because you may not be able to use it effectively. If this is your situation, employ all the positive strategies—distraction, redirection, and natural consequences—consistently, and refrain from using time-out.

You may also find that some of your friends and relatives who are unfamiliar with time-out regard it as unkind. Do not be influenced by this. Children do not suffer emotional damage from sitting alone for two or three minutes. It is ironic that many parents who see time-out as unkind see nothing wrong with spanking.

Other parents wonder if time-out is too artificial. If you worry about this, think about how other forms of time-out exist in our society. If you act out in school, you get detention. In sports, you get benched. Irresponsible drivers lose their licenses. If you break a law, you go to jail. The rights of others are important. If you seriously offend the group, you get kicked out. It makes more sense to teach children this connection with a milder, more temporary consequence.

How to Choose the Best Setting for Time-Out

There are a number of places you can use for time-out. Your choice depends on how well your child will sit. If your child will sit for a minute or two without problems, then a chair in an isolated area of the house will work fine. Do not refer to the chair as the "naughty chair," or say, "this is the place you sit when you are bad." Explain that the chair is for sitting and thinking. Use the same place all the time. Do not let your preschooler choose the location of the chair. Make sure that there is no view of the television from the chair, and that other children cannot run by and tease the child. The location needs to be isolated and boring. Many parents put the chair away after time-out is completed, having found that always having the chair out causes them to use time-out indiscriminately. It may also give your preschooler the idea that no matter what he does, time-out is inevitable.

If your child is resistant or unwilling to sit, then a more restrictive setting, such as a separate room, may be needed. Most bedrooms are too stimulating and fun. Use a bathroom, laundry room, utility room, or spare bedroom instead. Use your bedroom as a last resort. Remove all opportunities for self-amusement. Remove anything that is valuable. Make sure the room has a light. Place the time-out chair in this room.

The setting for time-out must be completely safe. If you use a separate room for time-out, make it childproof. Remove anything that might cause harm, including such items as soaps, cleaners, bleach, and toilet paper. Remove all dangerous items and breakable objects. You must feel confident that your preschooler is safe. Your child must believe that you are confident about the room being safe. Eliminate any doubts that make you feel uncomfortable. Your child may use these doubts against you, saying, "I'm scared. I'm afraid to be alone in here." Do not let these statements influence you; say, "There is nothing in the bathroom that will hurt you." It may be helpful to sit in the time-out room yourself for several minutes. Look around. Pretend you are an angry child. What could you say or do to make Mom or Dad never want to put you in time-out again?

The majority of parents I have worked with over the years use a bathroom for time-out. A spare bathroom is preferable. Your preschooler can sit on the toilet with the lid down or in a small chair.

What about the door—open or closed? That depends on your child. If your child can sit quietly, then the door can be left open. Many parents have found that leaving the door ajar about halfway works well. The risk here is that your child can get up and peek out, make noises for you to hear, or listen to other children having fun. If your preschooler is willing to comply with time-out with the door ajar, there is no problem. Explain to your child that the door can be left ajar as long as he remains quiet and cooperative. If he begins to act up, the door will be closed.

Many parents are uncomfortable with the idea of placing their preschooler in a room with the door closed. If you do not feel comfortable with the door being closed, leave the door open or slightly ajar. Some parents have used a childproof gate across the doorway. This is fine as long as your preschooler does time-out without manipulating. Do whatever is reasonable that works.

Since time-out for preschoolers requires only a few minutes, always provide nearby, constant supervision. A direct line of sight is best. That way you can consistently monitor the situation. It is always helpful to walk by and remind your preschooler that he is doing a good job. Say, "Thank you for sitting quietly. You are doing fine. Your time is almost over." A few passing words of encouragement go a long way.

Scott used the bathroom for time-out with five-year-old Lynn. Even though he thought he had done everything to make the bathroom safe and boring, Lynn entertained herself by playing with the water in the toilet bowl. Scott's remedy was to put a clamp on the toilet lid. A little creativity goes a long way. Scott did not abandon the whole idea of time-out just because there was a setback. He did not say what many parents might have said: "She is just having fun. Time-out doesn't work." He worked through the problem. He was committed to making time-out work.

There is one caution about the bathroom. Do not use the bathroom as your time-out setting for a child who is being toilet trained. This would be confusing. Do not use the bathroom for time-out with any child when another child is being toilet trained. You do not want your child to perceive the bathroom as a bad place.

The Time in Time-Out

How long your child spends in time-out depends on three factors. The first factor is age. For children between the ages of three and four, one or two minutes in time-out should be adequate. As they reach the age of four, up until age six, extend the time to two or three minutes. The longest a child this age should be asked to sit in time-out is five minutes. Using time-out consistently, not the length of the time-out, corrects misbehavior. Be consistent about the time, even though young children do not always understand the concept of time. Use a timer, such as a plastic egg timer. The child can connect the sand falling to when the time is over.

The second factor is your child's temperament. You may need to adjust the time to match your child's temperament. An energetic child who always has trouble being still may have difficulty completing a three-minute time-out. Use one or two minutes instead. A child who is stubborn and argumentative may need a full five minutes to calm down and realize that you mean business.

The third factor that contributes to how long your preschooler has to stay in time-out is how well he cooperates. You will need to explain how these ideas work when you first describe time-out to your children. There are two ideas to explain. Most parents use these two techniques in combination.

1 If your child goes to time-out willingly and sits quietly, you may let him out a minute early. In other words, time off for good behavior. Many parents find this strategy is extremely motivating, especially with children who like power, because it gives them some control over the time. Their preschoolers learn quickly that being cooperative pays off.

2 On the other hand, being uncooperative may add more time, perhaps another minute. You want time-out to work as smoothly as possible. If your child struggles on the way to time-out, stop and get his attention. Give him a verbal prompt and a choice: "If you cooperate, you have to sit for two minutes. If you struggle, you have to sit for three minutes. It is up to you. I hope you cooperate so your time will be shorter."

Christina did not always go to time-out on her own. She needed her mother to escort her to time-out. At times she would resist until her mother began prompting her, "You can go to time-out on your own. If you need my help, you will stay in time-out longer. If you can go by yourself, you will only need to stay for two minutes." Christina caught on to this immediately. Even when she was very upset, she would take herself to time-out right away to reduce the time.

Preschoolers often become sad or upset when they have done something wrong. They may feel that they have disappointed you and worry that you do not love them. This is a real fear that you need to take seriously. Your child may need reassurance that you love him. Say, "I love you, Jacob. I am sorry that you are sad. I am not mad at you. I do not like it when you do not obey. But I will always love you." Some preschoolers may ask for a hug. Hugging is always okay.

Children cry when they are unhappy and may do so during time-out. Here are some guidelines to handle crying and other forms of noise your child may make. If your child cries a little, ignore it and let the timer continue to run. Ignore any singing, humming, storytelling, or poetry recitals. If your child is sobbing, singing, or making noises to amuse himself, let the timer run. However, if the crying is designed to get you upset, do not start the timer. Wait for him to become quiet, telling him to notify you when he is ready to start the time.

If your child screams or has a tantrum while in time-out, ignore it. Tell your child that he has three minutes in time-out, and that you will start the timer when he is quiet. Ask your child to knock on the door when he is ready to start his time. All the time spent yelling and having a tantrum does not count toward the three minutes. Start the timer only when he is reasonably quiet.

The Priority Misbehavior

A priority misbehavior is a specific action that you consider inappropriate or problematic. You want to deal with this misbehavior now, and you want your preschooler to stop doing it now. The priority misbehavior you select must be very specific, such as not listening, arguing, talking back, or teasing. Terms such as obnoxious, mean, and rude are not good priority misbehaviors because they are not specific; they do not describe the misbehavior in a meaningful way.

You may need to practice being specific. If your children misbehave a lot, it is easy to lose sight of the actual misbehaviors, and you might find yourself saying things like, "My child is always in trouble." "He never does anything when I want him to." "She never has a good day." "He gets so obnoxious I could scream." "That child will never behave." If you find yourself thinking this way, consider exactly what it is that your child does, and describe it very concretely: "Carmen will not do things when asked," or "Jared hits his sister."

How to Explain Time-Out to Your Children

Sit down with each child separately and explain time-out. Timing and judgment are critical. Do not try to explain time-out shortly after a blowup. Do not explain time-out when you are angry, or when your child is angry. Choose a time when things are going well and your child is in a receptive mood. Explain that time-out is something that is going to help him behave and make good choices. Describe time-out as time sitting alone. Explain how the timer works. The timer will tell your child when time-out is over. If you suspect that your child may be un-cooperative, explain the consequences of these actions in more detail. Finally, describe the priority misbehavior to your child. Discuss this thoroughly and give examples. Be sure he understands the misbehavior.

Many parents have taught time-out procedures to their preschooler through role-playing. First, use one of your preschooler's dolls or stuffed animals. Then role-play an example or situation with your child. Practice the rules and procedures before you implement a real time-out. Here is an example of a father and mother explaining time-out to their five-year-old daughter, Julie.

Dad: "Julie, could you come here, please? Mom and I would like to talk with you about something."

Julie: "What, Dad?"

Mom: "You have been doing pretty well with your behavior lately in most things, but there are still times when you do not listen."

Dad: "We are going to help you listen better and make good choices."

Julie: "How?"

Mom: "By using time-out."

Dad: "When Mom or I ask you to do something, you need to listen to us. If you do not listen, we will remind you to make a good choice."

Mom: "If you still do not listen, you will go to time-out."

Julie: "What is time-out?"

Dad: "Time-out means going to the bathroom and sitting by yourself. If you go right away and you do not argue, you only have to sit for two minutes."

Julie: "What if I don't want to go?"

Mom: "If you argue or don't go right away, then you will have to sit for an extra minute."

Dad: "If you yell, or kick, or slam the bathroom door, then you will add another minute. Do you understand?"

Julie: "I think so."

Dad: "When you go to time-out, we will set the timer on the oven for two minutes. When you hear the buzzer, you can come out."

Mom: "But if you are noisy in there, or if you choose to have a tantrum in there, the time will not count. We will not start the timer until you are sitting quietly."

Dad: "So the sooner you sit quietly, the sooner you can come out."

Mom: "Do you understand how the timer works?"

Julie: "Yes."

Dad: "We hope that you won't have to go to time-out very often. The choice is yours. If you listen, you won't need to go in there. It is really up to you. Go get your teddy bear, and we will practice time-out with him. It will just be pretending this time."

Do not be surprised if your explanation does not go as smoothly as this example. Preschoolers need things repeated. Give your preschooler the best explanation you can. Write down what you are going to say to your child. Make a list of things you want to discuss ahead of time. Here is an outline that will help you stay on track when explaining time-out to your preschooler.

Explain these points:

- Time-out is going to help you behave (or make good choices).

- What time-out is—sitting for two minutes.

- How the time works—less time if you cooperate, more time if you do not.

- How the timer works—you can come out when the time is over.

- Describe and give an example of the priority misbehavior.

You must remember to:

- Choose a good time to talk.

- Ignore any negative comments from your child.

- Stay calm, no matter what happens.

- Role-play time-out—first with a doll or stuffed animal, and then with your preschooler.

How to Use Time-Out

When the priority misbehavior occurs, give your child a prompt to correct his behavior. If he continues to misbehave, send him to time-out. Stay calm. Be firm and assertive. Here is an example. The priority misbehavior is *not listening* the first time.

Mom: "Greg, would you please pick up your toys?"

Greg: "No. I am coloring a picture."

Mom: "Greg, you are not listening. Please pick up your toys. If you do not pick up your toys now, you will have to go to time-out. Please make a good choice. Be a good listener. Pick up your toys."

Once you tell your child that he has earned a time-out, do not change your mind. Some children will suddenly become obedient and cooperative, hoping you will be lenient. Do not be fooled.

Mom: "Greg, you are not listening. Please pick up your toys. If you do not pick up your toys now, you will have to go to time-out. Please make a good choice. Be a good listener. Pick up your toys."

Greg: "No. I don't want to pick them up. I didn't take them out."

Mom: "Greg, that is not listening. Go to time-out. You have two minutes."

Greg: "Okay. I'll pick up my toys now."

Mom: "No. First you have to go to time-out. You will pick up your toys after time-out."

Greg misbehaved by not listening and refusing to pick up his toys when asked. Mom provided Greg an opportunity to correct his misbehavior and make a better choice. When Greg refused, Mom correctly enforced time-out. Greg tried tempting her by conceding to do what Mom asked. Now he has decided that listening is better than time-out. Too late! Do not surrender to these attempts.

Only provide an opportunity to correct the misbehavior and make a better choice once, prior to telling your child to go to time-out. Once your preschooler has rejected the chance to correct his behavior, enforce the time-out. Once you have told your child to go to time-out, the opportunity to correct the misbehavior is over. There are no more chances. Send your child to time-out. If you give in, you will be encouraging your child to tease and plead and argue.

When you use time-out for the first time, begin with one misbehavior. Choose one misbehavior that you want to decrease. Do not choose the most troublesome misbehavior to start. Choose a more moderate problem. This will familiarize you and your child with time-out procedures before you attempt to tackle the bigger problems. Be consistent with this beginning misbehavior. Your success here sets the pattern.

When you have the first misbehavior under control, use time-out for a second misbehavior. Be cautious—you want your child to be successful. Moving ahead slowly is much safer than moving too quickly. Add new priority misbehaviors slowly and systematically to ensure feelings of success.

What to Say When Time-Out Is Over

The first thing you should say to your child after he completes time-out is, "Thank you for doing your time-out." It is perfectly acceptable to give your preschooler a hug and kiss. This reassures him that you love him. It also establishes a positive relationship, which will encourage better cooperation.

What you say next depends on why he went to time-out. If your preschooler was in time-out for misbehavior such as teasing, whining, bad language, or hitting, start fresh. Redirect him to an activity that will be more positive. Here is an example:

Sarah: (Teases her younger brother.)

Mom: "Sarah, please stop teasing your brother."

Sarah: (Continues to tease.)

Mom: "Sarah, stop teasing, or you will go to time-out. Make a good choice, please."

Sarah: (Continues to tease.)

Mom: "Sarah, go to time-out."

(Two minutes later, Sarah comes out of time-out.)

Mom: "Thank you for doing your time-out. Have you seen my purse anywhere?"

(Mom changes the subject—to start fresh.)

Do not lecture her on the issue of teasing. The time to explain right and wrong is later, when your daughter is more receptive. Here is what *not* to do:

(Sarah comes out of time-out.)

Mom: "Now aren't you sorry you were teasing your brother?"

Sarah: "No!"

Mom: "Then you march right back into time-out, and do not come out until you are sorry!"

Be careful about asking preschoolers to say they are sorry. Most three- and four-year-olds do not really understand what it means to be sorry for their actions. It is okay to teach the words, "I am sorry," and to rehearse apologies, but do not expect real remorse until age five or six, and even then they are usually expressing sorrow for being in trouble, rather than for doing something wrong or hurting someone's feelings. Many preschoolers do not understand that "I'm sorry" means "I will try not to do it again." In fact, it is not uncommon for a preschooler who does something wrong to say, "I'm sorry," and then repeat the misbehavior ten minutes later. A child who does this is just saying words, perhaps to get forgiveness and avoid punishment. Teach your preschoolers that being sorry means that you will not repeat the misbehavior. The best way to teach this is by being a good example. When you say you are sorry, you need to be sure not to repeat your misbehavior.

If your child went to time-out for refusing to do something, then he must do the task when he comes out of time-out. Going to time-out is not a substitute for doing what you are asked to do. If your son went to time-out for refusing to set the place mats on the table, repeat the request when he comes out. If he refuses, he receives another time-out. Do not let his refusal to help set the table delay dinner, since that would give him power. If you suspect that your son may not cooperate, ask him to set the place mats thirty minutes before dinnertime. This will give him plenty of time to correct his behavior.

Having household jobs teaches children responsibility, an opportunity to accomplish something, and feel proud. Be careful, however; children resent working if it becomes burdensome. They need responsibilities, but they also need to be children. They should not spend hours each day doing housework. Do not use time-out to make servants of your children.

How to Manage a Preschooler Who Refuses to Go to Time-Out

Managing your preschooler when she simply refuses to go to time-out is never easy. You want your preschooler to know that you mean what you say, but you do not want to play warden. The following sequence of strategies may help:

1. Take your preschooler by the hand and walk to time-out. Be firm but stay calm. As you walk, remind your preschooler that she can make a good decision. If your preschooler still refuses, it is acceptable to carry her to time-out. Be careful not to hurt your child or yourself.

2. If your preschooler will not stay in time-out, remind her that you will close the door.

3. If this reminder fails, then hold the door closed from the outside. This is not fun for anyone and should only be done as a last resort.

Holding a door closed is an intense physical and emotional drain. Both parents should take turns or have another adult nearby to call on for assistance. It makes more sense to hold the door closed for a few minutes than to give in. While you are holding the door closed, it is essential that you remain calm and in control of yourself and the situation. About once or twice a minute, remind your preschooler with a calm voice, "As soon as you are quiet, we will start the timer."

If you are uncomfortable with this technique, or if your child is too strong to control physically, you need a different approach. When your child refuses to go to time-out, wait a minute and ask again. If you are finding yourself getting angry, walk away and cool off for a few minutes. Do not argue or yell. When you repeat your request, give your child a minute to think about what is going to happen next. You must clearly explain the consequences: "Amanda, stop and think. Make a good choice. You are going to lose your Barbie dollhouse. You will still have to go to time-out. I am not going to argue with you. It's up to you. Please sit for three minutes and get it over." Sometimes preschoolers make poor decisions. Give them a minute to think. You want them to realize that three minutes in time-out is better than losing their treasure.

If your preschooler refuses to go to time-out after your second request, it's time to take away the privilege or activity or toy that is most loved by your child. If possible, choose something that you can lock up or put away. Things like Barbie toys, bicycles, trucks, computer games, and movie videos work well. Whatever your child's favorite plaything is, that's what you lock up.

If your son treasures his toy trucks, and he refuses to go to time-out, lock up his toy trucks. Keep them locked until he completes his three minutes of time-out. Some preschoolers will push you to the limit every time, hoping you will give in. They will refuse to go to time-out until you start to lock up the treasure. By the time you lock up the treasure, they have done the three minutes. Then you have to go unlock the treasure. You can be manipulated by this type of child. If you have a loophole in your plan, clever preschoolers will find it. You can correct this situation by keeping the treasure locked for a few hours or until the next day.

This backup strategy works well. Convince your preschooler that serving three minutes is better than losing his bicycle. And be aware that once you start taking privileges away, the misbehavior may escalate, because your preschooler may want to get even.

If you anticipate that your preschooler may refuse to go to time-out, discuss the backup procedures when you first explain time-out. Let's listen in on Julie and her parents again:

Julie: "What if I don't want to go to time-out?"

Dad: "We will lock up your Barbie dollhouse. You will get your dollhouse back when you do your time-out."

Mom: "If that doesn't help you make a better choice, then we will have to do something else, like locking up your dollhouse for a whole day."

Julie: "But that's not fair."

Dad: "Well, Julie, as I said before, the choice is yours. We hope we never have to lock up your dollhouse. We hope it never happens. But that is what we will do if we have to. That's a promise."

Whatever backup plan you develop, be sure that your preschooler's refusal to go to time-out costs your preschooler an inconvenience, not you. Do not threaten backup punishments that cost you more than they cost your child. Do not say, "We cannot go out for dinner until you do your time-out." This gives your preschooler control over you and the entire family.

Many parents are confused about taking a privilege away as a backup for time-out. Why not lock up the dollhouse from the beginning and forget time-out? Time-out is something that is short and easy to administer. It is something that makes punishment easier for you in the long run. Time-out is easier than locking up the toys several times a week. In addition, if you take too many toys away, your preschooler may become discouraged and give up trying to improve his behavior.

Time-Out Away from Home

Discipline begins at home. If you are positive and consistent, your child's behavior will improve at home and everywhere. But what about those ocasions when you are away from home and your child begins to misbehave?

One solution is to return home and send your preschooler to time-out. It sounds crazy, but chances are you will only have to do this once or twice, because it makes a lasting impression. Preschoolers have good memories.

An alternative would be to use the car or car seat, as four-year-old Kyle's mother did when they went to the bank. Kyle began to misbehave and continued doing so even after his mother reminded him to stop. She got out of line and took him to his car seat. He sat there for two minutes while Mom stood outside the car, watching him. He settled down, and they returned to the bank. This is a good example of consistency. Mom knew it was worth it to teach Kyle that misbehaving is not permitted. She was thinking about the future.

Establish a time-out setting at places you visit regularly. Use the bathroom at Grandma's. Use the laundry room at your friend's house. Teach your preschoolers that wherever they are, they need to behave. Be discreet when you use time-out away from home. Try to avoid embarrassing your child, as this will only increase resistance and create more misconduct.

Time-Out for Two

What should you do when two (or more) of your children misbehave at the same time? It is best to avoid discussions about who started it. This usually leads to more arguing and more disagreement. If both children have misbehaved, then both should go to time-out. Not together! One child sits while the other does time-out, and then they trade places. Flip a coin to see who goes first.

"I Don't Care if I Go to Time-Out"

What if your child says he doesn't care if he goes to time-out? Many clever children make statements like this. Ignore these remarks completely. This will not be easy. Do not start lecturing and moralizing. Do not respond with, "There must be something wrong with you if you don't care about going to time-out." Do not get trapped into believing everything your preschooler says.

Adjusting Time-Out

Earlier in this chapter I explained how many of today's parents have tried and failed with time-out. One of the most common reasons for these failures is the lack of record keeping. To assure success, you must keep a record or chart of your preschooler's time-outs. It is easy to be consistent with a new idea, just as it is easy to diet for three days. As the novelty wears off, we get lazy. Records or charts help you stay consistent. They will show that your child goes to time-out less and less. Looking at a chart will make you and your child feel successful, which will keep both of you motivated as you achieve your goal. A sample chart appears at the end of this chapter.

Count the number of time-outs per day or per week. If the number of time-outs goes down, the system is working fine. Do not be discouraged if your child's chart does not show improvement quickly. Some children need more time. Some children are persistent and resist change. Some children have several good days and then a few bad days. Some children may even misbehave more at first. They want you to think that no matter what you try to do, it won't work. It is as if they are saying, "I'll show you."

Record keeping or charting is important because the rate of improvement varies from child to child. Some preschoolers improve dramatically in less than a week. If this happens to your child, you will believe that time-out works well. Other preschoolers are more persistent in their misbehavior. With these children, improvement is much slower and more difficult to see on a day-to-day basis, and it may take several weeks before you see significant improvement. You will be tempted to stop using time-out and add it to the "We have tried everything" list. Your preschooler may average four time-outs a day the first week. At the end of two weeks, he may average three time-outs a day. While you may not feel like this is a huge improvement, it is in fact a 25 percent change for the better. A chart will keep you from being discouraged if large improvements do not occur right away. Believe me, there will be days that you will need all the encouragement you can get.

Many days may pass with no time-outs. Then several time-outs will occur within a few days. Some preschoolers test more than others. Every once in a while, your child will test you to see if anything has changed. He needs assurance that you still mean what you say. Charting will let you know if this happens with your preschooler.

Sometimes time-outs increase because you are having bad days. Maybe you have let your children get away with a bit more misbehavior than usual. You have not been as consistent as you need to be. Maybe your focus is negative—you have forgotten to look for good behavior. For most parents, time-out does not work because they are too impatient. We want quicker results for our hard work. Children learn to be more persistent than their parents. They know that if they are stubborn long enough, Mom and Dad will give in, just like all the other times. Keep charts on time-out for several weeks. With some children, a little improvement is all you get at first. If you are frustrated by the lack of improvement, ask yourself these questions:

1 Am I being consistent?

2 Am I following through every time the priority misbehavior occurs? You cannot skip a few times. If you only follow through when you feel like it, you will make the problem worse. You will be teaching your child that being persistent in a negative way pays off.

3 Am I getting angry when I use time-out? Some preschoolers want you to get angry. This is their goal. They would gladly serve several time-outs, as long as they can push your button each time. Getting you

angry may be a bigger reward than any amount of time-out. In other words, the punishment of time-out is outweighed by the reward of your anger.

4 Am I giving my child too much attention when I use time-out? Do not engage in long discussions and explanations. Do not let time-out pull you away from other children or other responsibilities for long talks. Three minutes in time-out is a good trade for some of Mom's or Dad's individual attention. If time-out seems more like a game than a punishment, you are giving too much attention.

5 Am I forgetting to be positive about good behavior? You cannot use time-out alone and expect it to work. Use time-out as part of a total plan. Spend more energy on the positive than the negative. If you only concentrate on misbehavior, time-out will not be as effective.

A parent recently told me that time-out changed her entire family. For years, she and her husband would yell and spank. The children would yell in return. Her son summed it up best: "I like time-out, Mom. It's better than what we used to do."

Time-out is a mild form of punishment that works. Use time-out with determination and planning. Arrange time-out in advance so that you teach your children how to predict the consequences of their behavior and make good decisions. Like everything else with your children, you must use time-out consistently. Provide preschoolers the opportunity to correct their misbehavior and make a good choice. Give your preschooler ample positive verbal reinforcement if he chooses to correct the misbehavior and cooperate rather than going to time-out. Be calm and in control of the situation when you use time-out. If you get angry, you are using time-out incorrectly.

•Y O U R   T U R N •

Preschool Time-Out Guidelines

What to do:

Determine the time-out setting—**safety first**.

Use a small chair in a boring place.

Identify the priority misbehavior you want to correct.

Use a timer (egg timers work well).

Start the time when your child is quiet (a little crying is okay).

Things to remember:

Use a record or chart to keep track of progress.

Use time-out as part of a total, positive plan.

Use time-out consistently.

Stay calm when you use time-out.

Initial episodes may be difficult.

Explain time-out to your child:

Time-out is going to help you make good choices.

Time-out means sitting and thinking about good choices.

You sit for two minutes.

You earn a minute off if you cooperate.

You may earn an extra minute if you do not cooperate.

Give an example of the misbehavior that will mean time-out.

Follow these steps with the child who refuses to go:

Take your preschooler by the hand and walk to time-out.

Remind your preschooler that he can make a good decision.

Carry your preschooler to time-out.

Give your preschooler a minute to think.

Take away the treasure.

When your child completes time-out:

Say, "Thank you for doing your time-out."

Start fresh—redirect (if the misbehavior is over);

or

Your child still has to do what is asked (if he went to time-out for refusing a request).

Time-Out Chart

Use this chart to keep a record of your preschooler's time-outs.

DATE	MINUTES	MISBEHAVIOR	COMMENTS

Each time your child receives a time-out, record the date, the minutes, the misbehavior and any comments. For example:

DATE	MINUTES	MISBEHAVIOR	COMMENTS
6/20	2	**Not listening**	**No problems going to time-out.**

| 6/20 | 3 | Not listening | Argued on the way—earned an extra minute. |
| 6/21 | 1 | Not listening | Did great— earned a minute off. |

How to Determine Priority Misbehaviors

Be specific when you think about priority misbehaviors. Being specific helps you focus. This exercise will help you practice being specific. Put an X in front of the statements that describe a specific misbehavior.

❏ 1. Corey hits his sister.

❏ 2. Kayla refuses to pick up her toys.

❏ 3. Joshua is obnoxious.

❏ 4. Justin is hyperactive.

❏ 5. Ryan is running through the house.

❏ 6. Brittany pinches her brother.

❏ 7. Erica argues when you ask her to do something.

Answers: 1, 2, 5, 6, and 7 are specific. Number 3 is not specific because of the word *obnoxious*. It does not describe the misbehavior in a meaningful way. This is also true for number 4. *Hyperactive* does not tell us exactly what Justin does when he misbehaves.

Suppose you planned to use time-out for Corey, Kayla, Ryan, Brittany, and Erica. How would you use positive feedback to strengthen an opposite, positive behavior for each of these children?

Corey: Compliment Corey when he plays nicely with his sister.

Kayla: Look for times when Kayla does pick up her toys. Thank her for doing her job.

Ryan: Compliment Ryan when he walks calmly through the house.

Brittany: Catch Brittany being gentle with her brother.

Erica: When Erica does something without an argument, draw her attention to it: "Thanks for listening without an argument."

Planning Improves Misbehavior

One of the most exasperating aspects of parenthood is managing misbehavior. When preschoolers misbehave, we often feel frustrated, disappointed, discouraged, and angry. When we are caught up in the midst of an episode of misbehavior, we are not always at our best. We may be angry or upset, and our use of reason often disappears. All we want is for the misbehavior to stop. Now! Here is a plan that will help you determine the most effective way of managing your preschooler's misbehavior.

Determine the Pattern of Misbehavior

Most misbehavior occurs as part of a pattern. Preschoolers develop one or more patterns of misbehavior to get what they want or to express an emotion. Four typical patterns of misbehavior occur in most children at least some of the time:

- Annoying misbehavior, such as whining, teasing, nagging, pouting, and tantrums.

- Disobedient misbehavior, such as not following rules or not obeying requests.

- Aggressive misbehavior, which can be verbal, such as name-calling, or physical, such as biting, kicking, hitting, throwing objects, or fighting.

- Defiant misbehavior, such as refusing to listen or arguing.

Decide the Purpose of the Misbehavior

Identifying the pattern of misbehavior is important because it helps you determine the purpose or function of the misbehavior. Although you can never be certain of the purpose of a preschooler's misbehavior, it usually is motivated by some purpose. Once you identify the misbehavior pattern, think about the purpose behind the misbehavior.

When misbehavior is annoying, children may be trying to get their way, to get you to give in, or to get you to change your mind. When children are disobedient, it may be because they are not motivated to do what you want. They may be motivated to do something else, such as playing with their toys or watching TV. Preschoolers who exhibit aggressive behavior are often expressing anger, frustration, or revenge. They may feel hurt or angry because they did not get their way, or because they believe that you or someone has done something mean to them. Preschoolers who are defiant are typically seeking control or power. They either do not want to do what you ask or want to do what you do not permit. These children are strong-willed.

Decide What to Say and Do

Since the purpose of most annoying behavior is to get you to give in or change your mind, one way to manage annoying behaviors is to ignore them. This does not mean to ignore the problem; learn to ignore the whining or teasing, but make sure you do not give in to demands. When your child throws a tantrum, she wants an audience. It is fine to say, "I am ignoring you." It is also helpful to use redirection. "My ears do not listen to whining; please ask in a polite voice." As a long-term solution, provide verbal reinforcement when your child is asking politely and speaking calmly.

When a child is being disobedient, give a firm warning to stop and tell him what action you will take if he chooses to continue: "Think about what you are doing. Please do what I asked. If not, you will have to take a time-out. You decide." In other words, give a firm warning and explain that this behavior is not a good idea. Then explain what he needs to do to make a better decision, and avoid punishment: "It is okay to not want to do it—but you still have to do it." "There will always be things we have to do that we don't want to do." As a long-term solution, recognize your preschooler when he is being obedient and respectful.

An effective way to manage verbal aggression such as name-calling and cussing is not to overreact. This is often difficult. It helps to talk with your preschooler during a calm moment and explain the consequences of name-calling—how words can hurt someone's feelings: "That is not nice. It is okay to be upset or angry, but it is not okay to use bad words. Bad words make children feel sad." As a long-term solution, reinforce replacement behaviors, such as properly expressing anger with appropriate words or pictures.

If your child becomes physically aggressive and bites, kicks, hits, throws things, or fights, you need to intervene quickly and stop the aggression. Remove your child if necessary. Then redirect your preschooler and explain that it is okay to be upset, but it is not okay to strike out: "That is not allowed. It is okay to be angry. But it is not okay to hit." It is essential to remind your child, *"Use your words."* Teach your preschooler to use words to express how he feels. If the pattern of aggression persists, take more deliberate action, such as a short time-out. Always explain the consequences of hitting or fighting. Someone could be hurt, either physically or emotionally. As a long-term solution, recognize your child when he does use words to explain how he feels, or when he uses words to resolve a problem. Look for situations when he is playing cooperatively, sharing, and speaking politely.

Children who are defiant and refuse to listen or obey are usually seeking control. Remain calm. If you get upset, your child wins. This is the victory he seeks. Be consistent. Be prepared to follow through immediately. Look for listening the first time. Say, "Thank you for listening the first time I asked you to pick up your toys. I appreciate it very much." Look for obedience: "Thank you for picking up your trucks without an argument."

It is especially important to remain calm when your preschooler wants to argue. Use redirection: "If you speak to me calmly, I will listen to what you have to say." If you find yourself getting dragged into an argument, remember to control yourself first. Say, "I need to calm down so we can talk more."

Developing an Action Plan

Think about your preschooler's misbehavior patterns. What are the recurring problems? What can you do to prevent these problems in the future? If your child argues, develop a plan to reduce arguing. If your child does not listen, develop a plan to promote good listening.

The following planning guide combines many of the ideas in this book into a set of specific strategies. This is a step-by-step method. Follow these steps, and behavior will improve.

Step 1: Establish your goal. How would you like things to be? What changes do you want to see in your children? When choosing a goal, base your decision on two factors: (1) Select a goal that offers a high chance of success. Your first plan must be successful. Success encourages more success. (2) Select a goal that contributes to the success of the whole family. This will encourage a positive family climate.

Goal: Adam and Whitney will get along with each other.

Step 2: Make a list of specific behaviors that you want to increase or decrease. What does getting along with each other really mean? What do you expect? These are your priority behaviors.

1. Adam and Whitney will argue *less*.

2. Adam and Whitney will tease each other *less*.

3. Adam and Whitney will share each other's toys *more*.

4. Adam and Whitney will call each other names *less*.

5. Adam and Whitney will cooperate *more*.

6. Adam and Whitney will be polite *more* often.

Step 3: Select one or two priority behaviors to work on first. Choose behaviors that are easy to correct. Quick success is important.

Step 4: Observe and keep a record for five days. Once you have selected priority behaviors, count the number of times the behaviors occur each day. Do not do anything to change the behaviors; simply

observe them. You need to know how often the behaviors are occurring before you carry out the rest of the plan. This will enable you to evaluate your success.

Assume that you have selected behaviors 1 and 3: Adam and Whitney will argue less, and Adam and Whitney will share each other's toys more. Count and record the number of times Adam and Whitney argue. Count and record the number of times they share toys. Do this for five days. Here is what this record might look like:

DAY	1	2	3	4	5
Share	0	1	0	2	1
Argue	5	6	7	5	6

This chart tells us that Adam and Whitney argue an average of six times a day. They share less than once a day.

You need to determine the current level of behavior before you begin applying consequences. These records are very important, since they will give you an accurate baseline to assess how well your plan is working. If you do not keep written records, you will be depending on your perception and memory. With some children, improvements come in small amounts and are not easily detected. At the start of the plan, Adam and Whitney are arguing an average of six times a day. Suppose that after a week, they are arguing five times a day. This is a small improvement, but it is still an improvement. If left to your perceptions, you would probably say the plan is not working. You would be wrong.

Step 5: Decide how you will intervene. What will you do to change the behaviors? What incentives will you use? What punishments will you use? Make a list of incentives and punishments. Ask your children for their ideas when you explain the plan. What incentives would they like to earn? Use charts, checklists, and menus of incentives to give your plan power.

Step 6: Explain the plan to your children. Tell them your goal. Explain the behaviors that you want to improve. Establish the rules, expec-

tations, and consequences. Clarify what you expect from them and what they can expect from you. Be positive about the plan. Tell them that this is something that is going to make everyone feel better. Tell them you are serious about the plan. You will follow through with punishments if they choose to misbehave.

"Children, I would like to talk to you about a new idea. I expect that from now on, you will be polite (nice) to each other. I also expect that you will share each other's toys. When you share and be polite, you can earn extra minutes at story time. If you break a rule, you will go to time-out for two minutes. This plan will help you behave and get along with each other. I know you can do a good job."

From that moment, the choice to behave is with Adam and Whitney. As a parent, you become a spectator, cheering for Adam and Whitney to be winners, to be successful. When the children break a rule, you won't need to engage in lengthy arguments; you simply enforce the consequence you have agreed upon. By setting up the rules in advance, you can remain on their side, rather than becoming the bad guy. You do not decide what happens—the children decide, when they choose whether or not to behave.

Use plenty of encouragement. When your children show improvements, point out how well they are doing. Make comments that increase their self-worth, like, "It's good to see you sharing. You should both be proud of your behavior."

Step 7: Evaluate. Is this plan working? Observe and keep a record, as you did in step 4. By comparing these two sets of records, you will be able to determine if your plan is effective. Get your children involved in charting. Post the chart in the kitchen. Do a new chart each week.

When your children show improvements, add another behavior but maintain the original ones as well. If there is additional improvement next week, add another. Be cautious; it is better to add new behaviors slowly. Do not rush the plan, or it may collapse. If there is no improvement after two weeks, adjust the plan.

Step 8: Adjust the plan. No improvement means the expectations are too high or the consequences are not motivating. If you think the ex-

pectations are too difficult, change them. If the children are unwilling to share each other's toys, you may change your expectation to taking turns while playing a game. Begin by playing the game with them. Model sharing and taking turns. Once they are successful, let them play a game alone. This expectation still emphasizes sharing and cooperation. As they learn to play more cooperatively, try sharing toys again.

The success of any plan depends on positive feedback and incentives. Children become tired of the same thing. Change the incentives to maintain a high level of motivation. If your children lose interest in story time, try a new incentive, such as happy faces or stickers on a chart. Overused incentives lack power.

You may be tempted to use stronger punishments if your plan shows no improvement. Stronger punishments seldom help, since they only discourage most preschoolers. Children show less effort, not more effort. It is better to be consistent with one small punishment and change the positive incentives.

When behaviors do not readily change, it is not because your child is terrible. It is not because you are a failure as a parent. When a behavior fails to change, it is because the system of expectations and consequences is not working properly.

Look at the plan and ask yourself: Should I make changes? Am I being consistent? Have I given the plan enough time? Am I staying calm? Are consequences administered quickly? Am I giving negative attention? Am I ignoring? Am I catching my children being good? These questions will help you determine where your plan can be improved.

•YOUR TURN•

Planning Guide for Improved Behavior

1. What behaviors do my children need to improve?

Goal: _____

_____

_____

2. List the specific behaviors you expect from your children.

_____

_____

_____

3. Choose one or two priority behaviors to change.

_____

_____

_____

4. Keep a record. Count the number of times the priority behaviors occur each day.

DAY	1	2	3	4	5

5. Decide what to do.

Replacements

Distractions

Incentives

Charts

Checklists

Punishments

6. Outline what you want to say when you explain the plan to your children. Make sure to consider ways to get your children more involved in the plan.

7. Evaluate. How will I know when the plan is working? Keep another record as you did in step 4. Count the number of times the priority behaviors occur each day.

DAY	1	2	3	4	5

8. Monitor and adjust the plan: What other consequences can you use? Ask yourself these questions:

Am I being consistent with positive feedback?

Have I given the plan enough time to work?

Am I following through with punishment?

Am I getting angry?

Am I yelling?

PART V

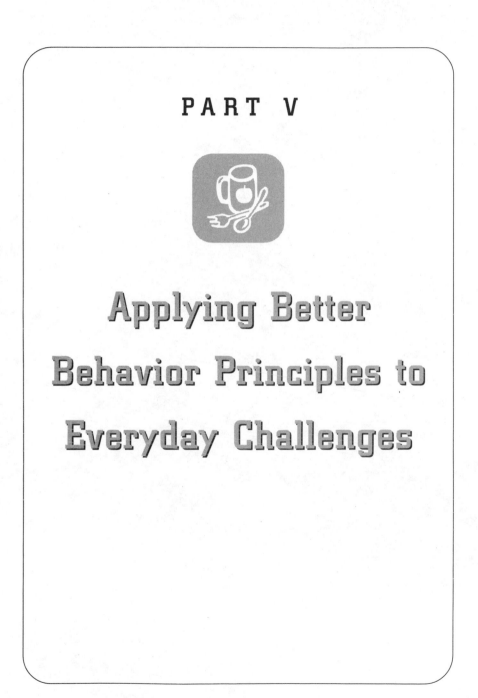

Applying Better Behavior Principles to Everyday Challenges

Common Challenges

Continual Attention Seeking

Eric: "Daddy, please come here."

Dad: "Yes, Eric."

Eric: "Look at my truck."

Dad: "What's the matter?"

Eric: "It has a thing right here."

Dad: "That is just a scratch. It is okay."

Eric: "Will you push it for me?"

Dad: "You are a big boy. You can do it."

Eric: "Where is my toy man?"

Dad: "It is right here."

Eric: "Where is my clay?"

Dad: "I don't know. It should be in that box."

Eric: "You're right, Dad. Will you make a dinosaur for me?"

Dad: "I have some work to do."

Eric: "Please, Daddy. I can't do it good. Will you do it?"

Dad: "I am sorry, Eric. I can't do it now. Maybe later."

Eric: (Cries out loud.) "I can't wait. You never play with me."

It is normal for preschoolers to want their parent's undivided attention, but attention seeking can become a problem when it is constant or demanding. One of the most common reasons for misbehavior in preschoolers is to gain attention. Even curious behavior, such as the "why—why—why" game, can become controlling.

Nora: "Where are we going?"

Mom: "To the grocery store."

Nora: "Why?"

Mom: "Because we need to buy some food."

Nora: "Why?"

Mom: "Because we need food to eat."

Nora: "Why?"

Mom: "Because food makes our bodies healthy."

Nora: "Why?"

The why game makes you feel like you are caught in an infinite loop with no escape and no logical conclusion. Play the game for a while and then stop with one of these statements: "That's how the world works," or "That is the best people can do," or "That's how God made it." Then redirect your child into a different conversation: "Is there anything you want at the grocery store?"

Clever preschoolers learn to make tragedies out of small concerns to get sympathy and attention. Excessive attention seeking can result in a situation where your preschooler dictates every aspect of your life, trapping you in a pattern in which she won't let you leave her side. She won't do anything without your sitting down and doing it with her.

Even though excessive or demanding attention seeking can be irritating and annoying, it may not be deliberate misbehavior, at least not at first. What begins as typical attention seeking, however, can escalate into shouted demands for attention or even full-blown tantrums if not managed correctly. When handled correctly, your preschooler's need for attention can be a helpful tool for improving behavior, when you pay attention to specific, proper behavior.

Do not try to eliminate your child's need for attention, but rather focus on eliminating those attention-seeking behaviors that are excessive or unacceptable. Recognize your preschooler's need but do not give in to the demands. Redirect him by reminding him that he can play well by himself—he has done it before. Then explain why you are not available and when you will be. Practice this strategy consistently, and your preschooler will be understanding and more cooperative.

> "Eric, I know that you want me to play with you. But I am busy paying bills right now. I know you can make something with your clay by yourself. If you can be patient for ten minutes, I'll be able to play with you then. I promise to make a handsome Tyrannosaurus. Would you like me to set the timer?"

Timers work well when preschoolers are impatient or waiting for you or something else. Ten minutes for an adult may seem like eternity to a preschooler. Timers help keep preschoolers from nagging you, "Is it time yet?" You can answer, "Did the timer go off?"

Parents often ask how much attention seeking is too much. That really depends on you. How much attention seeking can you tolerate—calmly, without getting irritated or angry? Preschoolers will take as much attention as you give them. Strike a balance between how much your preschoolers want and how much you can give. Even normal attention seeking can drive you crazy on some days.

When children do not receive attention in a positive way, they will get your attention any way they can. Do not let your preschooler's need for attention turn into demands for attention. When children do not receive enough attention for correct behavior, they resort to outbursts, tantrums, nagging, teasing, and other annoying behaviors. You need to give your preschoolers positive attention for positive behavior. This means encouraging your child or giving her hugs or a pat on the back. Not only will you be giving your child the attention she wants, you will also be fostering good behavior. When you give in to demands for attention, however, you are still giving your preschooler attention, but it is negative. Your child will learn to be more demanding of your attention. This begins a cycle or pattern in which your preschooler demands attention, and you give in; your preschooler demands attention again, and you give in again. . . . It won't take long for you to reach your frustration threshold.

The problem with this cycle is that it teaches children how to manipulate and get their way. They learn how to interrupt and control you, and that annoying behavior wins. Avoid the negative attention trap. Do not give in to negative demands; ignore them. This does not mean ignore the problem. It means ignore demands for negative attention. When your child misbehaves to get attention, ignore it. If your child does not stop in a minute or two, give him a reminder. Tell your child, "I do not listen to whining. When you stop, we'll talk." Wait another minute or two. If he still does not stop, then tell your child to stop or he will be punished: "Stop now, or you will go to time-out." If you must use time-out, stay calm. If you become angry, you lose. Your child will succeed in getting the negative attention that he was after.

Many parents have unintentionally and unknowingly taught their children to be negative attention seekers by continually focusing on the negative and ignoring the positive. Do not take good behavior for granted. When your preschooler demonstrates good behavior, recognize him for it. The more you notice, the more you will find. It is easy to catch children misbehaving. Turn this around. Catch him being good. Understanding these ideas is easy, but practicing them is difficult. Make the commitment. Your children are worth it, and so are you.

Whining, Nagging, and Tantrums

Jeffrey was almost three when he decided to have a tantrum because his mother, Nancy, would not give in to his whining demands. Jeffrey began to scream and shout at Nancy. She walked away. He ran after her and threw himself on the floor at her feet, kicking and screaming. Nancy asked him to stop and then took a giant step over the top of Jeffrey and continued to walk away. Jeffrey hopped to his feet, ran in front of his mother, and once again threw himself at her feet, screaming and kicking. Once again, Nancy asked him to stop, took a giant step over the top of Jeffrey, and continued to walk away. This time, Jeffrey looked at his mother and said, "You never let me get my way." "Not when you behave that way," replied Nancy.

Whining, nagging, and tantrums bring out the worst in a parent because these behaviors are so irritating and annoying. Children are experts at manipulating their parents. Some of it they come by naturally; some of it we teach them. Often we establish this pattern by the time a child is two years old. Whining, nagging, and tantrums may begin with your preschooler's inability to express himself. When children lack the language they need to express hunger, fears, frustrations, or wants, they may resort to communicating with their behavior, which often takes the form of a tantrum. If the tantrum is rewarded in any way, tantrums may become a pattern.

Perhaps the question I am most commonly asked by parents of preschoolers is, How do I stop my child from whining? There are two things to do: do not give in or reinforce the behavior, and redirect your child's misbehavior into correct behavior. Being consistent is crucial, and it is easy to inadvertently reinforce a child's whining. You only need to give in to whining once in a great while to establish it as a permanent pattern. Never give in to your children when they whine or tease to get their way. Never. That is the hard part. The temptation is to justify giving in. It is only one more cookie. It is only fifteen more minutes. It is only one more cartoon. These events are not the problem. The problem is that children learn that whining and teasing work. They win. This sets up a pattern that is difficult to change. In many children, these patterns can develop into disobedience and defiance. For parents, these patterns can lead to frustration and anger. Not managing whining correctly when children are at preschool age is one of the biggest mistakes we make as parents, and it plants the seed for larger problems later in life.

Redirecting is your strongest tool for correcting whining and teasing. Teach a replacement behavior; for example, "My ears don't listen to your whining (teasing, etc.). Please ask me in a polite voice, and then I will listen to you." The goal here is twofold: not giving in to the whining and teasing, and teaching and reinforcing the correct behavior, by saying, "Thank you for asking in a quiet voice." As with many types of behavior concerns in preschool children, the remedy is to focus on the opposite, correct behavior and build that with encouragement that aims at self-esteem: "You did it. Good for you. You should be proud of yourself." "Thank you for waiting while I was on the phone." This is a longterm approach that requires tremendous consistency and patience.

These suggestions require some language comprehension by your child. That is why whining can be so annoying in younger children—they do not always understand the reasons not to whine, no matter how much we explain it to them. This is frustrating. But once a child understands, use redirection and replacement.

Do not label your child a whiner, saying things like, "She always whines like that." "He nags more than any kid I have ever seen." Children believe what you tell them. If you refer to your child as a whiner, you will be planting the idea in his head that he will always be a child who whines.

If a child does not yet have the language comprehension, the same strategy should be used, with some modification. First, parents need to be patient. Young children require time and energy. Second, parents need to realize that in young children, crying and whining may be forms of communication. They may mean fatigue, hunger, or illness, for example. Parents need good judgment here. Is something causing the whining, or is it more calculating? If your child whines to avoid taking a bath, for instance, stay calm, do not give in, recognize your child's feeling, and restate the correct behavior: "I know you are upset right now, but you still need to take your bath." It is a good idea to encourage language development: "Take a deep breath." "Dry your tears." "Use your words." These techniques help children to learn the meaning of feelings and words. It is easy to give in to whining and teasing, especially after we have had a long day. Be firm and consistent. Do not give in. Think about the future. When a child gets what he wants by having an outburst, he learns there is a payoff for misbehaving. Once learned, this pattern is difficult to change. You change it by not giving in. Stop the payoff. As a long-term remedy, pay plenty of attention to correct behavior. That is always the best way to reduce negative behaviors.

Lying

"Julie, come here, please."

"What, Mom?"

"There is crayon all over this chair."

"I didn't do it."

Preschoolers use magical thinking to learn about the world. If a preschooler thinks something is true or says something is true, it magically becomes true. Most magical thinking applies to play, pretending to be Mommy or a fireman. But preschoolers also apply magical thinking to negative events, thinking, "If I wish a bad thing to go away, it will." When your preschooler sees that you are angry at something she did she may respond with "I didn't do it!" despite evidence to the contrary, such as the crayon in Julie's hand. Preschoolers are concrete thinkers: good people do good things, and bad people do bad things. So a preschooler's way of reasoning goes like this: My mommy won't love me if I am bad. I am not bad. I do not do bad things. Therefore, "I didn't do it!"

Every parent wants honest children. With the onset of magical thinking, parents of preschoolers are confronted with statements that appear dishonest. Exaggerations, embellished stories, and denial of what appears to be the truth are typical behaviors for preschoolers. Preschoolers exaggerate and embellish to feel more capable or grown up. When your son proclaims, "Hey, Dad. Look. I am as fast as Superman," it is his wishful thinking. He would love to be like Superman. Acknowledge his wish. "It would be a lot of fun to be as fast as Superman!"

Lying is difficult for parents to understand and accept. Preschoolers maintain their innocence for the same reasons adults do: to avoid a bad result. Adults know that lying is morally wrong, but preschoolers have not developed moral judgment yet. They are just beginning to learn about right and wrong. The child thinks, "Anything I say is okay as long as I avoid the bad result. Lying is okay because it keeps me out of trouble." A lie is a preschooler's best solution for the problem.

To teach your child better solutions, explain that telling the truth means using words to say what really happened, whereas telling a lie means saying something that did not happen. Yet this can be problematic; preschoolers have extreme difficulty discriminating fantasy from reality because so much of their life is about fantasy, make-believe, pretend play, fairy tales, or superheroes. Don't discourage your child's fantasies—you will only stifle creativity—but help your child discriminate fantasy from reality by talking about the difference between make-believe stories and lies. When you read a fantasy story, explain how the story helps you feel happy, it makes you think about happy ideas. When your child is lying, explain how her words do not make you happy.

"Julie, I understand that you do not want me to be upset with you for coloring on the chair. When you do not tell me the truth, when you do not say what really happened, I get more upset."

Discipline is a teaching process. Preschoolers need to be taught that being honest means telling the truth. Honesty establishes trusting relationships. Teach your preschooler to tell the truth by explaining that everyone makes mistakes: "When you make a mistake or do something wrong, tell me what really happened, and I will help you make it okay. Let's go clean the chair."

Manage your anger first. If you become angry when your child makes a mess, she will learn to lie to you to avoid blame and punishment. Make it safe for her to tell you the truth: "If you tell me the truth, I promise I will not be angry." Acknowledge how she may be feeling: "I know you may be afraid to tell me the truth because you know you should only color on paper, not chairs." Instead of punishing her for mistakes, praise her when she tells you the truth: "Thank you for telling me the truth." Remind her that she can tell you anything, and you will always love her. Focus on the solution to the problem at hand, such as what needs to happen to fix the situation or clean up the mess. Discuss what your child could do differently next time or how he might get your help. Do not lecture or blame.

Be proactive. If you do not want your preschooler playing with breakable treasures, keep them out of reach. If you don't want your child to use the paints unsupervised, store the paints out of reach.

Be a good model. If you want your child to understand that lying is not the right thing to do, do not lie to them or in front of them. Do not tell the person on the phone that Dad is not home when he is sitting on the couch. Do not tell the ticket seller at the amusement park that your child is two years old when she is three to get a reduced admission. The example you set provides your child the strongest model for what is right and what is wrong. When you make a mistake or use bad judgment, take responsibility. Apologize or resolve the situation.

Picky Eaters

Many children are selective about the foods they eat. It is normal for a preschooler to have a few favorite foods, lasting for days, weeks, or months, and then to abruptly abandon their favorites. A preschooler may request green beans at every meal, including breakfast, then suddenly label them "yuck." A preschooler may eat well for a few days, then nibble and pick for a week. It is rare for a preschooler to eat a variety of foods consistently.

Preschoolers are naturally resistant to trying new foods. This resistance can escalate into power struggles recurring three times a day, especially if you plead with or try to bribe your child to eat. Do not present too many new foods too quickly; instead, bring out new foods once or twice a week. Introduce new foods by encouraging your children to try them: "Please take one or two bites. You might be surprised!"

Make food child-friendly. Keep portions small. A plate piled high will discourage rather than encourage a child to try something new. Bite-size pieces or miniature versions have a natural appeal for preschoolers. Cut sandwiches into fun shapes using cookie cutters. Arrange fruits and vegetables like a face or in a special dish to add interest and excitement. Involve your child in selecting or preparing foods. If you can arrange time for gardening, show him how food grows. Lettuce, peas, melons, and carrots are fun crops to grow and eat. Participation improves motivation and interest in trying new foods.

Provide a variety of healthy foods from which your child can choose, which gives a young child the power to regulate his appetite. Be reasonable. If salmon is the main course for dinner, you may wish to provide your young children with an alternative that is more acceptable to their palate, perhaps fish sticks or peanut butter and jelly.

Teach good nutrition by example. When you eat healthful foods, you teach your children to eat them too. If you snack on candy between meals, you teach your children to want candy between meals. Your children will tend to eat the way you eat and behave the way you do regarding food. Family patterns teach attitudes about food that stay with your children into adulthood. Establish family meal nights, when all children are expected to be at the table. Turn off the television. Talk about your children's day. Establish a healthy relationship with your children regarding eating habits. This builds the foundation of eating patterns that guide your child to a healthier life.

Do not use food to coax children into good behavior. This practice can lead to adult eating problems. Consider the parent who uses a treat to comfort an unhappy child. While the treat will probably coax the child into a better mood, the youngster may learn that one way to get a treat is to act unhappy. Unhappiness is rewarded, and your child associates unhappiness with food. Whenever something unpleasant occurs, food will make the hurt go away. Occasional treats are fine. But do not use them to bribe.

Parents of young children often worry that their children are not getting enough to eat. Most children eat enough, but if you have a concern, check with your pediatrician. If your child is growing at a normal rate, he is eating fine. Your child's eating habits will improve naturally. By age ten, children start eating a more varied diet and become willing to try more foods, learning to eat most things. If you have a child who is a picky eater, talk to parents of teenagers. You will be amazed; most teenagers eat enough to make up for all they passed by as preschoolers.

Morning Routine

Preschoolers sense the times when you are vulnerable. The challenge for parents is to remain calm when you are in a hurry and your preschooler does not listen. Most parents start off by being patient and making polite requests of their preschooler:

Mom: "Ashley, we have to go. It is time to leave for preschool."

Ashley: (Says nothing in response.)

Mom: "Ashley. Please. Let's go."

Ashley: "I am drawing three billy goats. See."

Mom: "We have to go."

Ashley: "I am drawing now."

Mom: "You can draw when you get home later. We have to go now."

Then, if you are like many parents, you lose it. You get upset: "Stop drawing and get over here right now, or I will take away your color pencils!" This scenario occurs every morning all across the country. It is frustrating when children do not listen. It is even more annoying when you have a schedule to keep. Children do not have the same sense of urgency that adults have. This is a good thing—children should not be rushed. You, however, have to be to work on time. Stay calm and use reasoning: "Your teacher wants you be on time. She wants you to be there for the first song. My boss wants me to be to work on time, too. Let's go."

Get as many things ready the night before as possible. Put out clothing and shoes. Put them in the same place every night. Get lunches ready to be packed. Discuss the options for breakfast. Then have a consistent morning routine. Wake up at the same time. If you need time for yourself, get up fifteen minutes before waking your children. Once they are awake, give them a few minutes to stretch and wake up. Preschoolers need time to get their brains aroused and their bodies warmed up. Get washed and dressed. Eat breakfast. Take a few minutes to talk about having a pleasant day. Get everything together and go. It is best to have no distractions: no television, no drawing, no games. This will help your child stay focused. If your preschooler does not get started on an engrossing activity, you will have fewer problems leaving the house on time.

Be proactive. If you need to leave by 8:50 to be on time for preschool and work, aim for everyone being ready by 8:30, giving you and your child a fifteen- or twenty-minute cushion. In this way the inevitable delays and interruptions do not become behavior problems, and you have a few minutes to manage the crisis without feeling rushed or frustrated.

Many parents find it helpful to have a checklist for morning routine. Draw or cut out picture of things to be done: washing your face, getting dressed, making your bed, and so forth. Put each picture on a checklist. Be positive but firm. If your child gets everything done, put a sticker on the checklist for that day. And if your preschooler gets ready with time to spare, reward him by allowing him to push the button to open the garage door or some other special privilege. If your child's preschool has a playground, you can use the bonus of a few minutes of play before school starts as an added incentive for getting to school early.

Bedtime Routine

Most children will experience some difficulty either getting to sleep or staying asleep during their preschool years. Like other behaviors, consistency and clear expectations are essential. Procrastination and power struggles can be minimized by having a firm bedtime and a series of winding-down activities that start forty-five minutes to an hour prior to bedtime. Use calm activities, such as taking a bath and reading books, to prepare your child for going to sleep. Give time warnings at twenty

Morning Routine

	Monday	Tuesday	Wednesday	Thursday	Friday	Saturday	Sunday
Dress							
Wash Face + Comb Hair							
Eat							
Brush Teeth							
Make Bed							
Pack							

minutes and five minutes before bedtime. This will help your pre-schooler make the transition to bed successfully.

To minimize bedtime resistance, offer choices rather than giving orders. This will give your child a feeling of involvement. For example, "Do you want to wear your red or your blue pajamas tonight?" "Do you want to snuggle up with your teddy bear or your doggy?" or "Do you want Daddy or Mommy or both to help you with your bath tonight?"

Use a checklist to help motivate your preschooler to get ready for bed. As with your morning routine, use pictures to create a chart. Post the chart in your preschooler's bedroom. Begin the routine each evening at the same time. You need to be part of the routine by helping with cleanup, bath time, or reading stories. Both parents should be involved each night if possible, or take turns. This type of structure gives preschoolers a pattern to follow, which eases them into bed with fewer episodes of resistance and gives them a sense of safety and security. The last activity in the routine should be story time. That way, the more cooperative your preschoolers are with getting ready for bed, the more story time they can earn.

After completing the bedtime routine, leave your child's room. Establish a rule that your child is not to come out of his room. If he comes out, do not engage in long conversations. Keep your communication short and always escort him back to his bed. This will eliminate the potential for arguing, power struggles, and delay tactics.

If your preschooler is afraid of the dark, get a night-light. If he is having a bad dream, comfort him. (See the section on nightmares in chapter 20.) To improve the likelihood that your child will remain asleep all night, avoid letting him fall asleep while engaging in other activities. Children who fall asleep watching TV, listening to music, or while a parent reads a story are more likely to need assistance falling back to sleep during the middle of the night. Many children will ask for a parent to lie with them until they go to sleep. This can prolong their bedtime routine and contribute to difficulties sleeping alone throughout the night. If your child asks for someone to lie with her, redirect her by telling her that you will be back in a few minutes to check on her. Then return in a minute, then two, and then three, and by then she usually will be asleep. This gives your child the reassurance she needs to go to sleep on her own.

Bedtime can be a pleasant experience where parents and children

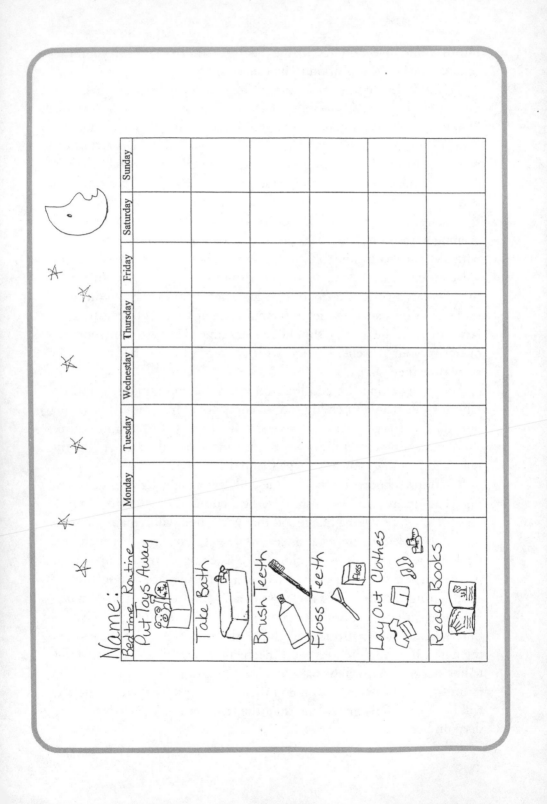

Name: _____

Bedtime Routine	Monday	Tuesday	Wednesday	Thursday	Friday	Saturday	Sunday
Put Toys Away							
Take Bath							
Brush Teeth							
Floss Teeth							
Lay Out Clothes							
Read Books							

share time talking and enjoying each other's company. Provide praise and encouragement when your child is going to bed and staying in bed. By using proactive strategies you can avoid bedtime struggles and stress.

Brushing and Flossing

Brushing and flossing need to be part of your preschooler's bedtime routine. Preschool children require parental assistance and supervision for proper toothbrushing, just as much as they do for bathing. It is helpful to have your preschooler choose the toothpaste that he likes best. Having two or three flavors to choose from can make brushing teeth an activity that involves a choice: "You need to brush your teeth to take care of them. Do you want mint or bubble gum toothpaste tonight?"

If possible, use a child's electric toothbrush with a built-in timer. This helps motivate your child to brush for a sufficient period of time. If you do not have an electric toothbrush with a timer, use an egg timer or small hourglass so your child brushes long enough. After your child brushes, you may need to take the brush in your hand and get the hard-to-reach places.

Flossing between children's teeth is necessary to clean below the gum line and to clean where a toothbrush cannot reach. Using a floss holder is easier than getting your fingers into your child's small mouth. Establish a routine that will help your child sit still for flossing. Julie's mom made it a little more fun by counting the teeth as she flossed them. When counting lost its novelty, she began counting in Spanish or saying the ABC's. Later Julie would choose a topic such as Halloween, animals, flowers, or dress-up items. This kind of activity distracts your preschooler and makes flossing more tolerable. Choosing the category got Julie's mind off the flossing. Preschoolers can begin to floss independently between their middle teeth on the top and bottom, where they can see in a mirror. Teaching your preschooler good dental habits not only prevents tooth decay, it also makes going to the dentist easier.

18

Sibling Strife

Preschoolers encounter conflicts for many reasons. They want the circumstances in their lives to be on their own terms, and they want the rules to fit their behavior, rather than molding their behavior to the rules. It is normal and natural for preschoolers to be self-centered, since they can only see their side of a situation and want everything to go their way. When they do not get what they want, they may become angry. It should not be surprising that anytime you put two or three preschoolers who think this way into the same confined space and tell them to play and have fun, you are likely to have some conflict.

Resolving Conflicts and Fights

What can you do to reduce the amount of conflict among your children? Use a conflict as an opportunity to learn. Teach your preschoolers acceptable ways of expressing disappointment and resentment. Encourage them to use their words to express anger and frustration. Show them how to manage their feelings without violating the other child.

"You know, Haley, it's okay to be angry at your brother for teasing you. But it is not okay to hit him. What else could you have done? Let's think about other things to do when you get angry."

This approach will not work if your child is still upset about the altercation. After a conflict, talk with your children about other ways to solve problems. Communication is always more effective when everyone has had time to cool off. It also helps to intervene early, before tempers erupt.

> "It sounds to me like you children have a disagreement. I believe that you can work this out for yourselves, and I hope you do. If you need my help, let me know. But if you can't solve this on your own, you will need to take a little break from each other for a while."

This type of message empowers your preschoolers to believe they can resolve their conflict. If you believe they can, they are likely to believe the same. Yet it also sets a limit. Knowing when to become involved and when to keep out takes judgment. As a rule, always encourage your children to solve their own conflicts. Give them time to do this. Then if you see that their conflict is escalating rather than being resolved, you may need to help them think of a solution. You may also want to separate them for a few minutes, to give them time to think. (See chapter 7.)

Do not try to reason with children when they are angry, and never take sides or try to determine who started the fight. Teach your preschoolers to respect other children. This is a skill that will be helpful when they become adolescents. Explain, for instance, "You do not have to agree with what your brother says. He sees it his way and you see it your way. But it's not okay to fight." In some situations, it can also help if you add something about seeing the conflict from the other child's point of view: "Each of you has a reason for thinking that you are right." Then have the children exchange their reasons and develop a compromise. Each child has to give a little so that both can be satisfied.

As a long-term prevention, focus on the positive social behaviors in your preschoolers. Compliment your children for getting along and playing together. Parents forget this. It is easy to take good behavior for granted. This is a mistake. Look for cooperation and sharing. Then recognize it: "I appreciate your playing together so well. Thank you. I hope you both feel proud of yourselves."

Perhaps the most important thing a parent can do to teach his children better methods of conflict resolution is to be a good example.

Model appropriate ways of solving the conflicts you encounter in your life—with your spouse, your boss, or your neighbor. Do not stockpile anger; express it constructively. Show your children that there are prudent ways to disagree. Model calmness, politeness, and respect for the other person. Remember to be patient. If your children have developed patterns of arguing and fighting, it will take time to change. Hang in there. They are worth it.

Older Siblings Picking on Younger Siblings

When conflicts arise between older and younger siblings, it is the older child who bears the responsibility for improving the situation. Start by talking to your older child. Speak with him alone, away from other children. Explain that you and his younger sibling really need his help, and that you understand that his younger sibling can be irritating. Yet, since he is older, you want to be able to count on him to be more responsible, to be a "good big brother or sister."

This will only work if the additional responsibility you place on the older sibling is matched by more respect and trust from you, and perhaps even more privileges: "I expect more because you are older; therefore you have more freedoms." Explain that helping his sibling by sharing and speaking politely is simply a nice thing to do. Encourage your older child to try complimenting his younger brother or sister once in a while. Stay positive with both children. Look for times when they show cooperation. They will continue to make progress.

Often, older children get upset with younger siblings because the younger child is "always bugging me." It is natural for younger children to emulate older siblings, as they desperately want to be like their older brother and sister. They may even take things that belong to their older siblings. It is therefore important that in addition to asking your older child's cooperation, you also support his maturity by speaking to your younger child as well. Explain that his older brother or sister will always be able to do things that he cannot do yet, but that when he is that age he will be able to do them too: "Your brother is five years older than you. Because he is older, he can ride his bike to the park. When you are nine, you will be able to ride your bike to the park, too."

It takes time to change these patterns, since it involves changes in children who have different levels of maturity. Think of these kinds of changes as very long-term goals for everyone in the family. Stay positive. Remember to reinforce your children when they cooperate, and they will continue to make progress.

Getting Ready for a New Baby

About a month after Samantha was born, Elliot said, "I don't feel of much importance anymore!" A few days later, Elliot and his mom were reading a story about a new baby. Near the middle of the story, someone asks the big brother of the new baby if he feels like no one loves him anymore. When Elliot's mom asked him, "Do you ever feel that way now?," he burst into tears; "Yes, Mommy. I feel that way all the time now." This scenario is not at all uncommon when a new baby enters the family. A new baby draws so much attention from everyone, young children often feel left out, replaced, and less loved. Tell your young children that you love them as much as the new baby. Read books to your preschooler before and after the arrival of a new baby. This will give your child a chance to share his feelings and fears.

When a new baby is expected, young siblings may feel jealous or worried that they are being replaced. Prepare preschool siblings by involving them in the experience. Let them feel the baby kick, talk to the baby, and look at the ultrasound pictures. Get out their baby pictures or movies and talk about all the care that they needed as an infant. Explain how they can be a big brother or sister and a helper when the baby arrives. Let them help set up the baby's room and pick out a few special toys or clothes.

Attending a sibling class offered by the hospital can help prepare preschoolers for becoming a big brother or big sister. These classes talk about what it will feel like to have a new baby in the house, and they also give some insight into all the care that newborns require. Many hospitals take the children to visit the nursery and a delivery room. The classes reassure the siblings that Mom will be well taken care of while she stays in the hospital. Most classes openly discuss how feelings of jealousy are normal. Children are taught how to recognize and express their need for attention through using their words rather than acting out.

Once the baby arrives, give your preschooler important jobs, such as opening gifts and trying out new toys. Have him help take care of the baby by getting diapers or picking out what the baby will wear. Thank him for his help. Being a helper gives preschoolers an important role and boosts their self-esteem. The more you can involve them, the greater their sense of belonging.

Preschool children will often regress to babyish behavior when a new baby arrives. This is a common reaction. They may start using baby talk, whining, or wetting the bed. It is important for parents to be consistent and understanding. Praise grown-up behavior: "Thank you for acting like a big sister." Make time for your preschooler by arranging one-on-one activities: "Sometimes you have to wait for your baby brother. Sometimes he has to wait for you." Put the baby in a carrier or infant seat so that you can read or play a game with your preschooler.

The frame of mind you establish between young siblings and the new baby is the foundation for their relationships in later childhood. Many problems with sibling competition and conflict that arise later can often be traced to feelings of jealousy over the new baby. Keep your preschoolers involved in the care of your newborn, and they will feel better about themselves and have a better relationship with both the baby and you during this period of transition.

Fair Is Not Always Equal
No parent ever wants to be accused of being unfair. We try to manage and attend to each child equally. This is difficult, since every child is unique. It is impossible to always treat each child exactly the same, and this may result in one of your children accusing you of being unfair. As a general rule, try to have balance. For example, if you have a special day with one child, have a special day with the others. Balance chores and privileges that coincide with age. Older children may have more to do, but in turn they have more freedom. Many parents have used birthdays as a marker for adding more privileges, more allowance, and more jobs around the house. When younger children complain that big sister goes to bed later, explain that when they are that age, their bedtime will be later, too: "You will have the same bedtime when you are seven."

At times you will make a decision about one of your children that you would decide differently for another. When this situation arises, make sure to explain it to your children. You might say, "I make the best decisions I can for each of you. I love you all. But you are each a little different. Sometimes what works for you may not work for your sister. I may be wrong. But I am making the best decision I can, based on what I know." Children may ask you whom you love more. Explain

that you love each child the same, and each for his own unique qualities. If this is an issue that concerns your children, you might want to
read *I Love You the Purplest,* by Barbara M. Joosse, together.

When a Child Is a Sore Loser

All children like to win. Unfortunately, when you play a game that is
competitive, there is a winner and one or more losers. If your preschooler wants to participate in this type of game, he must realize that
he may lose. A child of four is old enough to understand this lesson,
though it may be difficult. You can make it a little easier by minimizing
the importance of winning and enlarging the importance of fair play
and having fun. Playing by the rules, taking turns, cheering for others,
and laughing are all more important than winning. Once a child learns
these foundations, he will be ready for more competitive games.

When you play competitive games, choose games that are quick,
such as tic-tac-toe. Since a new game starts every few minutes, your preschooler has more chances to win and more opportunity to learn that
losing is not a big deal. You can show your child that if he loses, you
just start a new game, and maybe he'll win this time.

Another technique to teach preschoolers about winning and losing is
to play team games. Pair your child up with an adult so that if your
child's team loses, the adult partner can model appropriate ways to behave. The adult partner can also explain the rules of the game and why
games have rules. Once your child understands that rules organize the
game and help everyone understand it, he will be less tempted to try
and change them to avoid losing.

It is also important to spend time doing noncompetitive activities,
such as puzzles, Legos, blocks, crafts, or games like I Spy. These types of
activities allow children to learn social skills without the risk of losing.

When children get upset at losing or try to cheat, some parents are
tempted to scold or threaten, "If you don't play right, you won't have
any friends." It is fine to remind your child how important it is to play
fair, but do not tell him he will not have friends if he cheats. This will
plant the idea in his mind that because of this problem with playing
games, he may never have friends. Many children could interpret this
as, "Other children do not like me." You do not want your preschooler
to think this way.

Knowing when to comfort a preschooler who is upset at losing takes judgment. If your child is upset because he lost a game, it is natural for you to want to console him. However, the risk is that when your child loses and you are not there, he may have a harder time adjusting without your comfort. Keep your consolation brief: "I am sorry you are feeling sad about losing. Keep trying and have fun playing." When your preschooler loses and does not become upset, compliment him by building his self-esteem: "I am glad to see you were happy for your friend who won. Good for you! That shows you are really growing up. I hope you feel good about that."

19

From Comfort to Coping

Most children adopt a comfort object at some time during infancy or toddlerhood. Sometimes these favorite objects accompany them into the preschool years. Your child may have bonded with a special teddy bear, doll, or blanket that provides him with a sense of comfort and security, or may continue to be soothed by sucking his thumb or a pacifier. Young children use these methods to relieve stress and comfort themselves, especially when they are scared or tired.

As your child develops, his need for security objects will likely diminish on its own. If you want to encourage your child to become more independent, however, you could limit their use. For example, Tommy loved his blanket, which he referred to as his "Bubba." To prepare for preschool, his mother progressively put limits on where he could take his blanket. He could take it in the car but not into the store. When it was time to enter preschool, the "Bubba" stayed safely in his backpack or cubby during the first week, and then stayed home safely with Mom.

Jodie had a special doll she called "night-night baby." She had two identical dolls so that one could stay at day care with her pillow for naptime, and the other remain at home for bedtime. Just about the time Jodie turned four, a stuffed animal or doll replaced "night-night baby." Over time, these objects were used for company rather than for comfort.

If your preschooler continues to be overly attached to a security object or sucking his thumb, and you believe it is becoming a problem, help your child learn how to reduce his dependency. Do not tease your child about his attachment but rather appeal to his increasing desire to be a "big boy." Enlist the help of relatives and care providers in reinforcing his progress and effort. Be positive and supportive. Power struggles will create stress and increase your child's need for comfort rather than building self-confidence in his ability to cope.

Thumb Sucking

Most children who suck their thumbs quit before they enter preschool, yet some children continue to use thumb sucking as a form of self-soothing because it feels good. Although thumb sucking itself is not a problem, it can create dental problems, and like any other habit, it can be hard to break. Since most preschoolers have quit sucking their thumbs, a child who still does may be teased. If you have decided that it is time to encourage your child to stop this habit, use a positive, supportive approach. Parental pressure is more likely to create resistance than motivation.

Help your child be aware of his thumb sucking by calmly telling him, "John, you are sucking your thumb." This is important because it is a habit, and many children don't always know when they are doing it. A verbal reminder will help your preschooler, or you may want to use a "secret signal" to alert your child without embarrassing him in front of other children.

Jason loved the word *supercalifragilisticexpialidocious*. He picked it as the secret signal that his parents would use when they saw him thumb sucking. Because the word was so long, he enjoyed the challenge of getting his thumb out of his mouth before they finished saying the word. Using the secret signal allowed Jason's parents to cue him without embarrassment. Letting Jason choose the secret signal increased his desire to change and made it into a game.

Use praise and encouragement when your child is not sucking his thumb. This approach will reinforce his improved behavior change. Thank your child for being a big girl or boy. The privilege of chewing gum might also be used to motivate a preschooler to give up his thumb, since you cannot chew gum and suck your thumb at the same time. Be careful, however; you do not want to replace one habit with another. Use charts to reinforce your child. Stickers or smiley faces can be put on the chart when your child spends some time without sucking his thumb. (See chapter 11 for more information on using charts and checklists to increase your child's motivation.)

Choose a good time to begin your child's thumb-sucking program. Make sure it is a time when you can be consistent, with no special events or changes on the horizon, since these may increase fears and stress. If your child is still sucking his thumb at age five, you may want to discuss strategies with your child's doctor or dentist for changing his behavior to avoid affecting permanent teeth and jaw development.

Pacifiers

Pacifiers are easier to manage than thumbs. A thumb is always attached to your child's hand, while you can limit your child's access to pacifiers. When it becomes time to wean your child of them, begin by restricting the use of a pacifier to particular times of the day or specific activities. Here is one scenario: Three-year-old Christian wanted to have his pacifier in his mouth all the time, so much so that it began to interfere with his communication skills and limit his interactions with peers and adults. Christian's mother gradually restricted his pacifier use to bedtime or naptime, reducing his dependency. At other times, he was allowed to have it in his pocket, but not in his mouth. Reducing his pacifier use by setting limits and providing positive reinforcement made it a minor crisis the day it suddenly vanished.

Another way of weaning your child is through distraction. Emily's parents kept her busy with activities and made sure her pacifier was out of sight. Once Emily's pacifier use was limited, her parents proposed that they visit the store. They let Emily pick out a new toy to replace her pacifier. Emily exchanged her pacifier for a special doll. Some children are lucky enough to be visited by the "binky" fairy, who exchanges toys or goodies for "binkies" (pacifiers).

Since both thumb sucking and the use of pacifiers are ways in which your child has comforted and soothed himself, you will need to be particularly attentive to his fears and insecurities during this period. Make sure to be supportive and to encourage him to use his words to tell you what he is feeling. It is equally important that your child not feel that he is being punished, but rather that the removal of the pacifier and the end of thumb sucking are a positive part of growing up.

Toilet Training

Most children do not become completely toilet trained until they are between two and four years old. Even so, accidents are common beyond the preschool years. There are many books available to assist parents in teaching their child to use the toilet, and you may want to consult *What to Expect: The Toddler Years*, by Arlene Eisenberg, Heidi E. Murkoff, and Sandee E. Hathaway; *Touchpoints: Your Child's Emotional and Behavioral Development*, by T. Berry Brazelton, M.D.; or *Dr. Mom's Parenting Guide*, by Marianne Neifert, M.D. These books and others will help you familiarize yourself with the readiness signs to toilet training, and determine the right time to train your child and the strategy that would be most helpful.

Here are some of the readiness signs to look for:

- Able to follow directions.

- Shows some interest in using the potty, perhaps watching you.

- Knows wet and dry and wants to take a wet diaper off.

- Stays dry for two hours.

- Has bowel movements at about the same time each day.

- Realizes when she is about to go (watch her face or look for a squat!).

- Is willing and able to walk to and then sit on the potty.

Even when every sign seems solid, your child may still not be ready, and if she isn't ready, she won't be trained. Most experts in this field believe that children learn to use the potty in their own time. So don't worry about when it will happen, just let it happen, as you let crawling, walking, and drinking from a cup occur when your child is ready. If your child is older when she becomes trained, it does not mean you are an inadequate parent, any more than an early potty learner means a high IQ.

Keep in mind that preschool children can get so involved in what they are doing that they simply forget about going to the bathroom. Frequent reminders or a regular potty routine can help increase their awareness. Anticipate your child's toilet needs by encouraging him to use the potty before going somewhere. Pack extra clothing in case your child needs to change. Do not embarrass, scold, or punish your child for accidents. Toilet training is a learning process. All children have accidents, especially when they are tired or excited.

When asking your child to go potty, use statements such as, "It is time to go potty now." Questions such as "Do you want to go potty now?" are more likely to be met with "No!" Resist engaging in power struggles about using the potty. Children are motivated not by conflict but by the accomplishment of becoming more independent.

A potty chart can be an effective motivator for children who are learning to use the toilet. Create the chart with your child. Have him place a sticker or a stamp on the chart after he has gone to the potty. For most children, putting the sticker on the chart is recognition enough. Some children will be more motivated by working toward a goal. This type of reinforcement is most successful if the incentive is connected to the training. For example, Lacey stayed dry for three days, and her mother took her to the store to pick out some new "big girl" underwear.

Involve the entire family in your preschooler's potty success. When Ian would use the potty, he would get a stamp on his chart, and his younger sister would get a stamp on her hand. The parents would say, "This is because Ian is being such a big boy." Ian was doubly reinforced. The whole family celebrated.

Forrest's parents encouraged his awareness and desire to use the potty by putting a chart in the bathroom for everyone in the family to use. When Mom, Dad, or Sister used the potty, they put a stamp on the chart. When Forrest used the potty, he also put a stamp on the chart. Forrest's desire to be like everyone else increased his interest in using the potty and led to his speedy success.

Bed-Wetting

For many children, controlling their bladder through the entire night is beyond their physical capacity. As a result, bed-wetting is common during the preschool years. Since bed-wetting is not an intentional misbehavior, and children cannot control it, let your child know that you realize it was only an accident. Be understanding and supportive. Think of it this way. You would not ask a four-year-old to do long division—he does not yet have the mental capacity—but he will someday, when his brain is ready.

Potty
Chart

	Monday	Tuesday	Wednesday	Thursday	Friday	Saturday	Sunday	
MoM								
DaD								
Sissy								
Forrest								

If your child wets her bed on a reasonably regular basis, you may want to use a chart to emphasize your child's successes rather than failures. Using a positive approach will encourage your child to participate in bedtime routines that help reduce bed-wetting, such as using the bathroom before going to bed, not having drinks before bedtime, and being awakened to go potty before parents go to bed. Charting your child's dry nights will also enable you to measure her progress. This will encourage your child to feel good about herself and build her self-esteem.

Imaginary Friends

Having make-believe friends is common in preschool children because their creative thinking emerges during this period. By age three, most children begin to think symbolically, which is a sign of cognitive development. Being able to pretend and role-play helps young children with their emotional development.

Children work through their problems and conquer their fears through make-believe. Pretend play also helps them manage stress by giving them opportunities to practice controlling their emotions and impulses. An imaginary friend reflects a child's unique needs and often helps her cope with situations that she finds stressful, because she has control over her make-believe friend.

Imaginary friends can be playmates who are always available and agreeable. These invisible friends may help a preschooler share thoughts and feelings that he may otherwise find difficult to communicate. Listen to the messages the friends share, as often their concerns are also those of your child. Take note of the powers your child bestows upon his friend, as these may alert you to those things your child fears.

In most cases, peers replace imaginary friends, typically during the kindergarten year. Until then, parents need to show acceptance of imaginary friends, never disputing their existence. Let the young child enjoy his friend for imaginative play and emotional support. Pretend friends may test the limits of appropriate behavior, since your child may use his imaginary friend as a scapegoat or a protector. Many a mistake has been blamed on an imaginary friend. It is very important that you do not let the imaginary friend interfere with your preschooler taking responsibility for his own behavior.

Reducing Stress

Alternating physical activity with quiet times can reduce your preschooler's stress level. Going to the park, riding a bike, or kicking a ball are good releasers of excess energy and emotion. Likewise, listening to music or reading to your child can help her slow down and relax. A back rub, foot rub, or warm bath can also do wonders. If your child has trouble winding down, try putting away the bath toys and reading a story or playing music while she soaks in the tub.

You can also teach your child stress-reducing activities to use when she feels tense. Taking a deep breath will help a child calm herself when she is upset or anxious. Jamie taught Karen to breathe in slowly, hold her breath, count to two, and then breathe out slowly. Jamie also taught Karen to relax her muscles by tightening her arms, legs, or face muscles for a count of five and then releasing them. When Karen is having difficulty, she often uses these techniques on her own without being coached.

Young children sense the tension and stress that their families experience. Providing an unhurried schedule will help minimize the effects of stress on your children. It is also important that your child talk about her fears and concerns so that she can understand and work through them. Use story time before putting your child to bed to calm your child, as well as to read books that explain how small children can overcome fears.

Preschoolers and Trauma

A trauma or crisis can happen to anyone at any time, whether it be the result of a natural disaster, an automobile accident, suicide, or other sudden emotional loss. Common traumas for preschoolers include the death of a grandparent or the death of a pet. While emotional reactions vary with each child, these events can create tremendous stress and worry in preschoolers. Some children become angry and have outbursts, while others withdraw and become sad. Many preschoolers worry that harm may come to them and may regress to thumb sucking, bed-wetting, or nightmares and have trouble sleeping. Other children lose their appetites. These reactions may last weeks or months, and recur periodically for years.

Since you, as the parents, are the primary source of safety, security, and information during periods of trauma, your role is particularly important during this time. Do not lie about what happened, but only explain what they need to know. Provide support by talking about your feelings, which will help your preschoolers talk about their anger, fears, grief, or sadness. Knowing what to say is often difficult. When in doubt, reach out with a firm hug. Tell your child, "This is sad for both of us." If you believe that your child is not adjusting in spite of your best efforts, it may be helpful to talk with a professional.

Many children's books address traumatic events. It is important to read the story yourself before reading it to your child, to be sure the message is what you want to communicate. For example, if your daughter is concerned because her grandmother is ill, and you read a book to her in which a sick grandmother dies, you will not relieve but only increase your daughter's fears.

Raising Grandchildren

The number of children being raised by grandparents increases every year. This rising tide is the result of a variety of factors: parents who cannot afford to care or who have to work so many hours to make financial ends meet that they have nothing left for their children; parents who are in jail or addicted to drugs; and parents who have lost custody or abandoned their children.

No matter how much grandparents love their grandchildren, they are not their parents. Children know this, and feel abandoned or rejected by their parents. If you are raising your grandchildren, the most important idea you can communicate is that it is not their fault that they are living with Grandma and Grandpa instead of their parents. They are living with grandparents because of decisions that other people have made. Once children understand this, they feel better about themselves and are better equipped to withstand pressure, teasing, and questions about their "real" parents.

If you are a grandparent raising grandchildren, you have two jobs: grandparent and parent. As a grandparent, you need to be consoling and nurturing. As a parent, you need to be firm and consistent. Many grandparents feel guilty because their children are not involved in their grandchildren's lives, and they feel sorry for their grandchildren. These feelings are normal but should not get in the way of good discipline. Children still need guidance and limits in order to grow up mentally healthy.

When you enroll your preschoolers in school, be honest with school personnel from the beginning. Meet with the principal or teacher and explain why your grandchildren are living with you. If everyone knows the truth, there will be no need to ask questions that may lead to embarrassment or defensiveness.

The majority of children who are not being raised by their biological parents hope to be reunited with them someday. Let children know that it is okay to hope; be realistic and honest, but use judgment and discretion. There are some truths from which children need protection, at least until they are mature enough to comprehend the situation without emotional distress. If you are not sure about what to do, talk to a professional.

20

Preschool Fears

Preschool children often develop fears that reflect their budding imaginations. An active imagination can easily create monsters out of shadows, danger from common insects, and make a barking dog appear threatening. Young children have difficulty distinguishing between fantasy and reality. This is a normal developmental stage for children between three and five years of age. Fears reflect a preschooler's increased awareness of the world around him. As your preschooler grows and develops a better understanding of the world, he will be able to apply reason and logic to manage his imagination and alleviate his fears.

Common fears for preschoolers include the dark, dogs, insects, monsters, strangers, costumed characters, and being alone. Always acknowledge your child's fear; do not say, "There is nothing to be afraid of." Let your child know that it is okay to be afraid but that you are confident that he is safe. If you ignore your child's fears or make light of them, your child may keep his fears inside, where they may intensify and become more serious. Explain what is real and what is not, what could happen and what can never happen. Talking about what is make-believe and what is factual helps preschoolers learn to discriminate for themselves.

Imaginary fears are related to a preschooler's capacity to understand the world, and at this stage young children do not always have the ability to articulate their fears. Give your child words to describe what she might be afraid of. This is the first step on the road to overcoming her fears. For example, if your child wakes from a nightmare, you might ask, "Was there a giant in your dream?" Do not force your preschooler to confront her fear directly, as this can result in power struggles that can make the problem worse. If your child is afraid of the dark, use a night-light or allow her to have a flashlight in bed.

Help your child work through her fears by helping her attain mastery over what she dreads. Games and play can help a child become more comfortable and gain the confidence needed to control her fears and anxiety. If your child is afraid of bugs, you could read books about bugs, play with plastic bugs, draw pictures, and make up stories about bugs. Kristen was afraid of birds. Kristen's mother had her draw a picture of what she was scared of and then tear it up and throw it away. These techniques use the child's imagination to change her thoughts or perceptions, and therefore change her emotional experience. When a child has success overcoming one fear, her increased self-confidence and sense of accomplishment will help her to overcome other fears more easily.

Fears can also develop from a situation in which a child has been hurt or frightened. Fear of dogs often evolves from an experience of being knocked down by a dog, bitten, or alarmed by loud barking. Some fears may arise for other reasons. It is important to consider what is going on in your preschooler's life. Fears that seem unrelated are often the reaction to external stresses such as difficulty at school, the arrival of a new sibling, or a divorce. Once the underlying causes are identified and addressed, the fears will dissipate.

Separation

Fear of separation from parents is common among preschoolers. As a result, preschool children often demand excessive attention from their parents, follow their parents around, cling to their parents, cry, or have a tantrum when they are faced with separation.

Separation fear is developmental. It may arise spontaneously, or it may be due to a stress or change. Change is anxiety-provoking enough for adults, but for young children who have little or no control over their world, it can create extreme stress and anxiety. Moving to a new house, starting at a new day-care center or preschool, or the arrival of a new sibling can intensify fears and thus increase separation anxiety. Separation fear can also arise after an illness or accident.

Acknowledge your child's fears and feelings. Reassure him that you will come back. This requires patience and understanding, especially when you may be frustrated or feeling guilty about leaving your child. Provide a sense of safety and optimism. Remind your child that he is safe and that you love him. Do not be negative and say things such as, "You are too old to be crying like a baby when I take you to school. Act your age." Instead, focus on the positive and emphasize successes: "You did a great job when I dropped you off at day care today. I know it was a little scary for you. I was so proud of how you behaved. I know that you will do a good job again tomorrow." With practice and patience, your preschooler will become confident and independent.

Separation at Preschool

Getting yourself and your child ready for preschool takes careful preparation. Separation fear, concern about the unknown, and change in routine may result in your preschooler experiencing worry and insecurity about preschool. Your child may have difficulty saying good-bye. You may see regression, such as baby talk, toileting accidents, thumb sucking, and misbehavior. It is a time of great transition.

Many preschool programs begin their school year with a shorter first day, when the child is accompanied to the classroom by a parent. If your school does not make formal arrangements for a preschool orientation, call the teacher and ask if she will meet with you and your child for a short classroom visit.

Many good children's books are available to read with your child to learn about school and what to expect. Reading about school can help ease a child's anxiety. One such book is *The Kissing Hand,* by Audrey Penn, a story about a raccoon who did not want to go to school until his mother shared a secret— the kissing hand. The special kiss reassured him of her love and gave him the confidence he needed. This story allows you to create your own special kiss that your child can keep all day. Reading *The Kissing Hand* at night before preschool will give you the opportunity to talk through the morning routine, role-play what to expect, and reinforce the idea that when you leave, you will return.

On the first day of preschool, arrive early to help your child settle in before the entire class arrives. Get him involved in an activity. Always say good-bye. Do not sneak away, as this will damage your child's trust in you. Make sure that you are on time to pick up your child. Being punctual will keep him calm and enhance his feelings of safety and security. During the first weeks of school, spend one-on-one time with your child after school if possible.

Clinging, sadness, and crying when you drop your child off at school are common problems. Create a good-bye ritual for when you are leaving. It can be as simple as a special hug, kiss, or wave through the window. Whatever the routine, do it consistently. Predictability helps children feel secure. Rituals and routines also give them the ability to participate and have control over the situation. Establishing school-related routines such as laying out their clothes, planning their breakfast, or packing their lunch helps prepare children for school.

How your child will adjust to preschool may depend on his previous experience with separation and group activities. If your child has never been away from you, arrange for a friend whom your child trusts to watch him in your home or at hers. Doing this several times will ease your preschooler into the idea that it is okay to be without you. If your child has never been with a group of children, consider joining a play group before enrolling him in preschool. These opportunities will give your child a chance to practice.

Do not be surprised if your child seems to be adjusting to the separation and new environment of preschool, only to resist it after several weeks. This is common when the novelty of the new toys and friends becomes a routine. A child's comfort level may be improved by attending school with a favorite doll, stuffed animal, or other special item from home.

Children tend to reflect their parents' attitudes toward school. If you are having a hard time letting go, do not be surprised if your child has difficulty separating. Remember that young children pick up on their parents' worry or anxiety. Be confident. Preschool children will notice the tears that appear in a parent's eyes and the extra long hug during an emotional good-bye. Reassuring a child too much before a separation may leave him with the impression that you are concerned about his safety. He may begin to think that the situation is dangerous. Don't say things like, "Don't worry, you'll be fine," or "I will miss you so much while you're in school." Set a more positive tone by saying, "I'll see you in a little while. Have fun!" Long farewells only make children more anxious. They wonder whether you are going or not. If your child cries, and you continue to stay longer, you will reinforce the idea that if he

cries, you will stay. This often results in more tears the next time you drop him off.

Find out what special activities are planned. Talk with your child about them to generate excitement. If your child continues to have difficulty, ask the teacher to assist you by engaging your child in the classroom upon entering. The teacher can ask your child to help with preparations or involve him in an interesting activity.

Reach out to other parents and preschoolers who are distressed. You can help by inviting them on play dates. As the children become friends, they will be less frightened about separating at school because they will see a familiar face.

A preschooler's temperament may also influence how easily he adjusts to new situations. Some children embrace new situations more easily than others. If your child has difficulty adjusting, do not feel discouraged. It does not mean you have failed as a parent, only that he needs more time. A day will come when you arrive to pick up your preschooler and he tells you to go back home because he is not ready to leave yet.

New Situations

As children get older, imaginary fears are sometimes replaced by fears of new situations. New experiences can result in fears of failure, harm, or embarrassment. At about age five, children develop an awareness of life's realities. Children realize that people die and never come back. Tragedies in which children die may also arouse fears in your child. Encourage your children to use words to express their fears. Drawing pictures or writing a story can help children cope and build resiliency.

Some young children embrace new experiences with enthusiasm. Others are cautious or resist anything new and different. Your child's temperament strongly influences her disposition regarding new situations. Help a cautious child by talking through a new situation ahead of time, exploring what she might expect to see, feel, or experience. Role-play and have your preschooler practice at home or do a trial run. When you arrive at school or at another new place, have your child observe what is happening for a few minutes. Observing rather than participating can be an important first step for a child who is concerned about a new situation. It takes judgment to know when to gently push a child, and it may be necessary to give your child more time before introducing her to the new situation.

Nightmares

A child's first nightmares occur around three years of age. As pretend play becomes more complex, a child's ability to create mental images at nighttime emerges. Dreams are one way that children come to terms with strong emotions, and their nightmares tend to involve fear, anger, or aggression. Preschoolers have not learned how to cope with these negative emotions, and as a result they may wake up tearful and distraught.

Since bad dreams can be inspired by frightening stories, avoid scary movies and books, especially at night. Be aware that even if it is a children's movie or book, if it has frightening characters, it may lead to bad dreams. It is also best to avoid "I'm going to get you" games, even if your child is laughing and enjoying the attention. A relaxing bedtime routine gives a child a sense of order and security. Give him a warm bath, read a story, and spend some quiet time before putting him to bed.

When a child awakes during the night, comfort him by speaking in a soft, soothing voice to calm him down. Holding, cuddling, or patting your child can help him feel safe so he can go back to sleep. If your child wakes up many times during the night, remember to be patient. If a child senses a parent's distress, he will have more difficulty getting back to sleep.

When awakened by a bad dream, many children crawl into their parents' bed to feel safe. This is normal and common. It is only a problem if it is a problem for you, or if your child joins you in bed night after night. Everyone loses sleep. If this pattern develops, comfort your child and take him back to his bedroom. Stay a while, singing a soft song and rubbing his back. Reassure him that he is safe, and you will never let anything happen to him. Your ultimate goal is for your child to comfort himself back to sleep when he wakes up afraid. Be forewarned—this may take a long time, perhaps months.

Although your child's growing imagination is causing the nightmares, it is also a powerful tool in helping him cope with fears. Jessie helped her son Kylar learn how to comfort himself by teaching him how to hug his teddy bear while pretending that Mommy was hugging him. Kylar was taught to make a pretend movie of good thoughts in his mind. When the scary thoughts began, he would put in the happy tape. Jacob helped his daughter Jennie create a good ending to her dream.

The next day they talked and drew pictures about the happy ending. When Caitlin was frightened by the dark in her room, Mom made up a magic wand to wave around the room at nighttime to keep the monsters away.

If your child has nightmares often, think about what might be causing stress or anxiety in his life. Change or conflict can provoke fear and nightmares. By examining the situations in your preschooler's life, you may uncover events that are causing the fears or nightmares. When you do, try to eliminate them as much as possible.

Some preschool children experience night terrors. Night terrors, which are less common than nightmares, usually occur shortly after falling asleep rather than in the middle of the night. Your child may talk, cry, scream, shake, or stare. He may not be aware of your presence or your attempts to comfort him. Children who experience a night terror seem to go right back to sleep, but in fact they were never awake. Unlike a nightmare, a child does not remember a night terror. Do not try to wake a child who is having a night terror, but make sure he does not hurt himself if he sleepwalks. Allow him to relax and fall back into a peaceful sleep. Night terrors are more likely to occur when a child is overtired, so make sure your child is getting an adequate amount of sleep.

Doctor Visits

Going to the doctor often arouses fear and anxiety in preschool children. Since fear of the unknown contributes to this anxiety, find a book to help familiarize children with what happens when they visit the doctor. Substitute your doctor's name while you are reading the book to your child. Add or omit details as needed. Playing with a pretend doctor's kit can also help prepare your child for a doctor's appointment. Have your child give checkups to you and his stuffed animals.

Being examined by an unfamiliar grown-up can be frightening to young children. Acknowledge the fear, saying, "It is okay to be scared. I will be there with you." Reassure your child that you will stay with him. Shots are often the most dreaded part of a doctor's appointment. Never tell your child that it won't hurt. Some children become upset just hearing the word. It is better to use the word *pinch*. Emphasize that it will be over quickly, "Before you can count to three." Be honest with your child if a procedure will be uncomfortable. If you tell him it won't be painful and it is, he will be less likely to trust you in the future.

Provide praise and encouragement to your child throughout the appointment, especially if he is having difficulty. Do not criticize or belittle his fear, and be sure to encourage cooperation: "It is okay to cry. Thank you for holding still." Your support and understanding will help your preschooler gain confidence and influence his ability to cope in the future.

Plan something special to do after the appointment, like going out for ice cream or to a movie. Help your child focus on the upcoming event instead of what the doctor is doing. It may be helpful to bring a security toy such as a teddy bear for your child to hug for comfort. Alex brought his Elmo to the doctor's visit. He even explained Elmo's symptoms (which were his own) to the doctor, who examined both Elmo and the child.

Find a doctor who is good with children and knows how to make them feel comfortable. Many pediatricians will let children hold their instruments and explain what they will be doing before they do it. See the same doctor each time when possible. If your child has developed a relationship with the doctor, he will be more able to cope with an exam, especially when he is not feeling well. Emphasize that doctors are people who help us feel better.

Remember that no matter how well planned and positive you try to be, there may still be doctor's visits that are disastrous. Do not take this personally; take comfort in the fact that your child's doctor has had plenty of such visits and will not judge you to be a bad parent.

Dentist Appointments

As with going to the doctor, you need to talk to your child about the dentist visit before it occurs, explaining what will happen in simple terms: "The dentist will look in your mouth and count your teeth." Explain teeth cleaning as "tickling" to help children think of the vibration as pleasurable rather than scary. Ask your dentist what words he will be using when he talks to your child so that you can use the same words if your child asks you questions. You can also use these words when you read books with your child that describe going to the dentist and what to expect. Another way of preparing your child is to take your preschooler to your dentist appointment. By letting him watch you getting your teeth cleaned, he will see that you are not hurt.

Preschool children can be sensitive to having something done in their mouths. The sensations are often uncomfortable for them and may produce a gagging response. If your child gags easily, teach him to breathe through his nose and relax during the procedures. Some dentist's offices provide sunglasses for young children to wear to help dim the bright light that is shining in their faces. Bring your child's sunglasses along in case none are available and your child is particularly sensitive to bright light.

You may want to find a pediatric dentist for your preschooler, since they are trained in child development and behavior management techniques. Pediatric dentists describe to your child what he will feel, taste, hear, and touch before it happens. If you have had bad dental experiences that make you uncomfortable, try to keep your own anxiety from influencing your child. Preschoolers are masters at perceiving their parents' concerns. If you are unable to present a positive model, stay home and let your spouse go to the appointment with your child. If that is not possible, you might want to stay in the waiting room.

Scary Stuff at Halloween

Halloween can be a scary event for preschool children, especially since they are unable to discern fantasy from reality, and their naturally active imaginations create fears and anxiety. Prepare your preschooler for Halloween by talking about what she might see on television, at school, or in the community. Make sure to emphasize that what she sees is not real by using words that your preschooler understands such as *pretend, dress up,* and *make-believe.* For example, you might say, "Look at her, she is *pretending* to be a witch," rather than "Look at that witch!" Since many preschoolers do not understand that masks or costumes are pretend, have your child try on nonscary masks in front of a mirror to help her understand that putting on a mask does not change the person underneath.

You and your child should choose her costumes together and steer her away from anything that is scary. Select familiar characters such as Madeline, Pocahontas, Superman, or Batman, or familiar things such as a cat, ballerina, or fireman. Respect your child's wishes if she does not want to wear a costume or participate in trick-or-treating. If you do take your children trick-or-treating, go before sunset. Everything will seem less scary, and you will be less likely to meet up with older children wearing more frightening costumes. Trick-or-treating only at the homes of family or friends may also help the hesitant child feel safer. If your child wants to stay at home, ask her to help you pass out candy as a way of involving her in Halloween and building her confidence for next year.

21

Behavior in Public Places

 I have said it before, and here it is again: discipline begins at home, not in public. You must establish solid discipline in your home before you can begin to manage or correct misbehavior problems in public. We are more vulnerable in public, which makes us easier targets for whining and teasing. We get embarrassed more easily, so we have a greater inclination to give in—to stop the misbehavior and the accompanying embarrassment. This is always a great temptation and a mistake. Be consistent, be proactive, and emphasize cooperation, and you will neutralize many of the problems preschoolers can create in public.

Plan to be embarrassed once in a while. Preschoolers are famous for saying exactly what is on their mind. They have not yet developed a sense of personal censorship, nor do they know the meaning of being politically correct. Martha and three-year-old Stacie were grocery shopping. When a very large man came by, Stacie began shouting, "Hey, Mom, look at that fat man. Hey, Mom, have you ever seen a man as fat as that? Look at that fat man over there." This was truly an embarrassing situation, but not misconduct. This was an opportunity to teach. Martha spoke softly: "Yes, Stacie, that man is very big. But when you use the word 'fat,' you may hurt the man's feelings."

Betty's attempt to teach her child a little religious history completely backfired. It was the week before Easter, and there was a movie on TV about the life of Jesus. Betty encouraged her five-year-old, Josh, to watch the movie. After a few minutes, Josh lost interest. It was not a movie designed for young children, and Josh said it was boring. Betty was offended that Josh did not want to watch, so she insisted, which strengthened his resistance. They both became angry. After a while, Betty realized that no amount of struggling was going to make her son interested in this movie, so she got him engaged in another activity. A few weeks later, Betty took Josh to the doctor. The waiting room was packed with parents and children. Josh began interacting with another boy around the table of children's books. The other boy held up a book, saying, "Here is a book about Jesus." Remembering the boring movie, Josh proclaimed to everyone in the room, "Jesus! I hate Jesus!" Dozens of eyes seemed permanently fixed on Betty. "What are these people thinking about me?" she wondered as she grabbed a couple of books and asked Josh to sit next to her while she read. She announced to Josh, hoping everyone in the room would hear, "Josh, it is not nice to say you hate Jesus. You did not like the movie about Jesus." This was the most embarrassing moment of Betty's life, and as the parent of a preschooler you can no doubt relate your own excruciating episode. When facing an extremely awkward situation, remain calm and do not let your embarrassment trigger your anger. Use redirection. Think about ways to teach your child behavior that is appropriate for the situation.

Going Out to Eat

Twenty years ago it was unusual for families to go out to eat unless it was a fast food restaurant designed to accommodate children. Today it is much more common for parents to take their children to a wide variety of restaurants. Going out to eat can be a fun evening for the whole family or a reward for a child's good behavior. If the evening is a reward, allow the child to choose where to eat; otherwise, you will want to select a restaurant where the children have a few favorite foods from which to choose. Preschoolers eat foods they like better than foods they do not like. The place to struggle over trying new foods is at home, not in public. Select a restaurant that caters to families, with quick service and servers who are friendly to children, and if possible that provides young children with crayons and place mats with blank pictures for coloring. As a backup, always bring things to keep your preschooler busy at the table: crayons, color pencils, dolls, games, or books. Even with help from these activities, you still have to pay attention to your children. Play with them. Keep them engaged. When your child finishes coloring the place mat, turn it over and draw or play tic-tac-toe.

You may take several children out to eat for a party. Suppose you are taking a group of preschoolers out for pizza. You know the restaurant will be crowded. There are many video games and other expensive distractions. You want the children to have fun, but you do not want to spend all your time chasing them around. Anticipate problems. Should you let them play games before the pizza is ready? How many games should you allow them to play? How long should you stay after finishing the pizza? Think ahead. Then tell the children exactly what you expect. Lay down the ground rules before you leave the house. Let them know what happens if they do cooperate and what happens if they do not.

"We are going to Funtime Pizza for Jacob's birthday party. Each of you can play two video games while we are waiting for the pizza. If you listen to my directions, you can play two more games after we eat. I want you to have fun, but I also want you to behave. If you do a good job this time, I will want to take you again some day. It's up to you. We'll be leaving in ten minutes."

This also helps you stay on track. You won't have to second-guess yourself when you are under pressure. The plan is clear to everyone.

It is also important that your children understand that there will be occasions when you will go out without them. There are times when Mom and Dad need to have a romantic, peaceful, relaxing, leisurely meal, and leave the children home with a sitter. This is healthy not only for your marriage but for your children's growing independence.

Going to Religious Services

For preschool children, most religious services are too long. While they may be able to watch an hour-long children's movie with no fussing, at this age, an hour of religious service is another story. Children's movies are designed to capture and hold the attention of young children. Most religious services are for adults. Consider putting your preschooler in day care or Sunday school during the service. Many churches and synagogues offer teaching opportunities for young children during this time, so your children still receive the benefits of religious lessons. If your place of worship does not have day care, perhaps you could suggest starting one. If this option is not available, you may want to attend a place that offers child care, at least until your children are older.

Many places of worship provide dedicated "children's services," in which the entire ceremony is aimed at children. These services are typically shorter and often have special music and activities that engage or involve younger children. Some places offer combination services in which the children join in the first part and then are escorted to day care. If you can find this type of service, you will be able to share the experience of a religious service as a family, while avoiding the problem of bored and distracted children.

If you feel that your children are old enough to accompany you to the services, make sure you keep them busy with quiet activities. Consider choosing books that teach your values and ideals. Religious coloring books and crayons are an engaging option. You might take a drawing pad and ask your preschooler to draw a picture that relates to the theme of the service. Some preschoolers may become hungry during services. Prepare a non-sticky, non-crumbly snack that they may eat discreetly during the service. Be sure these activities and snacks are acceptable to your church and other members of the congregation.

It is also a good idea to include a special family time around going to service. You might go out to breakfast or make a special breakfast at home. Many families go for a family drive after their religious service. These special extra activities raise the value of going as a family and give preschoolers something to anticipate through the services.

Play Dates

A play date is a get-together with one or more other children. You gather at someone's home or at a public place like a park or restaurant. Children learn social skills, such as how to interact with others and use self-control, through play. Play dates require young children to share, take turns, and compromise. These behaviors are not easy for most preschoolers. That is why some play dates end in arguing, pushing, or tears. These conflicts are part of the learning process and help preschoolers discover how to take turns and resolve disagreements.

Whenever possible, allow preschoolers the opportunity to solve problems on their own. Get involved when rules need to be enforced:

"There is no name-calling or hitting at our house," for example. When needed, help the children focus on listening to each other and arriving at a solution. Be proactive. Plan ahead to minimize unnecessary conflicts. Provide toys that encourage cooperative play. Art or building projects and imaginative play such as dress-up are good noncompetitive choices for play dates. Special toys that are hard to share should be put away before guests arrive.

Children have more difficulty playing nicely together when they are hungry or tired. Plan to provide something to eat and drink. Involve the children in preparing a healthy snack. Weekends may be better than weekdays. Two hours is enough time for most preschoolers' play dates. Since sharing toys can be difficult enough without sharing a friend, a one-on-one play date works better than group play dates during the preschool years. There is less competition, and less likelihood of someone feeling left out.

Problems often occur when it is time to go home. Leaving a play date can often bring on tears and resistance. When Colleen arrived to pick up her daughter, Chelsea began to cry and screamed, "Go away, Mom," as she crawled under the coffee table. Provide a time warning. Telling children when the end of play time is approaching will lessen these departure difficulties: "We will be playing for fifteen more minutes. Please start cleaning up." This will help ease the transition because the children will not be in the middle of an activity when it is time to go.

If you suspect that your preschoolers will have difficulty ending a play date, try role-playing at home first. Role-play the events and explain how you expect your preschooler to behave when it is time to leave. This helps prepare your preschooler for what you expect.

Although children may be actively engaged during play dates, parental supervision is still required with preschool children. Provide abundant positive feedback when you see the children sharing, taking turns, and working out conflicts. Thank them for getting along. This will prevent most problems from getting started.

Shopping with Your Preschooler
The supermarket is the great unsung battlefield for children and parents. Think before you go. Do your preschoolers need to go with you? Can they stay home with your spouse or a sitter? Think about the shopping trip from your preschoolers' point of view. Will they have fun, or

will they struggle? Be realistic. If your preschoolers must go with you, be sure to set them up with a good attitude before you leave the house. Give them a pep talk. Build their self-esteem. Keep preschoolers engaged by allowing them to be helpers.

> "Come here, please, children. I will be going to the grocery store in a few minutes, and I am looking forward to your coming with me. I will need your help. I know you can be good helpers. I will need help holding the shopping list and putting things in the basket. Think about what you want to do. Maybe we can do it together or take turns."

Remember to make these trips as short as possible, minimizing opportunities for conflict or tantrums. If your child acts up, do not give in to her demands. If at all possible, it is better to leave the store without finishing your shopping than to give in. Your best strategy is to involve your child in the shopping: have her hold the shopping list or help you choose what kinds of fruits and vegetables to buy. By engaging your child, you can make shopping a fun rather than tedious activity.

Going to the Tool Store

Here is a lesson for parents who like to meander through hardware stores, as I do. If you assume that your children will enjoy all the things that intrigue you, think again. You can, however, make trips to the hardware store fun for both of you if you are proactive. Involve your child in projects around the house and give her a set of play tools. She will think tools are fun. Then when you go to the tool store, your child will take the lead. Let your child choose what aisle to go down. With a little guidance, you can still get through the aisles that you need. Stop and explain what things are and show your child how they work. Explain that the things you are buying are for the whole family. This plant is for Mom. This pipe is for Aaron's sink. This flashlight is for your room. At age three and four, your child will not comprehend everything, but she can enjoy herself if you focus on making the trip fun. This takes patience and time. Your trips to the tool store will be longer when you take your child, but it is worth the extra time. Believe it or not, there will be times when your child might say, "Dad, can we go to the tool store? We haven't been there in a long time."

Can I Have One of Those?

Preschoolers need to learn that they cannot always have what they want. This is an extremely difficult lesson, since most young children want everything they see. Stores are notorious for positioning items at child's-eye level and within reach. Be proactive and teach your preschoolers that they cannot always have everything they see. Phyllis, for example, would take James on practice trips to the toy store. She would explain the rules before leaving.

"How would you like to take a trip to the toy store?"
"Sure, Mom."
"We are going to look and play. But we are not going to buy anything."
"What do you mean?"
"We can go and have fun. But today is not for buying. Do you still want to go?"
"Yes."

They would go have fun at the toy store and leave without buying anything. James would often ask to buy something, just to see if Mom remembered. Phyllis would tell him not today, maybe some other day. She and James would take these practice trips about once a month. She was teaching her son that you cannot always buy what you want, but they had a lot of fun in the process.

Most four- to six-year-olds understand the concept of saving their own money, even through it is very difficult for them to do so. One strategy that helps teach children about saving is to suggest they save their money to buy things they see and want.

"Can I have one of those?"
"Not today."
"But I really want one."
"Then that is something you can save your allowance for."

Tips for Taking Children on Vacation

Taking preschoolers on vacation can be a special challenge. Children like routines; they help them feel safe, and they make life predictable. Vacations are meant to be a break from routine, especially for the par-

ents. Yet traveling with your preschooler can be a nightmare, starting with the plane or car trip. Would you confine your preschooler to three square feet of space for five hours? Of course not. It is unreasonable and unnatural, and it would be agonizing for your child. But that is exactly what you expect when you take your preschooler on long plane flights or long road trips, especially since you also want him to be quiet during the journey. Not all vacations need to be for the entire family, and when you have a preschooler, it is advisable for you to travel without children once in a while. Find someone you trust to baby-sit and then really get away from it all for a few days.

When you take your preschoolers with you, be sure the trip is appropriate for them. One mother described how she thought taking her two-year-old to the beach was going to be a splendid experience. Yet she spent the entire time washing sand from her daughter's eyes, ears, and mouth. Her daughter was too young for the beach, and the only thing that interested her was tossing sand into the air. Another mom and dad were surprised when their four- and six-year-old sons misbehaved at the Grand Canyon. The parents understood the canyon's timelessness and appreciated its beauty, but to their sons it was just a really big hole that they could not play in.

Plan your trips with your children and include activities for them to anticipate. Get their ideas about things they would like to do and see. Children who are involved in the planning have more ownership of the trip and will have more appreciation and fun. Show older preschool children how to follow the trip on the map so they can see the progress you are making. They will be less likely to bother you with, "Are we there yet?"

Use a favorite television program as a time reference. When Allison was four, her favorite program was *Barney*. When her family would travel, Dad would explain time in terms of *Barney* shows: "You know how long *Barney* is? We will stop in two more *Barney* shows." This technique works well because favorite programs appear to be over quickly from the preschooler's perspective. "That's fast, Dad." "You're right. We'll be there soon."

Have materials to occupy children's time and keep them engaged while traveling, such as headphones for audiotapes or CDs, books on tape, portable games, or handheld computer games. Also have plenty of materials for drawing and coloring. Create travel traditions, such as

singing songs or playing games such as I Spy. Keep a bag filled with new activities, such as storybooks, stickers, or dolls. Bring out surprises when your children are behaving well: "You are doing a good job of being patient. Thanks. Would you like to try one of these new games?"

Preschoolers become bored being strapped in their car seats. For long road trips, plan a thirty-minute stop every two hours. This lengthens the time between destinations but cuts down on stress. Stop where your children can have fun and release some energy. Instead of eating in a restaurant, get the food to go. Find a park and have a picnic, and make sure your children take the opportunity to run around and burn off excess energy. Preschool children need to eat more often than adults, so you need to pack extra snacks and juice.

When trips include nights in hotels, maintain the same bedtime routine you use at home. Bring along your children's favorite comfort toy or teddy. If you have been taking movies with a camcorder, play the videos at the end of each evening or ask your preschooler to draw a picture of his favorite thing that day. This will help your child to appreciate the difference between being at home and on vacation.

Each morning, explain your expectations for your preschooler's behavior before you leave. Get out a map and show him your itinerary, circling places where you plan to stop. Be sure to continually encourage your children throughout the trip: "I know it has been a long day in the car, you are being very patient. Thank you."

Traveling with small children is not like the carefree road trips from pre-child days. Adjust your expectations. Above all, remember to relax—you are on vacation.

22

Preschoolers, Aggression, and Anger

Few circumstances are more embarrassing or frustrating than when your normally well-behaved preschooler impulsively punches a playmate. Preschoolers can and do become aggressive, especially when they are feeling angry, hurt, disappointed, or frustrated. Some children become aggressive to gain attention or control. Aggressive behavior can be the young child's only way of asserting himself, especially when he is feeling vulnerable. This is often the case, as preschoolers tend to act out in this way when they are tired or hungry. Although aggressive behavior in preschoolers may not be a deliberate act of violence, aggressive behavior is never acceptable.

Some children become aggressive because it is the only way they know to solve problems. Teach your preschooler to solve problems with words and by compromising. This requires time and guidance. When a playmate refuses to share a toy, teach your child how to trade and take turns: "You trade for another toy, or take turns when Troy is ready." Redirect your child to another toy or activity until each child is ready to share. Many parents use a timer to indicate when it is time to trade.

Children who witness aggressive behavior in real life or see it on TV or in the movies tend to be more aggressive when they play. If you have a child who is consistently aggressive, eliminate his exposure to it in the media. If your child does see aggression on TV or in a movie, explain that hitting is not a nice way to act and that it is not the way to solve problems. Choose storybooks and movies that promote themes of kindness, respect for others, cooperation, and nonviolence.

Teach your preschooler to use words to express his needs and feelings. You may be tired of hearing this, but it is essential in the discipline process. Young children have a variety of feelings, just as adults do. Children need to be taught how to label and manage their feelings, especially anger.

Researchers now believe that all human babies are born with the same six emotions: happiness, surprise, sadness, disgust, fear, and anger. Infants do not have to learn these emotions. They are inborn. Children need to learn how to apply and manage these emotions, however. We learn this through our experience with the world around us.

Anger exists in everyone. Occasional anger is normal; chronic anger is not. The remainder of this chapter is to help you teach your preschoolers how to manage their occasional anger and keep it from becoming chronic anger, which may develop into aggressive behavior. There are also some ideas that will help you manage your own anger as well. (See chapter 13 for more on parental anger.)

It is helpful to think of anger as a secondary emotion; something upsets you, and then you become angry. Something happens to activate the anger. A child may experience teasing, hurt, failure, sadness, or rejection and become angry. Many preschoolers become angry when they do not get their way or when they believe that something is unfair.

Anger is part of our temperament. Temperament is inborn and describes our overall mood or disposition. Some parents have temperaments in which anger is more easily triggered, as do some children. Yet when children live with parents who become angry quickly and repeatedly, they learn to do the same thing. If a child sees a parent acting out his anger by screaming or hitting, he learns that this behavior is okay. When children live in a hostile or critical home, they become angry because of feelings of despair and hopelessness. Many children of divorce become angry because they feel alone or abandoned, having lost a solid connection with an adult or with their family.

Remember that no matter how diligently you apply the strategies that follow, a three-or four-year-old child is not capable of fully understanding how to control his anger. Your job over the next few years of his development is to teach him to identify his anger, understand its causes, and know how to channel it in acceptable and nonaggressive ways. This is a long-term goal and a lot of work.

Teach Anger Management

Teach your preschoolers to recognize and regulate their anger. In doing so, you need to explain that it is normal to feel angry, especially if someone has hurt your feelings, and that you may want to get even. Be clear that hitting or fighting not only doesn't solve the problem but also makes it worse, since being aggressive will only make the other person want to retaliate. Prepare your child to think and talk through the issues that are making her angry:

> "When you are angry with someone, you may think about hitting him. You feel like you want to hurt him because he did something to hurt you. But when you are feeling angry, the best thing to do is tell someone. Tell Dad or me. When you talk about anger, it helps you to feel better."

Teach your preschooler strategies that calm him, and how to redirect himself when he becomes angry. Do not try to teach calming techniques when your child is in the middle of an angry outburst. Instead, choose a time when your child is quiet and receptive. Practice techniques such as deep breathing, counting to ten, playing with a favorite toy, jumping on a trampoline, going to his room to take a rest, playing an appropriate computer game, or listening to relaxing music. When your child does become angry, use a verbal reminder or cue to help him calm down.

Jordan would often get angry when she did not get her way, so her father, Mark, taught her how to use deep breathing to calm down. He began by telling Jordan that deep breathing is an idea that many adults use to help calm down. Then he showed her what to do. He put his hand on his chest and took two deep breaths. Jordan did the same. When Mark would see Jordan getting upset, he would cue her by putting his hand on his chest and taking a deep breath. This would help Jordan remember to use deep breathing to calm down. He knew he was making progress when one day Jordan reminded him, "Dad, you are getting mad. Take a few deep breaths."

Role-playing is an excellent way to practice anger management and works with any age child older than three. Preschoolers call it pretending. Think of a situation that makes your preschooler angry and ask your child to brainstorm possible solutions with you. Then role-play the situation. A common preschool problem occurs when two or more children refuse to play with another. Here is an example of how you can use role-playing to teach your child how to resolve a situation in which other children will not allow her to play with them. Mother plays the antagonist.

Bobbi: "Can I play with you?"

Mother: "No. You can't play with us."

Bobbi: "Can I please play with you?"

Mother: "No."

Bobbi: "Okay. I'll go play with somebody else."

Practice role-playing several different situations; this helps children take what they learn from role-playing into the real world. After each role-playing activity, praise your preschooler for her effort and desire to learn to manage anger.

Teach your children to learn from their anger by talking with them after an episode of anger. Make sure to wait long enough for your child to calm down and be ready to talk and listen. Many parents want to rush into this discussion while the youngster is still angry. This can be a mistake, because it can reignite the anger. It may be helpful to say, "Let me know when you are ready to talk about this."

Begin your talk by asking your preschooler to remember what happened to get the anger started: "What was making you upset?" Then ask, "Can you say why this upset you so much?" If your child has trouble using words to describe what happened, you might want to offer some ideas, like, "It sounds like your friends did not want to play with you." Finally, you want to talk about alternatives. "What else could you have done?" For most preschoolers, simply talking about anger is a helpful way of learning about anger management.

Since many preschoolers have difficulty using words to describe how they feel, teach them to express anger with drawings. This helps them get started. Once they have a picture, you can ask about events and feelings.

Four-year-old Jack would lose his temper and get angry when something did not go his way. Susan had Jack pose for several pictures. In one picture he would smile; in another he would frown; in another he would make an angry face. Then Susan drew a picture of a thermometer on a large chart. She labeled the thermometer from bottom to top: calm, upset, angry, hot, and steaming. She taught Jack to choose a picture that showed his feelings and then place it on the thermometer. This enabled Jack to express himself and gave Susan a tool to begin talking with Jack about his anger.

Have clear limits and expectations about angry outbursts and aggressive behavior. If your preschooler begins to have a tantrum, remove him from the situation. Talk about his anger, but let him know that this behavior is not allowed: "I am sorry we have to leave the playground. I wish we could stay longer, too. It is okay to be upset. But it is not okay for you to behave this way." Then try distracting your child's attention. Give him something to look forward to when he calms down: "There are other fun things to do when we get home. What would you like to do?"

Hold boys and girls to the same level of expectations. Many parents excuse aggressive play in boys because they believe "boys will be boys." While it may be that boys are naturally more physical and aggressive, that is even more reason to teach them how to regulate their aggression.

None of these suggestions will work unless you model and practice anger management yourself. You cannot just tell your children what to do. You have to show them. You need to be a living example.

Bully-Proofing

Nearly every parent with a child in day care or preschool has been told her child has been the victim of biting, scratching, hitting, or hair pulling. An occasional aggressive act is normal; bullying is not. Bullying includes repeated acts of aggression or threats of aggression, or repeated teasing and taunting. Victims of bullying can become anxious and depressed, and may develop poor self-esteem. While most school bullying occurs in the upper grades, it can happen with preschoolers.

Preschoolers are not strong enough to handle a bully alone. They will need help from their parents and teachers. If you believe that your child has been the victim of a preschool bully, do not be afraid to get involved. Talk to the teacher, making sure to get all the details about the incidents before drawing conclusions. How often has it happened? Are there other victims? Does the preschool have written policies regarding repeated aggression? Bullying should never be tolerated.

Look to the teacher for guidance. What positive strategies are in place to teach all children that aggression and bullying are not acceptable? Many preschools include lessons on being a good friend, managing anger, and conflict resolution in their curriculum. Have the parents of the aggressive child been notified? It may be helpful to talk with the parents. Do not approach them as adversaries or challenge them to fix their child. Chances are they are already aware of the situation and are probably more concerned about it than you are. Let them know that you are willing to help in any way you can.

Would additional staff help? Many aggressive children require more adult supervision and engagement, especially during free play in the classroom or on the playground. An extra staff member could be used to provide guidance and instruction on proper play behavior, which would eventually replace the aggressive behavior. Extra staff would also provide quick intervention should aggressive behavior occur.

Talk with your child about preschool every day. Ask specific questions about the playground: "What happened at recess today?" "Whom did you play with?" Be sure to explain to your child that bullying is not okay: "If a child hurts you, make sure you tell the teacher. That is very important. Your teacher wants to know when children are not playing nicely." Encourage your child to play with children who are not aggressive: "Maybe you should play with Suzie tomorrow. She plays nicely. She does not hit." It may be helpful to phone Suzie's parents and arrange a mutual understanding about tomorrow's recess ahead of time.

The best approach for managing preschool bullies is for parents and teachers to work together to teach all children that aggressive behavior is not tolerated. Most preschools do this well. When all else fails, some preschools will dismiss a child who continues to be aggressive. If your child is being victimized and nothing seems to curb the bully's behavior, it may be time to look for another preschool, however.

What if the bully is your neighbor's or your friend's child, not a child at preschool? The same strategies apply. Do not be afraid to talk to the parent about your concerns and possible solutions: proper play behavior, anger management, and ways to resolve disagreements. Offer to have the children play at your home, where you can set up the rules and expectations. When the child arrives, explain, "At our house we play together. We take turns and share. We use our words when we disagree. We do not hit, kick, or bite. Since you are our guest, you can choose what to do first." As they play, provide plenty of verbal encouragement for proper behavior: playing together, sharing, taking turns, using polite language, Be sure there is adequate adult supervision to provide quick intervention if bullying begins.

What if your child is the bully? Since most preschoolers tend to become aggressive when they become angry, use the techniques in the first part of this chapter to teach your child appropriate ways to express and manage anger. Work with your child's teacher to develop positive strategies at preschool. Eliminate all aggressive or bullying behavior in your home and make sure older siblings are not victimizing your preschooler. Do not allow your preschooler to be exposed to aggression on television. Look for those times your child works through situations without anger or aggression, reinforcing and encouraging proper behavior.

Biting

Young children often use their mouths to learn about the world. They may bite as a source of comfort or as a way to express feelings of excitement, frustration, or anxiety. Most biting behavior has disappeared by the time a child reaches preschool age. If your preschooler is biting, however, identifying when and why he does so can help you prevent this behavior and teach him positive ways to express his feelings, wants, and needs.

Chad's mom identified two situations where he would bite: before naps and at the end of play dates. Reasoning that he was tired and easily frustrated at naptime, she began giving him a bath and reading books first. This calming routine helped him make the transition from playing to napping.

At the end of play dates, Chad would give his friends a good-bye hug and then a big bite. Mom taught Chad to give handshakes or high fives instead of hugs. This new behavior broke the habit of hugging and biting and also created more space between the children, so Chad's mouth was not within biting distance.

Some children bite because they lack the social skills to cope with conflict. If your child bites when he is frustrated, teach him to "use his words." Be consistent and always state firmly, "No biting, biting hurts." Follow through with a consequence such as sitting away from the other children for a few minutes or time-out. Do not get angry or overreact to the biting, as this may only reinforce the behavior. Provide verbal praise and encouragement when you see your child "using words" or playing nicely. Adult supervision is essential. Watch for signs of frustration and intervene immediately, before your child has a chance to bite. Use redirection or talk your preschooler through a problem-solving process: "If you are angry because Joshua took your truck, what can you say to him?"

Some children become easily overwhelmed or threatened. They may bite to gain control or to defend themselves or their possessions. If this is your situation, your child may be communicating that he needs a predictable routine and one-on-one attention to feel more safe and secure. Monitor your child's reactions to the setting. Too much activity, too many people, and lots of noise can overstimulate young children. Provide a calm and unhurried climate. Give your child choices to help him remain in control.

Roughhousing should be minimized, since young children often cannot distinguish when fun has crossed the line and someone has been hurt. Even playful nibbles on the neck and toes can give a child the wrong impression that biting is okay. Never hit or bite a child for biting. Nor should you use hot sauce or anything else to punish a biter. Teaching self-control is essential.

Temperament influences how a child copes with conflict and deals with frustration. If your child has a tendency to be aggressive, you need to examine your own parenting style. Do you get angry when you manage misbehaviors or solve conflicts? Do not spank your child or use physical force. Your parenting style can interact with your child's temperament and contribute to aggressive behavior. It is important to teach an aggressive child that biting or hitting is not how you get your way. Show your child how to compromise with other children rather than confronting them. Remain calm, using words and a soothing voice. This is especially important when your child has bitten someone. Negative attention can be reinforcing, increasing the likelihood that your child will bite again.

How to Avoid Escalating an Angry Child

Look at the list that follows and ask yourself how often you respond to your child's anger this way:

Losing your self-control.

Getting angry yourself.

Raising your voice.

Arguing.

Insisting that you are right.

Preaching or moralizing.

Making fun of your child.

Mimicking your child.

Calling names.

Speaking in generalities, such as "You always . . ."

Reminding your child of something else he did wrong.

Although many of these actions are commonplace among angry parents, they usually make the situation worse. It is important to avoid all of these, even if you have to tell your child you need a few minutes to calm down.

23

Choosing a Preschool

The term *preschool* suggests a time when children should learn the readiness skills that prepare them for success in school. How well a child does academically in elementary school, high school, and college is typically unrelated to the academic skills that they acquire in preschool. Yet preschool is the critical period in which children learn to manage the feelings and relationships that make them successful in life.

As you consider what type of preschool will enable your child to thrive, consider the following questions: What are my child's strengths and needs? What is his temperament, and how will it impact his ability to be independent and successful within the classroom structure? A shy child may need a program with less structure and more flexibility, while an energetic child may do better in a program with more structure and consistency. Finding the perfect program for your child may not be as important as finding a preschool that can adjust to meet the needs of each student. Quality preschool instruction will adjust to the developmental readiness of each child.

Different preschool programs have various philosophies of learning and discipline. Academic preschool programs emphasize early reading and beginning math skills. Instruction is primarily teacher-directed. The classroom may look like a traditional elementary classroom, with desks or tables for seatwork. Strict standards of discipline are often enforced, and learning social skills is secondary to mastering pre-academic skills.

Developmental preschools are less academic in their approach. They offer more hands-on, play-based learning activities. Opportunities to make choices are provided throughout the day. A circle time often brings the children together to sing, listen to a story, or engage in discussions. Imaginative play, creative play, and free play provide the settings for children to learn about themselves, their world, and relationships. Discipline is typically viewed as a teaching process in which the teacher facilitates social skill development by guiding the children to be aware of their feelings and those of others.

The basic philosophy of the program may not be as important as the interactions the staff have with the children. Before enrolling your child, take a morning to observe the classroom and the playground. Your own eyes and ears will provide the best information about how the staff communicate with the children and respond to their needs. Does it feel right? Trust your intuition about the people and the environment.

Here are some specific things you should do while considering a preschool:

1. Ask about the training of the staff. Do the teachers have degrees in early childhood education or development? Do they have teaching experience?

2. Is the program licensed by the state or accredited by the National Association for the Education of Young Children (NAEYC)?

3. What is the adult-to-child ratio? NAEYC recommends one adult for every seven to ten children, with a maximum group size of twenty for children three and four years of age.

4. Are there enough toys and appropriate materials available for all the children to be actively engaged? You can expect to see blocks, sand or water tables, toys, puzzles, books, art materials, and a playground with climbing equipment.

5. Is there ample space available for the children to move about, explore, and experiment?

6. How are parents involved? What is the school's visiting policy? Most preschool programs send home schedules of activities and

welcome parent participation, questions, and suggestions. Parent-teacher meetings should be held to discuss your child's progress.

7. What is the preschool's discipline policy? Look for a policy that is consistent with your home discipline.

8. Do the children seem happy and actively involved in interesting activities?

9. How do the teachers interact with the students? Do the teachers talk *with* the children or *at* the children? Look for teachers getting down to the child's level and showing patience, affection, and enthusiasm.

Since word of mouth is important and often helpful, ask friends or other parents in the neighborhood for their suggestions of preschools to visit. Do your research, but don't worry about choosing the *perfect* preschool. Although choosing a good preschool is important, many other decisions in your child's life will have greater importance.

Children with Special Needs

All children are challenging. A child with special needs provides everyone in her family with unique challenges, since this child may have delays in one or more areas of development. Common preschool delays occur in language development, self-help skills, or sensory-motor development. Most preschoolers with special needs are eligible for special services through their school district or other state agencies. These special services commonly include special education, speech and language therapy, occupational therapy, and physical therapy.

Most parents of special-needs preschoolers are very concerned with their child's delays and become directly involved in seeking professional help. At times, parents are so intent on improving their child's developmental gains that they overlook behavior problems and forget about discipline. This is a mistake; too often these children end up with misbehavior being a bigger obstacle to their learning than their developmental delay. A child's behavior can interfere with her ability to benefit from therapies and educational services, and limit her ability to participate in activities or interact with peers.

All children can learn, and all children can learn to behave. If you are a parent of a special-needs preschooler, teaching your child appropriate behavior is just as important as getting your child special services. All of the ideas in this book can be used with special-needs preschoolers. You will need to be even more positive, patient, and consistent, however. You need to provide immediate feedback and reinforcement. You have to plan ahead and be more proactive. While a typical preschooler might learn to share toys after three or four experiences, a special-needs preschooler may need more opportunities to learn. She may need more reminders, more redirection, more of your time, and more direct teaching.

The most important thing you can do for your special-needs preschooler is to educate yourself about your child's delays. Collect information about the most effective ways of teaching, as well as the best therapies. Educate yourself about your child; learn her strengths and weaknesses. Knowing your child's present level of performance will help you develop reasonable expectations for learning and behavior. The professionals who work with your child can help you learn more about her level of functioning. Ask them questions. What can she do right now? What needs to be taught next? Are there any specialized strategies or techniques that I can use at home?

Learn about "normal" development, especially if your special-needs child is your firstborn. You will find that many problems you encounter are typical to every child, not directly related to your child's delay. Learn to use language that your child can understand. Just as you would with any preschooler, use language to teach your child how to make good choices. Since many special-needs children have language delays and have difficulty understanding language, this can be a difficult process. If your child cannot understand the words and concepts you use, he will have more difficulty learning what you are trying to teach and how to make good choices. The following strategies will help: Get your child's attention before you speak to him. Give him simple directions, limiting the number of words you use and the number of choices you provide. Speak slowly. Show your preschooler what to do. Use hand-over-hand assistance as needed.

Martha described Chad as stubborn: "He will not do what I ask. I explain and explain and explain to him what he needs to do. I explain why he needs to do it. But he will just sit and look at me. I sometimes get mad and yell at him. He won't listen." Yet when Chad was evaluated by the special education staff, he was found to have severe auditory processing problems. He could not always understand sounds and words. The special education teacher helped Martha learn to use key words rather than lengthy directions and explanations. Martha also learned how to present visual cues, such as pictures and objects, to increase Chad's comprehension.

Many special-needs preschoolers have difficulty using words to express what they need or want. Expressive language includes word imitation, using the right word, knowledge of grammatical rules, and conversational skills. Some children with delayed expressive language skills have learned to use their behavior to communicate. They will have a tantrum or whine to get what they want. You may be tempted to give in to these behaviors to avoid frustration, but this will not help your child learn to communicate better. If your child is unable to use words to communicate, provide opportunities for your child to make choices by using gestures, pointing to objects, symbols, or pictures. If your child has moderate or severe language delays, talk to a speech/language pathologist about using a communication board or sign language. These accommodations can empower children with a functional way of communicating that is more appropriate than tantrums or whining.

Three-year-old Callie had not learned to communicate her wants and needs except by whining, crying, and having tantrums. When Callie started preschool, the special education staff needed to extinguish these behaviors before they could teach her. Callie learned how to communicate her wants and needs by using a communication board. As she learned how to communicate, she had greater control over her world and no longer needed to fuss. Gradually, Callie spent less time being upset and more time engaged in the classroom activities.

Provide your child with opportunities that require him to use his expressive communication skills. For example, present a milk carton and a juice carton and ask your child, "What do you want?" Give your child the drink he chooses. If he does not respond immediately, wait a few seconds and ask again. Accept any approximation of the correct sounds. Do not expect children with significant communication delays to use a complete sentence. A single word or sound might be acceptable, depending on your child's ability. Giving your child what he wants without some appropriate form of expression does not teach him to use acceptable communication skills. Giving in to whining and crying does not help your child learn to communicate or develop the social skills that will enable him to become more independent.

Many special-needs preschoolers have difficulty with articulation—the ability to produce sounds, words, and sentences. Your child may know the correct word, but be unable to say the word in a way that is understood. As you might imagine, this is very frustrating, and often results in behaviors that affect the child's social development. A frustrated child may scream, push, hit, pinch, or bite. If a child is unable to tell a playmate that he wants his toy truck back, he is likely to use physical force to get it back.

A speech/language pathologist can evaluate your preschooler's speech to determine if his sound errors require therapy now or will develop later. Speech/language pathologists can also provide you with specific recommendations that will help you teach your child how to manage his frustrations.

You can also help your child learn how to get what he wants without becoming aggressive. Show your child how to use words and gestures to communicate with his playmates and siblings. Use role-playing to rehearse and practice ways of communicating. Use plenty of positive reinforcement. Be consistent. This will give your child support while his articulation develops.

Some special-needs preschoolers have immature nervous systems that make it difficult for them to process and integrate the information they receive from their senses. Thus the information they receive from their hearing, sight, taste, touch, and movement systems can be overwhelming and overstimulating. Some children who have sensory processing concerns may have difficulty maintaining an optimal level of arousal. Others have difficulty paying attention, which impairs their ability to complete tasks and follow directions. These factors may affect their behavior and ability to learn. An evaluation by an occupational therapist can provide information that will help you determine if your preschooler's behaviors are the result of sensory integration difficulties. Special education teachers and occupational therapists can help design a plan to help a child with sensory issues.

If you have a special-needs preschooler, become actively involved in his education. Ask questions. Observe your child's classroom. This will help you learn strategies and techniques that you can use at home to help your child gain skills and improve his behavior. You may have ideas that will help your child's teacher work with him; make sure to share it. Any idea that works is a helpful idea.

Don't be afraid to set limits with special-needs preschoolers. Make eye contact and provide clear directions. Provide positive feedback and recognition when your child makes a good choice. Use mild and brief consequences when necessary. This will help your special-needs preschoolers develop an understanding of cause-and-effect relationships.

Have your special-needs preschooler pick up his toys just as you would a preschooler without special needs, even if your child's delays prevent him from doing 100 percent. It is important that he participates and tries. Remember that there may be situations when your child may not be able to understand what you are asking him to do. Repeat your directions and give your preschooler more time to respond. If he needs additional help, provide visual or physical assistance. Be specific when giving directions. Do say, "Put the blocks in the bucket." Don't say, "Clean up your room now." Use words and concepts that he understands.

Patterns of behavior that are established in early childhood can be very difficult to change. Be proactive; address concerns as they arise. Do not let your child's delay be an excuse for tolerating misbehavior. It may be easier for you to do things for your child than to teach the child to do it for himself. This type of enabling will not help your child become more independent. It can lead to decreased expectations. Often parents find it easier to give in to whining, crying, and refusing. Although this may be a short-term solution, it can create greater problems as the child gets older. A three-year-old who throws himself on the ground or hits when denied his way is easier to manage than a ten- or fifteen-year-old who is still using the same behaviors to get what he wants.

How to Find Help for Your Child

If you suspect that your child's development is delayed, call your local school district and participate in a Child Find screening. At a Child Find screening, a team of professionals will assess your child's skills and compare them to those of other children his age. A typical screening examines the areas of communication, motor, cognitive, social-emotional, adaptive, and sensory development.

Communication includes the ability to understand and use language. It includes speaking clearly, pointing to and naming pictures or objects, following directions, answering questions, carrying on a conversation, and relating events or retelling a story. Cognitive development refers to a child's ability to take in and organize information. It is measured by a preschooler's knowledge of pre-academic skills and problem-solving abilities. Adaptive development refers to a child's ability to use his communication, social, and motor skills to have his wants and needs met. Adaptive development includes self-help skills that enable a child to care for himself in the areas of feeding, dressing, bathing, and toileting. Social-emotional and behavioral development refers to a preschool child's play skill, coping behaviors, and interactions with others. Sensory development includes hearing, vision, and the processing of sensory information.

If the screening indicates that your child's skills are not within the expected range for a preschooler his age, a more comprehensive evaluation may be indicated. Children who are identified as special needs are eligible for special education and related services. This often includes a preschool program taught by specialists trained in child development and behavior management. It may also include related services such as speech/language, occupational therapy, or physical therapy. Preschool special education services within the United States are federally mandated. All three-to-five-year-old children who meet the eligibility criteria can receive special education services. If you have concerns about your child's development, do not wait until your child is in kindergarten. Early intervention is essential; a preschooler's brain is in a critical period of development. Behavior patterns established during the preschool years can influence your child's school success and his ability to become independent.

25

From Cookies to Car Keys

Living with preschoolers is never boring. They will always think of something that you are unprepared to handle. Being a parent is demanding, requiring countless sacrifices and continuous hard work. Fortunately, there are many rewards: the pride of achievement, the miracle of growth and development, and the warmth and affection. If your preschooler's misbehavior is depriving you of these rewards, you are being cheated. If you let misbehavior interfere, you are doing the work without the glory and being denied the pleasures of parenting. You deserve to enjoy your children.

Some parents avoid their children to escape the stress and irritated feelings. They send their children outside to play so they do not have to deal with them, and they cannot wait until the children go to bed. They see their children as a burden, resent them, and hope for the day when they leave home. This is a tragic waste of a precious opportunity. It can be avoided by practicing these points.

Principles to Practice

1 Be open to change in your children and yourself. Grow with your preschooler by seeking self-improvement, just as you expect your child to improve as he learns and develops. Do not limit your parenting style by thinking one way, even if that is contrary to the way you were raised.

2 Remember that successful discipline is built on a strong relationship. Build your child's self-esteem by encouraging him to feel happy inside because he did the right thing. Recognize proper behavior and do not give in to misbehavior. Reinforce polite requests, not whining, teasing, or tantrums. Reinforce calm voices, not arguments and power struggles. Call attention to positive qualities. Teach replacement behaviors.

3 Use language and reasoning to teach self-control to your preschoolers. Use words that a preschooler understands and that teach correct behavior. Read books with stories that teach lessons about life and values. Give positive directions rather than negative ones.

4 Remember that needs, wants, and emotions drive most behaviors in young children. Know the difference between mischief and misconduct. Preschoolers will get into difficulties and do things that are irritating and annoying. These actions are not always misbehavior.

5 Take time to teach and practice correct behavior. Preschoolers must know what you expect. Teach self-control by having self-control, and teach right from wrong by correct example.

6 Preschoolers believe what you tell them. Coach your children on ways to be successful by using plenty of encouragement. Seeing that you have faith and confidence in them will help your children face situations with resiliency and confidence.

7 Try to stay one step ahead by being proactive, anticipating problems, and planning transitions. Keep preschoolers enthusiastically engaged in positive activities.

8 Be firm but positive. Give your children consistent limits and structure. Children see these qualities as an expression of your love and concern. Use consequences that teach decision making. Do not punish when you are angry or to get even. Relate consequences to your child's choices. This teaches responsibility.

9 Tell your preschooler that you love him—frequently. Preschoolers need love and constant reassurance. Accept, value, and love your children just the way they are.

10 Provide a healthy and pleasant family climate by emphasizing each other's strengths and accepting each other's weaknesses. When you talk about values and goals, your children will learn to come to you with their problems. This will come in handy when they are teenagers.

Final Thoughts

Being a successful parent is hard work. Developing well-behaved children requires courage and patience. Trust yourself, since you know what is best for your children. Concentrate on the real issues: mental health, happiness, self-respect, and love for others.

I have been a parent for twenty-four years. It goes from cookies to car keys in what feels like just a few days. It is amazing how time evaporates. Do not waste a moment. Take time to appreciate every precious day with your children. Change the misbehavior and then have fun, laugh, play, and get involved with your children. It will keep you feeling young. These are the most valuable years of your life.

I do not remember where I was when I first read this poem, but it always inspires me to remember how important my behavior is to my children.

When You Thought I Wasn't Looking

When you thought I wasn't looking, I saw you hang my first
painting on the refrigerator, and I wanted to paint another one.
When you thought I wasn't looking, I saw you feed a stray cat, and
I thought it was good to be kind to animals.
When you thought I wasn't looking, I saw you make my favorite
cake just for me, and I knew that little things are very special.
When you thought I wasn't looking, I heard you say a prayer, and I
believed there is a God I could always talk to.
When you thought I wasn't looking, I felt you kiss me good night,
and I felt loved.
When you thought I wasn't looking, I saw tears come from your
eyes, and I learned that sometimes things hurt, but it's all right to
cry.
When you thought I wasn't looking, I saw that you cared and I
wanted to be everything that I could be.
When you thought I wasn't looking, I looked . . . and wanted to say
thanks for all the things I saw when you thought I wasn't
looking.

—AUTHOR UNKNOWN

Appendix: Children's Book List

Reading books to your preschoolers as a way of teaching them about issues in everyday life has been recommended throughout this book. Books help children make new discoveries about themselves and the world around them. They provide insight and comfort by explaining situations and feelings that may be unfamiliar and confusing.

When selecting books to read to your preschoolers, look for books with simple stories. At this age, children love words that rhyme and repeat. Look for characters with which your child can relate or identify. You will find many excellent books in the children's section of bookstores and libraries. Check with your child's preschool or other preschools in your community to see if they have a library of children's books or a recommended book list. Here are some good resources for children's books:

The New York Times Parent's Guide to the Best Books for Children
Eden Ross Lipson
Three Rivers Press, 2000
ISBN 0-8129-3018-5

The Read-Aloud Handbook
Jim Trelease
Penguin Books, 2001
ISBN 0-14-100161-5

Web sites for children's books (type exactly as printed):

Book Links   www.ala.org/BookLinks/
The Children's Literature Web Guide   www.acs.ucalgary.ca/~dkbrown/
Parent Soup   www.parentsoup.com
Parenting magazine   www.parenting.com
Parents magazine   www.parents.com
Penguin Putnam Inc.   www.penguinputnam.com

What follows is a list of picture books and storybooks that have been rec-ommended by preschool teachers or parents who have taken my workshops. These books can be used to address concerns you may have with your chil-dren. Either Dianne Heckman, a psychologist (and my wife), or I have read each of these books to verify its quality and intent. Always read a book in its entirety yourself before reading it to your children to make sure the content meets with your expectations and values and to reduce the risk that something in the book may be inappropriate. I have arranged this list by topic to make it easier to find books to address your child's particular needs.

Adoption
Adoption Is for Always by Linda Walvoord Girard
Although Celia reacts with anger and insecurity to having been adopted, her parents help her accept her feelings and celebrate their love for her by making her adoption day a family holiday.
Albert Whitman & Company, 1986   ISBN 0-8075-0187-5

The Day We Met by Phoebe Koehler
Mom and Dad recount the exciting day when they adopted their baby.
Aladdin Paperbacks, 1990   ISBN 0-689-80964-6

Families Are Different by Nina Pellegrini
An adopted Korean girl discovers that her classmates have different types of families.
Holiday House, 1991   ISBN 0-8234-0887-6

A Family for Jamie by Suzanne Bloom
Although Dan and Molly can make cookies and birdhouses, they cannot make a baby, so they adopt Jamie and share with him their life and love.
Clarkson N. Potter, 1991   ISBN 0-517-57492-6

Happy Adoption Day by John McCutcheon
Parents celebrate the day on which they adopted their child and continue to reassure the new addition to their family that he is wanted, loved, and very special.
Little, Brown and Company, 1996   ISBN 0-316-55455-3

How I Was Adopted by Joanna Cole
A young girl tells the story of how she came to be her parents' child through adoption.
Mulberry Books, 1999   ISBN 0-688-17055-2

I Love You Like Crazy Cakes by Rose Lewis
A woman describes how she went to China to adopt a special baby girl. Based on the author's own experiences.
Little, Brown and Company, 2000   ISBN 0-316-52538-3

Let's Talk About It: Adoption by Fred Rogers
This book discusses what it means to be part of a family and examines some feelings that adopted children may have.
G. P. Putnam's Sons, 1994   ISBN 0-698-11625-9

Tell Me Again: About the Night I Was Born by Jamie Lee Curtis
In this story a child pleads "Tell me again" about the night she was born and many other first-time experiences with the adoptive parents.
HarperCollins Publishers, 1999   ISBN 0-590-76481-0

Zachary's New Home by Geraldine M. Blomquist and Paul Blomquist
Zachary still remembers his "real" parents and finds that adjusting to life as Marie and Tom's adopted son is sometimes a painful reality.
Magination Press, 1990   ISBN 0-9455354-28-2

Baby-sitters / Day Care / Working Parents
Going to Day Care by Fred Rogers
The author describes the typical activities and feelings children can experience at a day-care center, including the conflicts and apprehensions involved in being away from home, along with the fun and excitement.
G. P. Putnam's Sons, 1987   ISBN 00-399-21237-X

It's OK! Tom, Ally, and the Baby-sitter by Beth Robbins
Tom's fear of the new baby-sitter begins to dissolve after she arrives and invites
Tom to play a game.
DK Publishing   ISBN 0-7894-7426-3

Let's Talk About Feelings: Nathan's Day at Preschool by Susan Conlin and Susan
    Levine Friedman
Nathan learns to emotionally negotiate the world of child care. The book includes a section at the back for parents on survival skills for children in child
care.
Parenting Press, 1991   ISBN 0-943990-60-2

My New Baby-Sitter by Christine Loomis
This book explores real-life care-giving situations with reassurance and insight
in a story for children; a "note to parents" offers advice about how to choose a
caregiver.
Morrow Junior Books, 1991   ISBN 0-688-0925-5

What to Expect When the Babysitter Comes by Heidi Murkoff
This book helps prepare your child for a baby-sitter by easing your child's anx-
ieties about the unknown.
Harper Festival, 2000   ISBN 0-694-01323-4

When Mommy and Daddy Go to Work by Joanna Cole
Carly is sad when her parents leave her at day care and go to work, but when
reminded that they'll be back later, she soon begins having fun with her
friends. A tips-for-parents page includes suggestions on how to make the transition easier for you and your child.
HarperCollins Publishers, 2001   ISBN 0-688-17044-7

Bedtime
Bedtime for Baby Bop by Donna Cooner, Ed.D.
This book takes Baby Bop through a nightly bedtime routine.
Barney Publishing, The Lyons Group, 1996   ISBN 1-57064-078-5

Ira Sleeps Over by Bernard Waber
Ira prepares to sleep over at his friend Reggie's house and struggles with whether
or not to bring his teddy bear.
Houghton Mifflin Company, 1972   ISBN 0-395-20503-4

What to Expect at Bedtime by Heidi Murkoff
This book explains reasons to go to bed and answers common questions such as "What happens when I am sleeping?" and "What if I wake up during the night?"
Harper Festival, 2000   ISBN 0-6940-1325-0

Winnie the Pooh's Bedtime Hummables by Amy Edgar
This board book includes a bedtime, bath, and story time routine.
Mouse Works, 2000   ISBN 0-7364-1020-1

Behavior
But I Wwaaannt It! by Dr. Laura Schlessinger
After his mother buys him all the stuffed animals he wants, a boy discovers what he truly wants.
Cliff Street Books, 2001   An Imprint of HarperCollins Publishers
ISBN 0-06-02775-6

Don't Touch! by Suzy Kline
When all the grown-ups constantly say "Don't touch!" Dan finds something he can safely squeeze, smash, and pound to his heart's content.
Albert Whitman & Company, 1985   ISBN 0-8075-1707-0

Elbert's Bad Word by Audrey Wood
After shocking the elegant garden party by using a bad word, Elbert learns some acceptable substitutes from a helpful wizard. In the book, the child's mouth is washed out with soap. This is not an appropriate response; however, the book illustrates the power of bad words and how to substitute more appropriate words.
Voyager Books, 1988   Harcourt Brace and Company
ISBN 0-15-201367-9

Let's Talk About Being Helpful by Joy Berry
Carlos learns why being helpful and doing what you are asked makes everyone happier.
Scholastic, 1996   ISBN 0-590-62385-0

Let's Talk About Being Patient by Joy Berry
This book describes what being impatient feels like and what you can do to help yourself be more patient.
Gold Star Publishing, 1999   ISBN 1-58634-055-7

Let's Talk About Feeling Frustrated by Joy Berry
This book describes times when it is easy to get frustrated, how a child might behave when he or she is frustrated, and what you can do that will make you feel better.
Gold Star Publishing, 1999   ISBN 1-58634-034-4

Let's Talk About Feeling Jealous by Joy Berry
This book describes jealousy, what you should not do when you feel jealous, and things you can do to make yourself feel better.
Gold Star Publishing, 1999   ISBN 1-58634-042-5

Let's Talk About Needing Attention by Joy Berry
This book describes how a child might feel when he needs more attention and gives examples of how to get positive attention.
Scholastic, 1996   ISBN 0-590-62424-5

Let's Talk About Saying No by Joy Berry
This book describes situations when a child should and should not say no and how to say no in an acceptable way.
Scholastic, 1996   ISBN 0-590-62425-3

Me First by Helen Lester
Pinderton the pig always manages to be first until he rushes for a sandwich and it turns out to be not the edible kind.
Houghton Mifflin Company, 1992   ISBN 0-395-72022-2

When I Feel Angry by Cornelia Maude Spelman
A little rabbit describes what makes her angry and the different ways she can control her anger.
Albert Whitman & Company, 2000   ISBN 0-8075-8888-1

Being Different
Clara Caterpillar by Pamela Duncan Edwards
By camouflaging herself, Clara Caterpillar, who becomes a cream-colored butterfly, courageously saves Catisha the crimson-colored butterfly from a hungry crow.
HarperCollins Publishers, 2001   ISBN 0-06-028995-3

It's Okay to Be Different by Todd Parr
Illustrations and brief text describe all kinds of differences that are "okay,"

such as "It's okay to be a different color," "It's okay to need some help," "It's okay to be adopted," and "It's okay to have a different nose."
Little, Brown and Company, 2001   ISBN 0-316-66603-3

The Legend of Spookley the Square Pumpkin by Joe Troiano
Spookley the pumpkin was different and all the other pumpkins teased him, until Spookley proved that being different can save the day!
Back Pack Books, 2001   Southern Lights Custom Publishing
ISBN 0-7607-2754-6

Why Am I Different? by Nora Simon
Portrays everyday situations in which children see themselves as "different" in family life, preferences, and aptitudes and yet feel that being different is all right.
Albert Whitman & Company, 1976   ISBN 0-8075-9076-2

Death and Grieving
Desser the Best Ever Cat by Maggie Smith
A child describes how Desser the cat had always been part of the family and how much he was loved even after he died.
Alfred A. Knopf, 2001   ISBN 0-375-81056-0

Goodbye Mousie by Robie H. Harris
A boy grieves for his dead pet Mousie, helps to bury him, and begins to come to terms with his loss.
Margaret K. McElderry Books, 2001   ISBN 0-689-83217-6

I Miss You by Pat Thomas
This book explores children's feelings and questions about death and helps children understand their loss and how to come to terms with their feelings. It includes a "how to use this book" page.
Barron's Educational Series, Inc., 2001   ISBN 0-7641-1764-5

"I Wish I Could Hold Your Hand . . ." A Child's Guide to Grief and Loss by Dr. Pat Palmer
This warm and comforting book gently helps grieving children identify their feelings—from denial and anger to guilt and sadness—and learn to accept and deal with them. The expressive illustrations and simple, direct writing help children discover that it is normal and natural to feel the pain of loss, and that they can help themselves to feel better.
Impact Publishers, 1994   ISBN 0-915166-82-8

I'll Always Love You by Hans Wilhelm
A child's sadness at the death of a beloved dog is tempered by the remembrance of saying every night, "I'll always love you."
Crown Publishers, 1985   ISBN 0-590-42744-X

It Must Hurt a Lot by Doris Stanford
This book describes a boy's reactions of anger, grief, and eventual acceptance when his dog dies. Includes suggestions to parents for helping a child deal with loss.
Multnomah Press, 1986   ISBN 0-88070-131-5

Lifetimes by Bryan Mellonie and Robert Ingpen
This book explains life and death in a sensitive, caring, beautiful way. It talks about beginnings and endings and conveys that dying is as much a part of living as being born.
Bantam Books, 1983   ISBN 0-553-34023-9

The Saddest Time by Norma Simon
This book explains death as the inevitable end of life and provides three situations in which children experience powerful emotions when someone close to them has died.
Albert Whitman & Company, 1986   ISBN 0-8075-7204-7

Stacy Had a Little Sister by Wendie C. Old
Stacy has mixed feelings about her new sister, Ashley, but when the baby dies of sudden infant death syndrome, Stacy is sad and misses her.
Albert Whitman & Company, 1995   ISBN 0-8075-7598-4

A Story for Hippo by Simon Puttock and Alison Bartlett
This book is about Monkey, whose friend Hippo dies, and how Monkey keeps the spirit of his cherished friend alive forever.
Scholastic, 2001   ISBN 0-439-26219-4

When a Pet Dies by Fred Rogers
This book explores the feelings of frustration, sadness, and loneliness that a youngster may feel when a pet dies.
Paperstar, 1998   ISBN 0-698-11666-6

When Dinosaurs Die by Laurie Krasny Brown and Marc Brown
Explains in simple language the feelings people may have regarding the death

of a loved one and the ways to honor the memory of someone who has died.
Little, Brown and Company, 1996   ISBN 0-316-11955-5

Divorce

At Daddy's on Saturdays by Linda Walvoord Girard
Although her parents' divorce causes her to feel anger, concern, and sadness,
Katie discovers that she can keep a loving relationship with her father even
though he lives apart from her.
Albert Whitman & Company, 1987   ISBN 0-8075-0475-0

Daddy Day, Daughter Day by Larry King and Chaia King
This book is unique in that it tells a story from both a child's and a father's
point of view.
Dove Kids, 1997   ISBN 0-7871-0490-6

Dinosaurs Divorce: A Guide for Changing Families by Laurie Krasny Brown and
Marc Brown
This book presents divorce words and what they mean and discusses why par-
ents divorce and what to expect after they divorce.
Little, Brown and Company, 1986   ISBN 0-316-10996-7

It's Not Your Fault, Koko Bear by Vicki Lansky
Koko Bear learns what divorce means, how to deal with changes, how to recognize and deal with feelings, and that divorce is not Koko's fault. Each page
includes helpful tips for parents.
Book Peddlers, 1998   ISBN 0-916773-47-7

Let's Talk About It: Divorce by Fred Rogers
This book discusses how even though a mother and father are no longer living
together, they can still love their children and give them the secure feeling that
comes from being a part of a caring family.
Paperstar, 1998   ISBN 0-698-11670-4

Mama and Daddy Bear's Divorce by Cornelia Maude Spelman
Dinah Bear feels sad and scared when her parents say they are going to divorce. In time, Dinah learns that while Daddy isn't living with them anymore,
many of the best things stay the same.
Albert Whitman & Company, 1998   ISBN 0-8075-5222-4

Two Homes to Live In by Barbara Shook Hazen
A little girl explains how she came to terms with her parents' divorce.
Human Sciences Press, 1983   ISBN 0-89885-173-4

Fears / Being Afraid

Can't You Sleep Little Bear by Martin Waddell
When bedtime comes, Little Bear is afraid of the dark, until Big Bear brings
him light and love.
Candlewick Press, 1994   ISBN 1-56402-262-5

Franklin and the Thunderstorm by Paulette Bourgeois and Brenda Clark
Franklin worries about the weather because he is afraid of storms. In this book
he learns about thunder and lightning.
Scholastic, 1998   ISBN 0-590-02635-6

It's OK! Tom's Afraid of the Dark by Beth Robbins
Tom, a young cat, overcomes his fear of the dark by using his imagination to
think about good things rather than bad ones.
DK Publishing, 2001   ISBN 0-7894-7420-4

Jessica and the Wolf: A Story for Children Who Have Bad Dreams by Ted Lobby,
    M.S.W.
With her parents' support, Jessica finds the strength and self-reliance to con-
quer a recurring bad dream.
Magination Press, 1990   ISBN 0-945-35422-3

Let's Talk About Feeling Afraid by Joy Berry
This book describes situations when a child may feel afraid, what the child's
body might feel, and how to resolve the fear or get assistance.
Scholastic, 1995   ISBN 0-590-62384-2

Scary Night Visitors: A Story for Children with Bedtime Fears by Irene Wineman
    Marcus and Paul Marcus, Ph.D.
When Davey realizes that his scary nighttime visitors are really his angry feelings about his little sister projected into the world, he feels free to express his
anger in a healthy way.
Magination Press, 1990   ISBN 0-945354-26-6

The Bad Dream by Jim Aylesworth
When a little boy is awakened by a bad dream, his parents comfort him by reminding him that nightmares are not real.
Albert Whitman & Company, 1985   ISBN 0-8075-0506-4

Feelings

Double-Dip Feelings: Stories to Help Children Understand Emotions by Barbara
    S. Cain, M.S.W.
This book discusses how natural it is to feel contradictory emotions. It presents situations, such as the first day of school, the birth of a sibling, or a move to a new house, and identifies two emotions each event is likely to elicit.
Magination Press, 1990   ISBN 0-945354-20-7

Feelings from Sadness to Happiness by Nuria Roca
With help from this book, children can start naming many feelings they have. Parents will find guidelines and suggestions to help their children understand their feelings.
Barron's Educational Series, 2001   ISBN 0-7641-1840-4

Growing Up Is Hard by Dr. Laura Schlessinger
When a young boy has a day where nothing goes right, his father helps him deal with his feelings and see that things will change as he grows up.
Cliff Street Books, 2001   An Imprint of HarperCollins Publishers
ISBN 0-06-029200-8

I Know I Made It Happen by Lynn Bennett Blackburn
This book gently explores children's feelings about guilt when people get in an accident or get sick, get old, and die, or get divorced. It emphasizes that wishes, thoughts, and words don't make bad things happen. The book includes a section on helping children know they did not make them happen.
Centering Corporation, 1991   ISBN 1-56123-016-2

Let's Talk About Feeling Disappointed by Joy Berry
This book describes how a child might feel disappointed and things they can do to feel better.
Gold Star Publishing, 1999   ISBN 1-58634-043-3

Let's Talk About Feeling Angry by Joy Berry
This book describes why a child might feel angry, and what he or she might do to handle anger in a positive way.
Scholastic, 1995   ISBN 0-590-62386-9

Let's Talk About Feeling Sad by Joy Berry
This book describes how a child might feel sad and what he can do to make
himself feel better.
Scholastic, 1996   ISBN 0-590-62387-7

Nobody's Perfect, Not Even My Mother by Norma Simon
A young child learns that nobody's perfect, yet people can be wonderful just
the same.
Albert Whitman & Company, 1981   ISBN 0-8075-5707-2

Today I Feel Silly and Other Moods That Make My Day by Jamie Lee Curtis
A child's emotions range from silliness to anger to excitement, coloring and
changing each day.
Joanna Cotler Books, 1998   An Imprint of HarperCollins Publishers
ISBN 0-06-024560-3

When I Feel Angry by Cornelia Maude Spelman
A little rabbit describes what makes her angry and the different ways she can
control her anger. A note to parents includes helpful tips for teaching children
to manage their anger.
Albert Whitman & Company, 2000   ISBN 0-8075-8888-1

Friendship / Sharing
Edsel: The Elephant Who Learned to Share by Sunny Griffin
Edsel the elephant learns that sharing feels good.
Landoll's, 1993   ISBN 1-56987-095-0

Let's Talk About Playing with Others by Joy Berry
This book describes how a child might feel when others won't play with him
and explains how to be considerate.
Gold Star Publishing, 1999   ISBN 1-58634-060-3

How to Be a Friend by Laurie Krasny Brown and Marc Brown
Dinosaur characters illustrate the value of friends, how to make friends, and
how to be and not be a good friend.
Little, Brown and Company, 1998   ISBN 0-316-11153-8

Sorry by Sam McBratney
This book is a story about being best friends and when to say sorry.
HarperCollins Publishers, 2000   ISBN 0-06-028686-5

That Toad is Mine! by Barbara Shook Hazen
Two friends who are good at sharing become upset when they are unable to agree on how to share a toad they find.
Harper Festival, 1998   ISBN 0-694-01035-9

What to Expect at a Playdate by Heidi Murkoff
This book will help your child understand how play dates work and help you make them a successful social-skills experience.
Harper Festival, 2001   ISBN 0-694-01330-7

Honesty
The Empty Pot by Demi
When Ping admits that he is the only child in China unable to grow a flower from the seeds distributed by the Emperor, he is rewarded for his honesty.
Henry Holt and Company, 1996   ISBN 0-8050-4900-2

Hospital / Doctor / Dentist
It's OK! Tom and Ally Visit the Doctor by Beth Robbins
When cat siblings Tom and Ally visit the doctor for a checkup, Tom is scared of receiving a shot, but soon realizes that there is nothing to fear.
DK Publishing, 2001   ISBN 0-7894-7428-X

Going to the Dentist by Fred Rogers
This book prepares a child for his first visit to the dentist by describing the procedures, equipment, and staff involved in a dental examination. It includes tips on keeping teeth clean.
G. P. Putnam's Sons, 1989   ISBN 0-399-21636-7

Going to the Hospital by Fred Rogers
This book describes what happens during a stay in the hospital, including some common forms of medical treatment.
Paperstar, 1997   ISBN 0-698-11574-0

What to Expect When You Go to the Doctor by Heidi Murkoff
This book helps children understand who doctors are, what they do, and why we go to them for checkups.
Harper Festival, 2000   ISBN 0-694-01324-2

My Friend the Dentist by Jane Werner Watson, Robert E. Switzer, M.D., and
J. Cotter Hirschberg, M.D.
This book describes, simply, a visit to the dentist's office, how teeth are filled
and cleaned, and what to do to have good, healthy teeth.
Crown Publishers, 1987   ISBN 0-517-56484-X

Listening
In a Minute by Virginia Miller
Ba is a small bear who wants to play, but George is busy with housework. Ba is
a pest, getting in the way and wanting attention, until George yells in a big
voice, "In a minute!" Ba tries to wait, but by the time George is ready, Ba has
figured out that *play* means joining in the fun of carrying the firewood, bringing in the laundry, and sweeping the floor.
Candlewick Press, 2001   ISBN 0-7636-1270-7

Listen Buddy by Helen Lester
A lop-eared rabbit named Buddy finds himself in trouble with the Scruffy
Varmint because he never listens.
Houghton Mifflin Company, 1995   ISBN 0-395-72361-2

Love and Relationships
Love You Forever by Robert Munsch
This book is the story of how a little boy goes through the stages of childhood
and becomes a man. It is also about the enduring nature of parents' love and
how it crosses generations.
Firefly Books, 1991   ISBN 0-920668-37-2

I Love You as Much by Laura Krauss Melmed
A variety of mothers tell their children how much they love them.
Lothrop, Lee and Shepard Books, 1993   ISBN 0-688-11718-X

Mama, Do You Love Me? by Barbara M. Joosse
A child living in the Arctic learns that a mother's love is unconditional.
Chronicle Books, 1991   ISBN 0-87701-759-X

Why Do You Love Me? by Dr. Laura Schlessinger
A young boy asks his mother why she loves him and learns that her love is un-
conditional.
Cliff Street Books, 2001   An Imprint of HarperCollins Publishers
ISBN 0-06-027866-8

Manners

Eddycat Introduces . . . Mannersville by Ada Barnett
When Buddy Brown Bear moves into Mannersville, he finds the entire town full of friendly, polite animals who know how to behave properly. The book includes a parent guide for teaching etiquette.
Gareth Stevens Publishing, 1993   ISBN 0-8368-0939-4

Joshua's Book of Manners by Alona Frankel
Joshua learns manners and the magic words "please," "thank you," "bless you," and "excuse me." This book provides practice for a child to learn what the correct response is.
HarperCollins Publishers, 2000   ISBN 0-694-01380-3

Oops! Excuse Me Please! by Bob McGrath
A collection of twenty-eight vignettes illustrating good manners, covering such topics as proper etiquette, following the Golden Rule, and memorizing correct phrases. A note to parents is included.
Barron's Educational Series, 1998   ISBN 0-7641-5083-9

Perfect Pigs by Marc Brown and Stephen Krensky
This book is a simple introduction to good manners children should use with family, friends, and pets, at school, during meals, on the phone, during games, at parties, and in public places.
Little, Brown and Company, 1983   ISBN 0-316-11080-9

Moving

The Berenstain Bears' Moving Day by Stan and Jan Berenstain
The Berenstain Bears pack up and move to another home and adjust to their new neighborhood.
Random House, 1981   ISBN 0-394-84838-1

Franklin's Bad Day by Paulette Bourgeois and Brenda Clark
Franklin is sad and mad because one of his best friends moved away. He learns how to share his feelings by writing and calling.
Scholastic, 1997   ISBN 0-590-69332-8

Moving by Fred Rogers
This book describes in detail the process of moving, as well as the irritation and uncertainty, the sorrow and the excitement.
G. P. Putnam's Sons, 1987   ISBN 0-399-21383-X

New Baby

It's OK! Tom, Ally, and the New Baby by Beth Robbins
Feline siblings Tom and Ally feel both excited a little worried when they hear
there will be a new baby in their family.
DK Publishing, 2001   ISBN 0-7894-7430-1

The New Baby by Fred Rogers
This book explains the needs of toddlers faced with a new baby in the family,
and some of the changes and disruptions the baby can cause in the life of the
older brother or sister.
G. P. Putnam's Sons, 1985   ISBN 0-399-211236-1

The New Baby at Your House by Joanna Cole
This book describes the activities and changes involved in having a new baby
in the house and the feelings experienced by the older brothers and sister. The
book includes a good note-to-parents section.
Mulberry Books, 1998   An Imprint of William Morrow and Company
ISBN 0-688-16698-9

Our Teacher's Having a Baby by Eve Bunting
As the months pass during first-grade-teacher Mrs. Neal's pregnancy, her class
gets involved writing letters to the baby, thinking up possible names for it, and
designing a baby room on the bulletin board. This book discusses the fears
children can have about their teacher leaving to have a baby and never coming
back.
Clarion Books, 1992   ISBN 0-395-60470-2

Sam Is My Half Brother by Lizi Boyd
A young girl, fearful that her newborn half brother will get all the attention, is
reassured of her father's love. This book also addresses how stepchildren who
do not live together can stay connected.
Puffin Books, 1992   ISBN 0-14-054190-X

What to Expect When Mommy's Having a Baby by Heidi Murkoff
This book addresses questions your child may have (but may not be able to
clearly express) and serves as a jumping-off point for further discussion and di-
alogue about how a baby is created, how it grows, and ultimately how it comes
to join the family.
Harper Festival, 2000   ISBN 0-694-01321-8

Pacifiers

Bye-Bye, Pacifier by Louise Gikow
Baby Piggy loves to use her pacifier. Then one day her nanny asks Piggy if she can play without it. Piggy sees her friends playing without pacifiers and realizes that she doesn't need one either.
Golden Books, 1999   ISBN 0-3071-3468-7

Little Bunny's Pacifier Plan by Maribeth Boelts
Little Bunny gradually learns to give up his pacifier.
Albert Whitman & Company, 1999   ISBN 0-8075-4581-3

Pacifier Days: A Fond Farewell (Berenstain Bears Baby Board Books) by Stan Berenstain
Nothing comes between the Berenstain Baby Bears and their "passies." But the Baby Bears are growing up and are about to learn that there's more to life than pacifiers.
Random House, 1999   ISBN 0-6798-9336-9

Self-Esteem

Sad, Sad William by Gitte Spee
William, a big bear, feels far from beautiful and different from everyone else, until his friends convince him he does have a talent to be proud of and that makes him special.
Gareth Stevens Publishing, 1995   ISBN 0-8368-1607-2

You Are Special by Max Lucado
Punchinello's opinion of himself changes after talking to his creator.
Crossway Books, 1997   ISBN 0-89107-931-9

Separation Anxiety / Preschool

Into the Great Forest: A Story for Children Away from Parents for the First Time by Irene Wineman Marcus and Paul Marcus, Ph.D.
Reluctant to leave home for his first day of school, a young boy has a reassuring dream in which he leaves his royal parents for an adventure in the forest and returns safely to the castle.
Magination Press, 1992   ISBN 0-945354-39-8

It's OK! Tom's First Day at School by Beth Robbins
On the first day of school, a young cat named Tom worries about his teacher, his classmates, and finding his way around.
DK Publishing, 2001   ISBN 0-7894-7422-0

Wemberly Worried by Kevin Henkes
A mouse named Wemberly, who worries about everything, finds that she has a whole list of things to worry about when she faces the first day of nursery school.
Greenwillow Books, 2000   ISBN 0-688-17027-7

What to Expect at Preschool by Heidi Murkoff
This book introduces children to the basic aspects of preschool: what the classroom will look like, what teachers do, and what happens in a typical preschool day.
Harper Festival, 2001   ISBN 0-694-01326-9

Sexuality and Reproduction

What's the Big Secret? Talking About Sex with Girls and Boys by Laurie Krasny Brown, Ed.D., and Marc Brown
This book answers some of the most common questions about sex and development.
Little, Brown and Company, 1997   ISBN 0-316-10183-4

When You Were Inside Mommy by Joanna Cole
This book introduces young children to the concepts of pregnancy and childbirth. A note-to-parents section provides tips on answering children's questions about birth.
HarperCollins Publishers, 2001   ISBN 0-688-17043-9

So That's How I Was Born! by Dr. Robert Brooks
When Joey's friend Lisa tells him how babies are born, he asks his mother and father to tell him how he was really born.
Aladdin Paperbacks, 1983   An Imprint of Simon and Schuster
ISBN 0-6717-8344-0

Shyness

The Kissing Hand by Audrey Penn
When Chester the raccoon is reluctant to go to kindergarten for the first time, his mother teaches him a secret way to carry her love with him.
Child and Family Press, 1993   Child Welfare League of America, Inc.
ISBN 0-87868-585-5

Shrinking Violet by Cari Best
Violet, who is very shy and hates for anyone to look at her in school, finally comes out of her shell when she is cast as Lady Space in a play about the solar system and saves the production from disaster.
Farrar, Straus & Giroux, 2001   ISBN 0-374-36882-1

Let's Talk About Being Shy by Marianne Johnston
This is a book you might want to read to a five- or six-year-old. The book uses two stories to help children understand shyness.
Hazelden Information and Education, 1997   ISBN 1-5683-8222-7

Edward Unready for School by Rosemary Wells
Edward, a shy young bear unready for play school, feels out of place surrounded by students who are ready, busy, and happy.
Dial Books for Young Readers, 1995   ISBN 0-8037-1884-5

Sibling Rivalry

I Love You the Purplest by Barbara M. Joosse
A wise and loving mother reassures two brothers that each has a special place in her heart.
Chronicle Books, 1996   ISBN 0-439-07723-0

The Birth-Order Blues by Joan Drescher
A school newspaper reporter surveys kids on how they feel about being born first, last, or in the middle of their family's hierarchy.
Viking, 1993   ISBN 0-670-83621-4

Single-Parent Families

Do I Have A Daddy? by Jeanne Warren Lindsay
A single mother explains to her son that his daddy left soon after he was born. The book includes a section with suggestions for answering the question "Do I have a daddy?"
Morning Glory Press, 2000   ISBN 1-8853-5663-3

I Wish I Had My Father by Norma Simon
Father's Day is tough for a boy whose father left him years ago and never communicates with him.
Albert Whitman & Company, 1983   ISBN 0-8075-3522-2

Love Is a Family by Roma Downey
Lily worries about what others will think when she brings just her mother to family fun night at school. The story shows children that family should not be defined by mother, father, and child, but by love.
Regan Books, 2001   ISBN 0-06-039374-2

Special Needs / Disabilities

Andy and His Yellow Frisbee by Mary Thompson
The new girl at school tries to befriend Andy, an autistic boy who spends every recess by himself, spinning a yellow Frisbee under the watchful eye of his older sister.
Woodbine House, 1996   ISBN 0-833149-83-2

Even Little Kids Get Diabetes by Connie White Pirner
A young girl who has had diabetes since she was two years old describes her adjustments to the disease.
Albert Whitman & Company, 1991   ISBN 0-8075-2158-2

He's My Brother by Joe Lasker
A young boy describes the school and home experiences of his younger brother who has a learning disability.
General Publishing, 1974   ISBN 0-8075-3218-5

Talking to Angels by Esther Watson
Christina is autistic. Her sister describes how she sees the world in a different way than most people.
Harcourt Brace and Company, 1996   ISBN 0-15-201077-7

My Brother Sammy by Becky Edwards and David Armitage
A boy describes some of the many feelings he has about his brother Sammy, who is autistic.
The Millbrook Press, 1999   ISBN 0-7613-0439-8

Veronica's First Year by Jean Sasso Rheingrover
Nine-year-old Nathan helps welcome his baby sister, who has Down syndrome, into the family and eagerly anticipates the day when she will be able to ride his tricycle.
Albert Whitman & Company, 1996   ISBN 0-8075-8474-6

We'll Paint the Octopus Red by Stephanie Stuve-Bodeen
Emma and her father discuss what they will do when the new baby arrives, but they adjust their expectations when he is born with Down syndrome.
Woodbine House, 1998   ISBN 1-890-627-06-2

What About Me? When Brothers and Sisters Get Sick by Allen Peterkin, M.D.
Laura experiences conflicting emotions when her brother becomes seriously ill.

This book includes suggestions for parents to help their well children cope with a chronically ill sibling.
Magination Press, 1992   ISBN 0-945354049-5

What's Wrong with Timmy? by Maria Shriver
After Kate asks her mom questions about a boy she meets who seems different, she learns that he is more like her than it first appears.
Little, Brown and Company, 2001   ISBN: 0-3162-3337-4

Stepfamilies
Let's Talk About It: Stepfamilies by Fred Rogers
This book discusses the changes involved in becoming part of a stepfamily and ways to deal with the new situation.
G. P. Putnam's Sons, 1997   ISBN 0-399-23145-5

My New Mom and Me by Betty Ren Wright
After a young girl's widowed father remarries, her cat helps her make a few important discoveries about herself.
Steck-Vaughn Company, 1992   ISBN 0-8114-7154-3

Thumbsucking
David Decides About Thumbsucking: A Story for Children, A Guide for Parents by Susan Heitler, Ph.D.
This is a very positive story that encourages children to quit thumb sucking. It includes a section for parents.
Reading Matters, 1996   ISBN 0-9614-7802-0

Harold's Hideaway Thumb by Harriet Sonnenschein
Harold, a bunny, has outgrown most baby things, but his thumb is hard to relinquish. The parents here are nicely nonjudgmental, while Harold provides a good model of solving one's own problem in one's own time.
Aladdin Paperbacks, 1993   ISBN 0-6717-9602-X

Little Thumb by Wand Dionne
Little Thumb encourages children to put their thumbs to better use.
Pelican Publishing, 2001   ISBN 1-5655-4754-3

Toilet Training

Going to the Potty by Fred Rogers
Parent and child can read together about the way children develop from the experience of eliminating waste from their body and about the positive aspect of using the toilet.
Paperstar, 1997   ISBN 0-698-115775-9

What to Expect When You Use the Potty by Heidi Murkoff
This book will answer your child's questions about the process of using the toilet. It will help remove some of the potential stumbling blocks to success, including anxiety, shame, and fear.
HarperCollins Publishers, 2000   ISBN 0-694-01322-6

Index

adaptive development, 276
aggression, 259–67
  biting, 265–66
  bullying, 263–65
  escalation of, 267
  temperament and, 266
anger management, 155–63
  blaming child and, 159
  components of, 156
  defusing anger in, 159
  delay strategy in, 159
  exercises for, 162–63
  expectations in, 156–57
  guilt in, 159
  modeling of, 156–57
  punishment in, 144–45
  repetitive anger in, 155–56, 157
  responding to child's anger in, 159–60
  spanking in, 168–69
  taking responsibility in, 157–59
  teaching of, 261–63
  temperament and, 260
  time-out in, 175
  tips for avoiding frustration in, 160–61
  tips and strategies for, 161–62
  trigger events in, 156
  see also aggression

attention, getting child's, 25–26
attention seeking, 209–12

bedtime routine, 219–23
bed-wetting, 8, 235–37
biting, 265–66
books:
  child's temperament and, 44
  distraction strategy and, 87
  as gifts, 74
  list of, 281–302
  reading to child from, 71–75
  vacations and, 74–75
Brazelton, T. Berry, 234
bribery, 91, 100–101, 218
brushing and flossing, 223
bullying, 263–65

cause and effect, 20, 80, 109, 141
charts, 131–38, 200–201, 204, 205, 232–33
  goals and, 135
  guidelines and techniques for, 131–33, 138
  posting of, 133
  potty, 235, 236, 237
  redirection of behavior with, 135
  sample, 133–34

charts (*continued*)
   success, progress and, 135
   time-out and, 190–91, 193, 194–95
checklists, 136–37
   in bedtime routine, 221, 222
   in morning routine, 219, 220
   pre-time-out, 172
   rules and, 140
   sample, 137
Child Find screening, 275–76
cognitive development, 275–76
compromise, 10
conscience, 81–82
consistency, 33, 102, 103–14
   cause and effect seen in, 109
   challenges to, 113
   commitment to, 113–14
   and giving in a little, 104–5
   importance of, 103–4
   love and, 114
   narrowing the list for, 110–11
   negative persistence and, 104–5
   between parents, 110
   patience and, 112
   in punishment, 114, 146
   reminding oneself about, 111–12
   rules and, 141, 146
   in setting limits, 107–8
   in spanking, 167–68
   stalling statements and, 107–8
   strategies for, 109–14
   threats, warnings and, 105–7
   time of day and, 112–13
   time-out and, 175, 191, 193
   in time warnings, 106–7
   transition activities and, 106–7
conversation, evolution of, 19
cooperation, 10
Cosby, Bill, 30, 39
cues, nonverbal, 36

decision making, 117
   consequences and, 141–42, 145
dental habits, 223
dentist visits, 248–49
development, types of, 275–76
discipline, 176, 250
   being proactive in, 84–85

bribery vs., 91, 100–101
choices for child in, 85
compromise and, 90–91
conscience in, 81–82
consistency in, 10
definitions of, 23, 53, 79–80
distraction strategy in, 86–87
guilt control in, 91–92
and making excuses for child, 91
negotiating and, 90–91
parental unity in, 110
positive behaviors in, 82–83
in preschool, 268–69
purpose of, 33
redirecting behavior in, 87–88
routine and, 85
rules in, 81, 83–84
self-control in, 81
self-esteem in, 278
as teaching process, 79–81
in teaching right from wrong, 81–82
time of day and, 112–13
timing start of, 112
transition activities in, 88–90
see also punishment; spanking; teaching;
   time-out strategy
distraction strategy:
   discipline and, 86–87
   tantrums and, 86
Dr. Mom's Parenting Guide (Neifert), 234
doctor visits, 247–48

eating habits, 216–18
Eisenberg, Arlene, 234
evolution of conversation, 19
extended families, 11
extinction strategy, 101–2, 152

family climate, 57–61, 279
   humor and, 58, 59
   improvement of, 58–61
   motivation and, 57–61
   parents and, 57
   questionnaire for, 60–61
fear:
   of dentist visits, 248–49
   of doctor visits, 247–48
   Halloween and, 249

of new situations, 245
nightmares and, 246–47
of separation, 242–45
temperament and, 245
feedback:
    positive, *see* positive feedback
    verbal, 24
food, 216–18
fortune cookie technique, 24–25

goals:
    charts and, 135
    establishment of, 200
    motivation and, 56
grandchildren, 239–40
guilt, 91–92, 159

Halloween, 249
Hathaway, Sandee E., 234

I Love You the Purplest (Joosse), 229
imaginary friends, 237
incentives, 132–33

Joosse, Barbara M., 29

Kissing Hand, The (Penn), 243

labeling, 44
language, 17–37, 62, 214
    "are you whining?" approach to, 33
    attentiveness and, 25–31
    bad, 31–33, 63–64
    from birth to three, 18–19
    in communicating with child, 22–23,
        26–28, 36
    in evolution of conversation, 19
    expression in, 18
    in giving directions, 30–31, 36–37
    good listening skills and, 23–25, 35–36
    interruptions and, 34–35
    learning of, 17–18
    in learning problems, 20–21
    in learning self-control, 35–36
    motivation and, 54
    nonverbal cues and, 36
    "please use your words" strategy and,
        21–22

in preschool years, 19–23
in social skills, 20, 22
in teaching correct behavior, 23–25
learning, 62–75
    through experimentation, 67–68
    through fantasy and make-believe, 70–71
    by imitation, 62–67
    integration and, 68–70
    of language, 17–18
    to misbehave, 100–101
    to parent, 9–10, 62–63
    of self-control, 35–36
    through stories, 71–75
    by special-needs preschoolers, 272–75
libraries, 74–75
limits, testing of, 4
listening, 23–25
    child's lack of, 6, 24, 25–31, 97–98
love, 10–11, 279
    consistency and, 114
    self-esteem and, 46–47
lying, 214–16

magical thinking, 215
Manhattan Museum for Children, 19
misbehavior:
    bribery and, 91, 100–101
    deciding what to say or do about, 198–99
    determining pattern of, 197–98
    extinction strategy for, 101–2
    laughter and, 51–52
    learning of, 100–101
    making excuses for, 91
    not listening as, 6, 24, 25–31, 97–98
    parental modeling and, 98–99
    of parents, 63–65
    priority, 180–81, 195–96
    record keeping and, 200–201, 204, 205
    redirecting strategy for, 5, 87–88,
        99–100, 101, 118, 142
    replacement technique for, 118–20
    after rewards, 121
    temperament in, 43
    threats and, 97–98
    see also consistency; discipline; public
        behavior; time-out strategy; *specific
        misbehaviors*
morning routine, 218–19

motivation, 53–61
  "beat the clock" strategy in, 55–56
  charts and checklists in, 136
  encouragement in, 122
  external, 53, 54
  family climate in, 57–61
  goals and incentives in, 56
  increasing of, 54–58
  interest and, 55, 60
  internal, 53, 57
  language of, 54
  positive feedback in, 119–20
  self-esteem in, 54
  shaping or sequencing strategy in, 55–57
  success stressed in, 54
  verbal encouragement in, 56–57
Murkoff, Heidi E., 234

nagging, 212–14
Neifert, Marianne, 234
nightmares, 246–47
night terrors, 247

pacifiers, 233
parents, parenting:
  changing behavior of, 11–13
  consistency between, 110
  cultural changes and, 11
  disagreement between, 10
  family climate and, 57
  by grandparents, 239–40
  guiding voice of, 82
  learning and, 9–10, 62–63
  misbehavior of, 63–65
  as models, 5, 24, 35, 48, 62–67
parent trap, 95
patience, 13, 102
Penn, Audrey, 243
persistence, 102
  nurturing, 49
  temperament and, 40, 41–42
picky eaters, 216–18
Pinker, Steven, 17
planning, 197–203
play dates, 253–54
positive feedback, 117–19, 141, 203
  activities and incentives for, 124–25,
    127–28

  exercises for, 128–29
  list of incentives for, 126–28
  motivation and, 119–20
  punishment vs., 153–54
  reinforcement with, 123–25
  self-esteem and, 117, 120
  self-reward and, 120, 121
  tangible incentives and, 125, 126–27
  verbal encouragement and, 120–21,
    123–24, 126
preschool:
  discipline in, 268–69
  fear of separation and, 243–45
  selection of, 268–70
preschoolers:
  comfort objects of, 231–32
  communicating with, 26–28
  imaginary friends of, 237
  magical thinking of, 215
  new foods and, 217
  principles to practice with, 277–79
  with special needs, *see* special-needs
    preschoolers
  trauma and, 238–39
  unconscious messages and, 121–22
public behavior, 250–58
  in eating out, 251–52
  in play dates, 253–54
  at religious services, 252–53
  in shopping, 254–56
  on vacations, 256–58
punishment, 142–54, 203
  anger in, 144–45
  as chosen by child, 147–48
  consistency in, 114, 146
  deliberate misbehavior and, 152–53
  embarrassment in, 145–46
  explaining purpose of, 144–45
  immediacy of, 147
  positive feedback vs., 153–54
  questions to ask prior to, 151
  realistic, 147–48
  as revenge, 145, 168–69
  rules and, 142–45
  simple vs. harsh, 146–47
  threats, warnings and, 105
  see also discipline; spanking; time-out
    strategy

reading stories, 71–75
record keeping:
    of misbehaviors, 200–201, 204, 205
    time-out and, 190–91, 193, 194–95
    see also charts; checklists
redirecting, 5, 25, 99–100, 101, 118, 135,
        142, 213–14
    discipline and, 87–88
    tantrums and, 87–88
    warnings and, 106
religious services, 252–53
replacement behavior, 118–20, 213–14,
        278
responsibility, encouraging, 124
role-playing, 42, 83
    in anger management, 262
    in explaining time-out, 181–82
rules, 171
    consistency and, 141, 146
    discipline and, 181, 183–84
    explaining of, 81
    punishment and, 142–45
    simplifying of, 83–84
    teaching of, 81, 83–84

sarcasm:
    preschoolers and, 58
    self-esteem and, 92
self-control, 20, 23, 81, 278
    language in, 35–36
    readiness skills for, 35
    teaching of, 81
    verbal reinforcement of, 51
self-esteem, development of, 45–52,
        213–14, 278
    accepting disappointments in, 49–50
    compassion in, 48
    embarrassment in, 48–49, 91–92
    false praise in, 51
    family climate in, 57
    giving choices in, 47–48
    "good helper" strategy in, 47–48
    guilt control in, 91–92
    laughter and humor in, 51–52
    love and, 46–47
    motivation in, 54
    new skills in, 48–49
    positive feedback in, 117, 120

sarcasm in, 92
spanking in, 167, 168
success and failure in, 45–46
trust in, 50–52
validation in, 46–47
sensory development, 276
separation, fear of, 242–45
sequencing strategy, 55–57
    reading to child and, 73
shaping strategy, 55–57
shopping, 254–56
shyness, 42–43, 122
siblings, sibling conflict, 22, 224–30
    competitive games and, 229–30
    fairness and, 228–29
    new baby and, 227–28
    older vs. younger, 226–27
    resolving of, 224–26
    sore losers in, 229–30
social-emotional development, 276
spanking, 164–70
    anger in, 168–69
    child safety in, 169–70
    child's self-control and, 165, 166
    consistency and, 167–68
    effects of, 166–67
    embarrassment in, 167, 169
    impulsive, 167–68
    questions to ask oneself about,
        164–65
    self-esteem and, 167, 168
    slap-on-hand technique in, 167
    see also discipline; punishment
special-needs preschoolers, 271–76
    finding help for, 275–76
    language development and, 272–74
    sensory processing by, 274–75
stories, reading, 71–75
stress, reducing, 238
superheroes, 71

tantrums, 18–19, 68, 94–95, 119, 146, 198,
        211, 212–14
    distraction strategy for, 86
    extinction strategy for, 101–2
    parent trap and, 95
    redirecting activity and, 87–88
    time warning strategy for, 88–89

teaching:
  of anger management, 261–63
  discipline and, 79–81
  expectations and, 81
  of positive behavior, 82–83
  redirection and, 87–88
  of right from wrong, 81–82
  rules and, 81, 83–84
  of self-control, 81
temperament, 38–44, 245
  activity levels and, 39
  aggression and, 266
  anger and, 260
  in children's books, 44
  definition of, 38
  energetic, 40–42
  new situations and, 245
  parenting style and, 44
  "perfect child" image and, 44
  persistent, 40, 41–42
  shy, 42–43, 122
  strategies for matching of, 43–44
  time-out and, 172, 179
  types of, 39–40
threats, warnings vs., 105–7
thumb sucking, 232–33
time-out strategy, 9, 25, 171–96
  adjusting of, 190–92
  anger and, 175
  apologies and, 185–86
  away from home, 189
  charting improvement in, 190–91, 193,
    194–95
  common mistakes in, 174–76
  at completion of, 185–86, 194
  consistency in, 175, 191, 193
  crying and, 180
  deciding to use, 171–76
  determining priority misbehavior for,
    180–81, 195–96
  explaining of, 181–83, 193
  giving instructions on, 174
  guidelines for, 193–94
  impulsive use of, 175
  lack of improvement with, 191–92

language and, 174
length of, 178–80
making choices with, 173–74
overview of, 174
record keeping and, 190–91, 193,
    194–95
resistance to, 175, 187–89, 193–94
safety and, 177, 193
setting for, 177–78, 193
temperament and, 172, 179
for two, 189–90
time warnings, 88–90
  consistency and, 106–7
  in morning and bedtime routines,
    219–21
  tantrums and, 88–89
toilet training, 8, 234–35
*Touchpoints: Your Child's Emotional and
    Behavioral Development* (Brazelton),
    234
transition activities:
  consistency and, 106–7
  discipline and, 88–90
trauma, 238–39
trust, 123
  environmental, 50–51
  relationship, 50–51
  self-esteem and, 50–52

vacations, 256–58

warnings:
  threats vs., 105–7
  time, 88–90, 106–7, 219–21
What to Expect: The Toddler Years (Eisenberg,
    Murkoff, and Hathaway), 234
When You Thought I Wasn't Looking, 280
whining, 68, 93–95, 119, 198, 212–14
  distraction strategy and, 86
  extinction strategy and, 101–2
  parent trap and, 95
  redirecting activity and, 87–88
  time warning strategy and, 88–89
"why-why-why" game, 210
Words and Rules (Pinker), 17–18